Tits Up

ALSO BY SARAH THORNTON

33 Artists in 3 Acts

Seven Days in the Art World

Club Cultures: Music, Media and Subcultural Capital

Tits Up

WHAT SEX WORKERS, MILK BANKERS,
PLASTIC SURGEONS, BRA DESIGNERS, AND
WITCHES TELL US ABOUT BREASTS

SARAH THORNTON

W. W. NORTON & COMPANY
Independent Publishers Since 1923

Tits Up is a work of nonfiction. Individual names and potentially identifying details have been altered in some cases, and some accounts are composites.

Copyright © 2024 by Sarah Thornton

For information about permission to reproduce selections from this book, write to Permissions, W. W. Norton & Company, Inc., 500 Fifth Avenue, New York, NY 10110

For information about special discounts for bulk purchases, please contact W. W. Norton Special Sales at specialsales@wwnorton.com or 800-233-4830

Manufacturing by Lake Book Manufacturing
Book design by Chris Welch
Production manager: Lauren Abbate

ISBN 978-0-393-88102-8

W. W. Norton & Company, Inc., 500 Fifth Avenue, New York, N.Y. 10110
www.wwnorton.com

W. W. Norton & Company Ltd., 15 Carlisle Street, London W1D 3BS

1 2 3 4 5 6 7 8 9 0

Jessica

+

Otto

+

Cora

+

Echo

CONTENTS

Introduction: Reclaiming a Part of Womanhood   1

1. Hardworking Tits   29

2. Lifesaving Jugs   73

3. Treasured Chests   111

4. Active Apexes   153

5. Holy Mammaries   205

Conclusion: Toward a Liberated Rack   247

Acknowledgments   255
Notes   259
Bibliography   285
Illustration Credits   303
Index   307

Tits Up

Reclaiming
a Part of
Womanhood

Absence Makes the Heart Grow Fonder

During a holiday dinner a few years ago, the conversation turned to my boobs. No one in the family thought I should call them Bert and Ernie. My mother suggested Thelma and Louise; my daughter recommended her favorite comedians, Tina and Amy; my wife advocated Venus and Serena. My father, then seventy-seven, and my son, twenty-two, exchanged eye rolls. They were new, these silicone aliens, and they didn't feel female or even human. Nature gave me my first pair, while a high-ranking plastic surgeon had installed these impostors.

When I stood naked in front of a mirror, I thought: the rack on that woman looks pretty good. However, when I put on clothes and moved around, I felt estranged from my chest. I had never questioned the gender I was assigned at birth, but I now had a visceral inkling of the dissonance that a trans person might feel about unwelcome parts. Having a body that misrepresents one's sense of self is unnerving.

I had a double mastectomy in 2018 and, without much thought, opted for the reconstruction covered by my health insurance.[1] Rumor had it that my surgeon, a soft-spoken man at the top of his field, was a weekend painter—a doctor with an aesthetic sense. I told him that I wanted "lesbian yoga boobs," meaning something between an A and B cup. "Think of them as A+ boobs," I quipped. So, imagine my confusion and dismay when I was measured for my first bra post-surgery and discovered that my dysmorphia had a physical foundation. Bert and Ernie were, in fact, Ds.

The good news was that I didn't have invasive cancer, but a load of rogue cells known as ductal carcinoma in situ (DCIS). Seven years of stressful biopsies were over and danger had been excised. Be grateful and ignore the Muppets, I told myself. Unfortunately, the psychology of having breasts is rarely so straightforward. With the mastectomy, I'd lost something inchoate, a vague mood linked to my gut instincts—my breast perception, for lack of a better phrase. Before the implants, when I was cold or anxious or near a fearful height, when I was about to menstruate or had the potential to be aroused, my breasts would let me know. They had sensation and even a modicum of subjectivity. By contrast, these inanimate implants were blank. They were also too cumbersome and conspicuous for the person I thought of as me.

As an art history undergraduate, I was exposed to thirty thousand years of topless Venuses, nursing Madonnas, disheveled mistresses, and feminist self-portraits. Yet now, thirty years later, overcome by the identity pivot spurred by my new chest, one figure kept marching through my head: Liberty, particularly as depicted in Eugène Delacroix's *Lib-*

Liberty misleads.

erty Leading the People. In this 1830 painting, a powerhouse of a woman holds a French flag in one hand and a rifle in the other. She is no victim of wardrobe malfunction; her two bare breasts affirm her bravery and symbolize the wholesome truth of democracy. But the work embodies a high-pitched irony. Despite their pleas and manifestos, women were denied the right to vote, own property, control their earnings, and gain entry to education. This Liberty is a decoy—a fictitious female who helps keep actual women in their place.

While Liberty's bosom fused politics and aesthetics in novel ways specific to nineteenth-century nation-building, the shape and size of her breasts were nothing new. For millennia, the European ideal has been roughly the size of an apple, whether it was the medieval crab apple or the baroque Bramley. With the significant exception of gloriously busty Hindu goddesses, beauty was associated with modest breasts. After World War II, the ideal American boob started to inflate. Was the mega-bust a perverse offshoot of the hyper-visualization of the body, brought about by pinups and Hollywood movies? Or was it the embodiment of a gender-polarizing ideology that sought to push women back into the home when men returned from military duty? During World War II, when American government propaganda incited women to help with the war effort, Rosie the Riveter had flirtatiously feminine eyelashes but a barely visible bosom.

Big breasts, as Rosie suggests, get in the way. They're a pain in the ass. Since my new set arrived, I've been banging them into door frames, passersby in crowded streets, and men in elevators. Without full sensation, I often don't know until it is too late that my numb nipples are poking into strangers or, worse, familiars.

Prior to reconstructive surgery, the only time my boobs had been unwieldy Ds was postpartum. I recall breastfeeding in the middle of the night, pondering the etymology of the word "nurse," feeling connected to an ancient sisterhood of life-givers. Stupid with sleep deprivation, I also spent many hours empathizing with cows, puzzling over

Rosie, an iconic working woman.

the existential strangeness that humans are called mammals when only women have mammary glands that make a nourishing supply of milk. In an androcentric world of man-made classifications, which generally emphasize the superiority of men, why this anomaly? Male breasts are decorative but useless. Indeed, for centuries, evolutionists pondered the mystery of the male nipple.[2]

Although nothing made me feel more like an animal than breast-feeding, the act did not come naturally. It wasn't quite "an exhausting servitude," as Simone de Beauvoir once wrote, but it was certainly a duty.[3] Breast milk, I read, was "liquid gold." It would bolster my baby's immune system, lessen his chance of allergies, and possibly even

increase his IQ. Having been raised on fresh produce and home cook-
ing, I was suspicious of the powdered fast food called formula.

With my second child, a girl, I developed a bad case of mastitis, an
infection that resulted in recurrent fevers and green secretions. For a
month, I pumped with a handheld device and cried over spilt milk as
I threw the "expressions" of my left breast down the drain. Due to the
infection's persistence, I was referred to a specialist—an older English
gentleman—in Harley Street, London. When I removed my heavily
padded nursing bra, my jugs were so engorged that one of them shot
out a jet spray of milk, hitting him on the collar. He was not amused. In
his profession, he must have been sprayed before, but he acted like it
was a uniquely grotesque affront. Why are lactating women simultaneously virtuous and distasteful?

This doctor was a relic, but at least he recommended antibiotics
rather than puppies, which, in the eighteenth century, were sometimes
placed on the engorged breasts of women with "childbed fever" to draw
off the bad milk. Such was the fate of Mary Wollstonecraft, the founder
of English feminism who, inspired by the French Revolution, wrote *A
Vindication of the Rights of Woman* in 1792.[4] Wollstonecraft died, aged
thirty-eight, shortly after giving birth to her daughter, Mary Shelley,
who went on to write the first medical horror story, *Frankenstein*.

My first personal experience of death was due to breast cancer. My
maternal grandmother died in 1971 when I was five; I was shocked to
see my British stiff-upper-lip mother cry. With this history, the decision
to part with my breasts was not that hard. After seven biopsies over
seven years and the continued discovery of dynamic masses of atypical
cells, my doctors had reached the point where they couldn't be sure
that I didn't have cancer. After two hematomas, a bruised rib, and an
inflamed vein, I'd developed a fear and loathing of mammograms and
biopsies. I had what they call "surveillance fatigue"; a double mastectomy felt like the only rational way forward.

In the month leading up to my surgery, I was anxious and remorseful. I usually swim indoors, but for their final outing, my breasts and I went to the Claremont Hotel in the Oakland Hills, which has two 25-yard pools. On that sunny Monday afternoon, as I swam my seventy-two lengths, I thanked them for being there. I apologized for failing to love them enough and asked them to forgive me for letting them go. Yes, it was weird. They swayed obliviously, alive to the moment but unaware of their impending doom. If they'd had the power of speech, their demands would have been simple: Let us float free. Release us from this imprisoning bikini!

Two days later, my breasts had departed for the mysterious afterlife of human tissue. Under my pectoral muscles, my surgeon had installed two saline-filled pillows called expanders, placeholders for my impending implants, which hurt like hell. While they squatted in my chest, I went back and forth on email with a friend, whose trans child had just had gender-affirming top surgery. Our correspondence made me wonder: breast reconstruction, breast augmentation, and chest feminization are parallel plastic surgeries. Why do they have three distinct labels? Although my implant installation went by the name reconstruction, it was so similar to what a trans woman might undergo that my operation could be called a gender re-affirmation or re-feminization surgery. I was being outfitted with unambiguous, man-made "evidence" of my womanhood.

The day of my reconstructive surgery was unexpectedly enjoyable. Teams of conscientious, warm, smart people swooped in and showered me with reassuring attention. While I sat on a wheelie bed in a front-opening hospital gown, the anesthetist asked me nuanced questions about drugs, then parted with the promise that this would be the best general anesthetic I'd ever had.

The highlight of this pre-op drama came when my plastic surgeon showed up with a black sharpie and a hushed entourage of deputies and assistants. He asked me to stand up and then, with his left hand, he drew a short vertical line in the center of my chest, two long swooping lines in the creases under my former mammaries, and then half-moons along the top of each areola. The saggier breast, which had had mastitis and seven biopsies—"left is for loser," I clowned gloomily—received a larger moon, suggesting that more skin would be cut away from it. Then he signed his initials over one and then the other breast, laying claim to his responsibilities.

After a bedridden week in which I watched every episode of *The Handmaid's Tale*, I discovered that my round implants, measured in cubic centimeters, were from the "number 1 plastic surgery portfolio," as Allergan advertised its Natrelle collection. Describing their corporate mission as "the science of rejuvenation," Allergan claimed to "shape the future with you." The language made me feel like a confused cyborg, resistant to my new and improved parts.

Only after Bert and Ernie Natrelle moved in did I wonder about my original breasts. Why did I know so little about them? What kind of life did they lead? What had I lost?

To my recollection, they made their debut on a summer's day in the mid-1970s. Not yet a teenager, I imagined that my new assets might become a potent symbol of adult self-possession or a source of mesmerizing power. I remember vividly the best-selling poster of the period, published in 1976, depicting the decade's premier sex symbol Farrah Fawcett in a one-piece Norma Kamali bathing suit that rejoiced in her unshackled, laissez-faire nipples (see image on page 1).

When I was fifteen, however, my breasts underwent a sobering blow. Tired of babysitting, I took a job as a busser at the local golf club. The kitchen's autocratic ruler was the head chef, who drank on the job. One lunchtime, I was walking through the kitchen with a tray loaded with clean cups and saucers when he obstructed my path and planted his palms on my breasts. His eyes blazed smugly. We knew that I would be the one to get in trouble if I dropped the tray, smashing the china. It was a sad day for my top half—a humiliating initiation to sexual aggression.

About a year later at a sleepover, my boobs were again manhandled without my consent. My school friend and I were sleeping on couches in the living room of her sister's downtown apartment. In the middle of the night, I woke up to a giant naked man (the older sister's much older boyfriend) whose huge hands were rummaging in my pajama top. I rolled over and told him to go back to bed in as authoritative a voice as I could muster. He was so high that his eyes were devoid of consciousness. For an interminable hour, I lay on my stomach, scared stiff, while he wandered around the living room.

For decades, I forgot about those vacant eyes . . . until Brett Kavanaugh's confirmation to the Supreme Court. Like Christine Blasey Ford, I'd had sleep disturbances—indeed, chronic insomnia—for several years. My assaulter probably had little or no recall, and I didn't tell my parents. Two insights reactivated by the #MeToo movement are the power of speaking out and the value of consciousness-raising. So here I am, delving into the personal as a means of figuring out the political.

I was sixteen, still a virgin, and my breasts had become defeated fools—boobs in the literal sense—that needed to be buried under oversized sweaters. Oh, how I wish that "boobs" had some of the power and self-determination of "assholes" and "cunts." When I observe women who relish their cleavage, I am delighted by their good fortune. Breasts and chests are the front and center of body positivity.

For many years, I held a haughty feminist prejudice against boob jobs, which I associated with insecurity, vanity, and a slavish desire to appeal to men. However, my gender re-affirmation surgery has wiped away that judgment. A few people have implied that I'm a femme conformist, who should have resisted reconstruction and taken the braver route of going flat. However, I've never managed to achieve, let alone maintain, a politically correct identity. It only seems fair to give my sisters some slack. Breast augmentation is the number one plastic surgery in the world.[5] Is it a survival tactic in a patriarchal society where beliefs are embodied? Or a way that women try to wrest control over the perceived meanings of their flesh?

Which brings me back to my 34Ds. Finally, the day arrived for my follow-up appointment, to which I wore a T-shirt that said, "We rise by lifting others." I assured my surgeon that I understood that my new boobs looked good, but I also tried to convey how they didn't feel right. The implants were under my muscles, so they swung into my armpits when I did a chaturanga, or yoga push-up. This "animation," as surgeons call it, compounded the feeling that my breasts were bulky and cartoony.

My plastic surgeon, in turn, explained three things. First, even months after the surgery, it was possible that my breasts were still swollen. Second, a primary part of his job with nipple-sparing mastectomies like mine was to keep the nipple in the center of my breast. Third, he had to be careful to "fill the pocket" without cutting too much away in order to avoid "skin death." As he spoke, I had a déjà vu; we'd had this conversation before. I'd lost my grip on its contents during my post-operative opioid haze. I empathized with the difficulties of his craft but was perplexed that state-of-the-art medical practice had given me the boobs of a lactating mother rather than the small dignified orbs of my middle-aged dreams. Something was wrong with the system.

One of my neighbors had breast reconstruction four times. Her breasts were always too big until she found Dr. Carolyn Chang, a surgeon she described as "a petite woman who understood my desire for a cute B cup." Through the art world, I learned that Chang worked on a lot of the most expensive racks in the San Francisco Bay Area, and curious about what she would make of my bust, I obtained a consultation with her. Her white-walled office was strewn with art and photography books that suggested that she was a fashion-conscious scholar of attractiveness.

During my topless exam, Dr. Chang moved her head around, assessing my shape from angled perspectives, as if she were an artist preparing to sculpt from life. She assured me that, objectively, this was an excellent result. Minimal scars. A naturalistic shape. No excessive rippling. When I mentioned my discomfort with their size, she nodded kindly. She lifted my right breast, then my left, as if calculating their exact weights with her hand. She tested their density and bounce by applying gentle pressure with three fingers at their sides and centers. Then she looked me in the eye and inhaled deeply before saying, "The enemy of good is better."

In a follow-up call, Dr. Chang put it more bluntly. "A mastectomy is an amputation. Losing a body part is a severe trauma. Amputees wear prostheses to make them feel normal," she explained. "But it takes time." With these words, I realized that Bert and Ernie, those alien goofballs, were already being absorbed into a revised me, a human with plastic parts who had embarked on a new quest. I now had an overwhelming desire to understand the multifarious meanings and uses of breasts.

Demystifying and Appreciating the Ladies

How is it that we look at breasts so much but reflect on them so little? Mine had been hanging out under my nose for forty years before I began to contemplate their significance. While reflecting on the history of my own boobs, I decided to become a titty connoisseur. I started by reading all the scholarship I could find, and then I went in search of fresh insights by interviewing a broad range of professionals. After sixty formal interrogations, I had discovered five clusters of breast specialists with whom I resolved to spend more time. Together, these diverse experts offer a pentagon of wisdom about this elemental body part. I watched them work, gathered their insights, and explored how their environments impact the perceived worth of breasts. I discovered many fundamental and peculiar realities during what became a four-year research expedition.

Breasts are so misunderstood and underappreciated, so marginalized from histories of humanity and evolution, and so engulfed in male chauvinist myths that I need to share a few well-documented truths to clear our heads for the journey ahead.

Breasts feed

From an evolutionary perspective, the only purpose of breasts is to nourish newborns. The term "mammary gland" derives from the Latin word *mammae*, which means breast, sounds like "mama," and likely originated in baby talk. Before artificial breast milk substitutes, or "formulas," babies would die without access to human milk. In the past, if a mother died in childbirth, a volunteer allomother or hired wet nurse had to step in to feed the infant.

Breasts are at the root of our humanity

As *Homo sapiens*, we are distinguished from other animals by our sociality and complex array of communication skills. "Lactation turns out to be a key player in the evolution of animals who [are] both social and intelligent," affirms Sarah Blaffer Hrdy in her book *Mother Nature: Maternal Instincts and How They Shape the Human Species*.[6] Indeed, the dependence of human babies on their mother's milk for survival means that they develop neural networks related to the ability to love and be loved.

Breasts are primary

The notion that breasts are "secondary sexual characteristics," like facial hair, is flawed. Breasts are integral to human reproduction. As Cat Bohannon's *Eve: How the Female Body Drove 200 Million Years of Human Evolution* recounts, the first threat to a human life is dehydration, followed by infection. Breast milk averts both problems by being 90 percent maternally purified water with thousands of ingredients that bolster the immune system and the microbiome.[7] Without lactation, 200,000 years of human reproduction would not have happened. No breasts, no offspring.

Breasts are not universally erotic

Anthropological evidence makes clear that erotic attraction to breasts is culture-specific. In Indigenous communities in tropical climates where women wear no clothing above the waist and breastfeed openly, breasts belong to babies. Katherine Dettwyler, who did extensive ethnographic research in Mali, West Africa, discovered that both genders were "bemused" that an adult man might put his mouth on a woman's breast as a form of foreplay. They found it "unnatural" that adults were sexually attracted to women's breasts.[8]

The sexualized breast began life as a French perversion

The erotic breast developed alongside the popularity of wet-nursing in France during the Renaissance, about six hundred years ago. The delegation of breastfeeding to wet nurses enabled the aristocracy to have more children (lactation can suppress ovulation) and allowed a birthing mother's breasts to retain a more youthful shape. Unclaimed by infants, breasts could become the possession, fetish, and status symbol of husbands and lovers.

Starting in the 1500s, French kings commissioned paintings depicting the pristine, weightless breasts of the mistresses who had borne their children next to the heavy jugs of the wet nurses who fed them.[9] By the mid-1800s in Paris, the market in maternal milk had become a significant business wherein agencies helped shopkeepers and other urban *petit bourgeois* to place their babies with rural women who nursed for a fee.[10] In other European countries, wet-nursing ebbed and flowed with the political climate. To this day, French women are less likely to breastfeed than women from other nations, and Paris is still a leader in the seductive lacy lingerie business.[11]

Formula may have affected heterosexual foreplay

In the early twentieth century, momentum behind the eroticization of breasts started to globalize with the arrival of pasteurized formula delivered in glass bottles. With the rise of bottle-feeding, breastfeeding became *déclassé*, associated with families who couldn't afford to

Betty Grable's expensive legs.

buy breast milk substitutes. Curiously, the social echelons of formula bear a striking resemblance to the social stratification of sexualized breasts. The famous Kinsey report on *Sexual Behavior in the Human Male,* published in 1948, offers intriguing evidence. While 82 percent of college-educated men made "mouth contact" with their wife's breasts during foreplay, only 33 percent of men without high school diplomas did the same.[12] When lesbians were surveyed in a related report, a mere 24 percent reported caressing their partner's breasts, and yet 95 percent of this "female homosexual" group achieved orgasm—a much higher proportion than the women engaged in het-

Marilyn Monroe with her "bosom companions."

erosexual activity.[13] These data points suggest that breast-related sexual activity is a learned behavior of greater appeal to men.

Twentieth-century sexual fetishes moved from legs to breasts

In the first half of the twentieth century, legs were arguably the most eroticized part of a woman's body. After having been covered for centuries by floor-length skirts, the spectacle of legs had the power to arouse. Between 1942 and 1951, for example, Betty Grable was America's highest-paid actress and most popular sex symbol. She was so celebrated for her legs that 20th Century–Fox insured them for a million dollars. By 1953, a benchmark year in the sexualization of breasts, Marilyn Monroe had become Hollywood's premier bombshell,[14] starring in the immensely successful *Gentlemen Prefer Blondes* and appearing topless in the inaugural issue of *Playboy*. Within a few years, Monroe's bust was so famous that it was treated like her sidekick. In the poster for *Some Like It Hot*, the actress's nipples are at eye level with her costars, Tony Curtis and Jack Lemmon, who were promoted as "bosom companions."

Inflated busts were an American fashion from 1953 to 2007

While breasts are a resolute part of Western erotic life, the fifty-year arc of mainstream America's obsession with big breasts starts with the instant success of *Playboy* magazine in 1953 and runs through to the final episode of *Baywatch* in 2001, the television show that featured Pamela Anderson as a buxom blonde lifeguard. This period idealized supersized breasts in the same way that the porn industry valorized large penises. It glamorized and globalized the punchy sexualization of tits. Since 2007, surgical breast augmentations have declined.[15] While breasts continue to jiggle and bounce across our screens, they do so without the same energy or perverse thrill. Exactly how this relates to women's real embodiment today is a theme that runs through *Tits Up*.

Global beauty ideals are divergent

The late twentieth century saw a proliferation of ethnocentric attempts by male scholars to transform this American craze for large, round breasts into an evolutionary "law of nature" applicable to all people at all times.[16] However, not only was this archetype of attractiveness unrelated to the reality of women's chests, it never prevailed in Africa. For instance, in Dogon wood carvings from Mali, the ideal consists of long, conical breasts. By contrast, the paradigm in much of Asia has been a flat chest, as is evident in the traditional clothing of both Japanese

The conical ideal of the
Dogon peoples.

Breast binding, an East Asian route to beauty.

geishas and Chinese noblewomen, which minimized curves through breast binding.[17] To the degree that the big round bust went global, it was perceived as an "Americanization" brought about by the influence of Hollywood.[18]

Most women don't appreciate their breasts

"Most American women hate their breasts," a designer of intimates and swimwear told me in an interview.[19] The statement is hyperbolic but also well informed. As a creator of garments that hug, hold, and adorn busts, she devours all available market research, attends focus groups of women talking about their breasts, analyzes customer product reviews, and scours lingerie-related social media daily. While "hate" is too strong a word, it is accurate to say that a majority of American women are dissatisfied with, indifferent to, or ambivalent about their breasts.[20] The over-sexualization of our chests would appear to inspire hypercritical focus or sullen dismissal in many women. Either way, the objectification of breasts has profound, if unconscious, subjective effect.[21]

Appreciation is about both understanding and increasing value. In these pages, I aim to shed light on breasts in ways that improve women's esteem for their torsos. That doesn't mean that every paragraph is a cheery rollick. As any good practitioner of narrative therapy will confirm, one has to identify negative perspectives in order to put them in the rearview mirror. If breasts are associated with weakness, these accounts may help readers to reframe them as sources of strength. At the very least, I trust that *Tits Up* will expand and deepen the stories we tell ourselves about our bodies. At its most ambitious, this book hopes to lift breasts out of disgrace and escort them into a realm of enlightened pride. Breasts are key emblems of femininity, so their status impacts women's overall status. In appreciating the value of women's top halves, *Tits Up* attempts to contribute to the continued ascent of women.

Speech Acts and Sites of Research

The expression "tits up" is American showbiz slang for "good luck," cried out by one woman to another as she goes on stage. "Tits up" reminds a sister to stand up, pull her shoulders back, and succeed. In *Mother Camp*, a landmark ethnography of 1960s gay culture, Esther Newton recounts that drag queens would say "tits up" to command a fellow performer to get into character before going on stage.[22] Since 2017, the phrase has been popularized by the Amazon Prime show *The Marvelous Mrs. Maisel*. In my old hometown of London, "tits up" means something has gone "belly up," like a lifeless fish floating in water. It's possible that the positive American meaning of "tits up" arose independently, a physical migration of "chin up," or it could be that theatrical people flipped the dead metaphor, making ironic use of the British idiom in the manner of "break a leg." To my British friends, I say, this book is part of a movement that predicts male supremacy will—eventually—go tits up.

The English language boasts over seven hundred expressions for female mammary glands, most of which are spoken by men.[23] In this book, I seek to reclaim a few words for women's top halves, shifting their connotations into more affirmative, woman-owned territory.[24] At first, the word "breast" may appear neutral. It is respectful, but also sterilized, medicalized, and privatized. It is associated with cancer and, to a lesser extent, infant nutrition.

While I was brought up using the colloquialism "boob," I now feel conflicted about it. The term has the virtue of being jovial and unthreatening, but it also suggests that breasts are foolish and embarrassing.[25] Booby prizes are for losers, and booby traps are for victims. When a television program is mindless, we refer to the boob tube. Also, "boob" skews white. The expression most commonly used among Black women in America is "titty," an affectionate term without explicit links to stupidity or disgrace.

"Tits" is the number-one word for breasts on the Internet. It's a man's word that I encourage women to use. Without reclaiming this sexualized slang, we have little hope of repossessing the body part. "Tits" may be immodest, but they are not inane or ill at ease. When uttered by women, "tits" can be out and proud—shame-free rather than shameless. For me, talking about "tits" is not just about word choice. It's a "speech act" with implied politics and hopeful cultural effects.

Each of the five chapters in *Tits Up: What Sex Workers, Milk Bankers, Plastic Surgeons, Bra Designers, and Witches Tell Us about Breasts* revolves around a different cluster of experts in a discrete milieu. The locations that serve as the hub of each chapter are, in order, a strip club, a human milk bank, a surgery center, an apparel prototype fit room, and a witches' restorative retreat in the California redwoods. Breasts have multiple meanings that depend on context and the jargon used in those different environments.

Chapter 1, "Hardworking Tits," is set in a "titty bar," where I explore the role of breasts in sex work. While sitting with strippers and watching their stage shows, I reflect on my interviews with prostitutes, digital madams or bookers, burlesque dancers, and sex-worker-rights activists. As professionals whose livelihood depends on the art of seduction, these performers are highly self-conscious about breasts and their effects. ("Prostitution is a performance in private," a self-declared "happy hooker" told me.[26]) In this world, tits are eroticized, monetized, and subject to à la carte menus. Moreover, sex workers often have raw, unfiltered interactions with their clients, so they hear comments and grapple with behavior that wives, girlfriends, sisters, and office coworkers do not encounter.

Chapter 2, "Lifesaving Jugs," focuses on breastfeeding and the oldest human milk bank in America. The chapter starts with a handful of high-capacity breast milk donors, whose largesse saves the lives of premature infants in neonatal intensive care units and improves the health of adopted babies and other infants whose parents cannot breastfeed.

Women with thousands of ounces of excess breast milk, whose daily lives are inundated with nursing and pumping, have much to say about breasts. Then I follow the milk to the bank, where it is pasteurized for distribution, to understand the banker's point of view. I also encounter a mammal-milk lawyer and a super successful lactation consultant. In this chapter, I reclaim the word "jugs" because it's a rare English example of slang that pays tribute to the primary function of breasts as purveyors of hydration and nourishment.[27]

Chapter 3, "Treasured Chests," investigates the perspectives of plastic surgeons. In America and internationally, over 90 percent of cosmetic surgery is performed on women, and breasts are the number one location for these elective surgeries.[28] Set in the operating room, the narrative arc of this chapter follows an explantation (implant removal) and breast lift (an upward-trending surgery), but it also considers how augmentations, reductions, reconstructions, upper body lifts, and trans top surgeries enhance people's sense of self. Along the way, it explores the changing philosophies and geometries that plastic surgeons use to make what they see as a beautiful boob.

Chapter 4, "Active Apexes," goes behind the scenes with bra designers, or "bra engineers," the fit models upon whom they sculpt their wares, and the lingerie models who display the garments in photographs. While looking at the concerns of designers of traditional "constructed" bras, sports bras, and swimwear, I consider the impact of dress reform on women's health and fitness. The word "nipple" is taboo in a corporate environment, so intimate and activewear designers use the term "apex." Indeed, censorship of the pointy summits of breasts is a primary function of bras. This leads me to ask exactly what is so offensive about women's nipples and to explore the relevance of "free the nipple" activism.

Finally, chapter 5, "Holy Mammaries," investigates the spiritual significance of breasts with body-positive nature worshippers and authorities from other religious traditions. Over a long weekend during summer solstice, I attended a pagan retreat where I participated in consciousness-raising sessions and eco-feminist rituals meant to improve the wellness of those assembled. The insights of these women, most of whom identify as witches, were generally evidence-based, influenced by their day jobs as therapists, nurse practitioners, and educators. As an art enthusiast, I was fascinated by their perspectives on matriarchal icons, such as the ancient Greek and Hindu goddesses, Buddhist bodhisattvas, and Christ's mother, Mary. I also found it easy to ally myself with their love of the wilderness, which includes a healthy reverence for the sacred wonder of their own unruly bodies.

Tits Up concentrates on real bodies in real time and space. It offers a grounded experience as an alternative to the breasts represented in the media. It also explores breasts from their owners' perspectives. We are engulfed in masculine views that rarely admit their gender-specific origin and masquerade as neutral. Margaret Miles, an interviewee who was the first woman to become a tenured professor in Harvard's Divinity School, was part of the 1980s battle for degrees in women's studies. As she told me, "At Harvard, they used to say, 'But we don't have a Men's Studies program,' and then we'd say, 'Excuse me, this whole damn place is a Men's Studies program!'"

Tits Up favors enriching, enabling stories. If someone wonders why my discussion of Christianity in "Holy Mammaries" avoids the story of Saint Agatha and the many other martyrs whose breasts were sliced off their living bodies as a form of torture, my response is that we are already served a daily diet of misogyny.[29] Adding to it, in my opinion, is good for neither our mental health nor our empowerment. Reporting on sexism and misogyny is essential, but repeating it like a mantra is not a strategy for change. I see optimism as a discipline and a self-fulfilling prophecy. So, if someone wonders why a book on boobs has no pornography chapter, my reply is clear. *Tits Up* investigates sex work in real life. It focuses on women's perspectives rather than the male gaze and seeks out unanticipated forms of feminine bodily autonomy.

True to my training as an ethnographer (a participant observer and in-depth interviewer in the anthropological tradition), I aim to be as open-minded and accepting as I can. First, judgment gets in the way of vigorous research. It clouds your vision and impedes understanding. It's hard to gather facts when you're tripping over your own opinions. Second, breasts are already entangled in moralizing webs related to taste. It is difficult to disentangle both visceral reactions and political convictions from biases related to class, race, ethnicity, and religion, not to mention one's position on sprawling spectrums of gender and sexuality. Finally, judgment shatters affiliations and factionalizes people. It inhibits the formation of a bigger, broader, more inclusive women's movement. In a plural world, it is naive to imagine that only one road leads to progress. I see many routes to better femme futures.[30] Indeed, the more groundbreaking and unpredictable paths we take, the better our chances of advancement.

The Top Half of Women's Liberation

Breasts have *not* been a key issue for the women's movement. When it comes to the female body, feminists have tended to focus on vaginas, wombs, and uteruses.[31] As symbols of both subordinate sexiness and the historic subservience of mothers, breasts have been disconcerting. They seemed to be visible obstacles to equality, associated with nature and nurture rather than reason and power. Victorian suffragists understood this intuitively. They hid their busts under diagonal banners inscribed with slogans like "Votes for Women."

When concern for women's rights was revived in the 1970s, feminists were fiercely antagonistic to any whiff of "essentialist" ideas that reduced women to their biological functions. As a result, motherhood and specifically breastfeeding were swept to the side. But the vast majority of the world's adult women are or will become mothers. As Vanessa Olorenshaw, the author of *Liberating Motherhood*, writes,

The suffragist uniform.

"There are three big things that women can do that men can't: create life, give birth, and breastfeed. We need to proclaim our power rather than be ashamed."[32]

Also relevant to the feminist discomfort with breasts is the fact that women's liberation has often been cast as freedom from an oppressive monolith called femininity. Although second-wave feminists occasionally admitted that femininity was a subtle aesthetic that could be creative and pleasurable, they ultimately saw it as false consciousness, "decorative and frivolous," and the "ultimate restriction on freedom of mind."[33] As trans feminist Julia Serano argues, this "anti-femininity tendency may represent the feminist movement's single greatest tactical error."[34]

In devaluing femininity, the women's movement inadvertently depreciated our bosoms. While noting that the sexual objectification of tits can be dehumanizing, many feminists yielded to patriarchal discourses that trivialize our chests. They brushed breasts aside as irrelevant to our emancipation. Even the symbolic tossing of bras in a "freedom trashcan" outside the Miss America pageant in 1968, which was reported in the media as "bra burning," was arguably more anti-bra than pro-boob.

Trans activism, however, has recently shifted the place of breasts and chests in definitions of gender. By de-emphasizing the sex we're assigned at birth, it rejects the gender-concluding function of genitalia.

Gender is ever more about self-presentation and the visible top halves of our bodies. This is one reason why "top surgery" is often the only surgery undergone by a trans man (whose physical destination is masculinity) and why trans women often delight in the burgeoning breasts that result from taking estrogen. Put another way, the hierarchy between so-called primary and secondary sexual characteristics is in the process of being overturned.

The old distinctions between physical "sex" and social "gender" are also being eroded as research into the human genome makes clear that the environment is embedded in our genes—nurture is inextricable from nature—and that biological sex is related to an anarchy of about sixty genes "scattered haphazardly throughout the genome."[35] Masculinity and femininity are increasingly understood as embodied expressions over which we only have so much conscious control. As Chase Strangio of the American Civil Liberties Union (ACLU) explained to me: "Sex and gender are not discrete in the sense that one is real, fixed, and related to body parts while the other is constructed, behavioral, and performative. They're both dynamic, contingent, and basically inseparable."[36]

Trans activists Laverne Cox and Chase Strangio.

I think this reappraisal of gender is a great opportunity for cis women—those who were assigned female at birth and still identify as women. I recently reread Kate Millett's 1970 classic, *Sexual Politics*. Millett doesn't pay much attention to breasts, but she comments usefully on the strategies of women's liberation. American feminists formally proposed women's suffrage in 1848 but were not enfranchised until 1920. The vote was "the red herring of the revolution—a wasteful drain on the energy of seventy years," writes Millett. "Because the opposition was so monolithic . . . the vote took on disproportionate importance. When the ballot was won, the feminist movement collapsed in what can only be described as exhaustion."[37] If they had spread their energies, fighting for things like better jobs, equal pay, and the criminalization of domestic violence, women would have improved their station more effectively and perhaps still have eventually gotten the vote. Millett's account makes me wonder: Was the vote to first-wave feminists what abortion has been to feminists since the 1970s? Given the Supreme Court's overturning of *Roe v. Wade*, it might be productive to think outside the box about bodily autonomy. I am confident that a collective effort to repossess and redefine breasts will have positive repercussions for women's liberation.

Tits Up explores beauty, health, respect, self-esteem, self-determination, humanness, and equality. I hope the book sheds light on breasts in ways that elevate their value, not just because I believe in some happy, shiny body positivity, but because these organs are emblematic of womanhood. Put another way, the status of breasts—not to mention tits, titties, jugs, racks, and apexes—is integral to women's social position. For as long as breasts are disparaged as silly boobs, we will remain the "second sex."

1

Hardworking Tits

The bouncer at the Condor Club, a historic titty bar, welcomes me with a hug. A sentinel with a good memory for regulars, he nods to the cashier to waive my cover charge. Inside, four strippers sit around the edges of the otherwise empty room. Two peer through giant false eyelashes at their phones. One dancer, eyes closed, indulges in a seated power nap. The fourth has glow-in-the-dark acrylic nails wrapped around an old-fashioned glass. Her jaded demeanor suggests that she would be an expert on the subject I'm here to investigate—the role of breasts in sex work.

Back in 1964, Carol Doda, an outgoing waitress, shocked patrons by wearing only a bikini bottom while she did the Twist and the Swim. She didn't strip or tease; her completely bare breasts swung in time to rock 'n' roll. By these means, the Condor launched a "nationwide craze" of nonchalant toplessness, a revolution in commercial entertainment that put precious burlesque out of business.[1] Nowadays, the venue is owned by Déjà Vu, the largest strip club operator in the world, with major real estate holdings in red-light districts all over the United States.[2]

DJ Bling interrupts his playlist of hip-hop tracks about sex, drugs, and wealth to announce, "Barbie, up next. Barbie!" This part of the multiroom club is arranged like a cabaret, with large booths lining the walls and cocktail tables next to the mirror-backed stage. The track lighting glows red—a hue said to flatter skin of all colors.

Barbie emerges from an area at the back of the club lined with cubicles for private lap dances.[3] With long blond hair and a pink bikini, she teeters on her 8-inch-high Pleaser platforms. During the course of my investigation into the public performance of breasts, Barbie has become a key informant. She walks around the pole, swishing her recently fitted hair extensions. Her "hairography," as dancers call it, moves to the beat of a rap track about marijuana, guns, and "banging." "The music is like white noise to me," she explained in an interview earlier. "When I notice the lyrics—'bitches sucking dick' or whatever—I remind myself that the music is a part of the game we use for our benefit. It helps create a space that builds men up and when they feel powerful, they spend money."

At twenty-nine, Barbie is one of the oldest entertainers here, but she evinces unfettered innocence. More of an actress than a dancer, she moves through a series of poses, or "tableau images," as she calls them. Her favorite movie is the 1998 spoof-horror flick *Bride of Chucky*, whose heroine is a murderous doll. "I've always enjoyed performing the doll," she said. "I like that uncanny feeling. You're perfect and beautiful, but also cold and scary."

A typical stripper set consists of two or three songs; only the final one is topless. Barbie hugs the pole with her buttocks, arches her back, then slithers into the splits. With a quick swivel, she is in a V-shape, looking through her legs at three lone men, recent arrivals, sitting in an unlit area favored by aloof voyeurs. Serenely, she attempts to make eye contact with each of them individually. One man squirms and looks away. Another decides it's time to check his text messages. Only the third, who wears a yellow Golden State Warriors baseball cap, rises to the challenge of her gaze, locking into an ocular exchange that might lead to a transaction. Feminist theories of the male gaze emerged from film studies, not live performances where the women on stage could actually stare back.[4] "Eye contact makes both of us more vulnerable," Barbie told me. "Most customers think of us as objects, so when we focus on them, they're confronted with our humanity."

When Barbie turns away from her prey, she looks at me out of the corner of her eye with a conspiratorial grin. Barbie was homeschooled by her mother, a Wiccan or modern pagan, who raised her to be wary

Barbie, a "domme disguised as a sub."

of men. "Don't trust them; train them," she told her daughter. Barbie describes her mother as a "misandrist" (misandry, I learned after
looking it up, is the hatred of men, the inverse of misogyny). A self-
declared "intersectional feminist," Barbie disdains Sex Worker Exclusionary Radical Feminists, also known as SWERFs.[5] Barbie is clever but
pretends she has "boobs for brains," as she put it. She also enjoys being
sexually dominant while masquerading as submissive; in stripper slang,
she's a "domme disguised as a sub." The media cliché of a dominatrix
is a goth in black leather with dyed black hair. By contrast, Barbie's
dream-domme look is a life-sized version of the Mattel plastic figure
wearing pink and white latex with a glittering whacking paddle.

Barbie's admirer in the baseball cap moves to a seat within tipping
distance of the stage. When she turns her gaze toward him, he starts
sprinkling her with single one-dollar bills, then throws a wad into the
air to "make it rain." She rewards him by crawling catlike in his direction. The macro-political world of the strip club favors an explicit style

of male supremacy, but individual strippers exploit every ounce of their interpersonal micro-power to game the system and extract from it what they can.[6]

Strippers, as professional manipulators of male desire, are acutely aware of the dynamics of patriarchy. Sitting here, I've come to respect their position on the frontline, observing their shrewd navigation of the global gender war. In the past, I might have assumed that they pandered to patriarchy, but I've come to see this perspective as prudish and thoughtlessly classist. A professor friend who visited the Condor once told me that she found the scene to be "revolting." My riposte was blunt: disgust is a privilege. Worse still, it gets in the way of building a feistier political movement that is in touch with the socioeconomic ground upon which all sorts of women walk and march in protest.[7]

Barbie's third track is "Candy Shop," a mid-tempo classic by 50 Cent about a brothel. Barbie turns around to show her fingers unhooking the clasp of her top in the middle of her back. She drops the garment unceremoniously, then swirls to offer up her small, shapely tits. In this environment, the revelation of nakedness stimulates desire and suggests availability. As such, the strip is integral to marketing the lap dances, which I've learned are the night's main moneymakers. Lap dances evolved out of the practice of dancers sitting on patrons' laps, grinding and "dry-humping" for extra tips. In the 1990s, the custom became a formal part of many strip clubs' business models. However, in some American cities, lap dances are regarded as prostitution and outlawed.

Barbie keeps detailed spreadsheets of her strip club earnings. She also works two daytime jobs: one designing and selling circus apparel, the other as a nanny. The latter surprised me, as strippers have a reputation for being proudly undomesticated, resistant to the tedium of being a housewife. When I asked her about being a nanny *and* a stripper, Barbie said, "They're not as different as you think. Drunk men are children."

o o

As I ponder the linguistic parallels between baby/sitting and lap/danc-
ing, RedBone sashays through the Condor's front door.[8] A dancer
with twenty-five years of experience in the sex industry, RedBone has
agreed to help me as an expert observer (see image on page 29). The
term "RedBone" is slang for a light-skinned African American. In high
school, a cute boy once hollered, "Hey, RedBone, you're beautiful." The
positive reception stuck with her, so she chose it as a stage name and
rhetorical bulletproof vest. "It made me feel sexy, coveted, and more
confident about performing solo on stage," she explains.

RedBone is wearing a lumberjack plaid coat, no makeup. You would
never guess that this shy tomboy was the reigning Princess of the Burlesque Hall of Fame, where her sparkling on-stage persona is, as she
puts it, "high femme, a little rough."[9] For her winning performance
in Las Vegas, RedBone danced to "Jungle Fever" by the Chakachas, a
global 1970s jazz-funk hit banned by the BBC due to its heavy breathing and moaning. Wearing a sequined dress with a peekaboo opening
that drew attention to her cleavage, she performed an elaborate strip
wherein she eventually swung her bikini top over her head like a lasso
before casting it aside and shimmying in turquoise pasties. Her tits
were always on the move, too active to be demystified.

In this nocturnal world, "tits" is a technical term for an eroticized
and monetized body part. A thousand-year-old variant on "teats" that
could derive from the ancient Proto-Indo-European *tata*, "tits" was
well-established lusty slang by the time burlesque and other "tits and
ass" entertainments proliferated in the early twentieth century.[10] Nowadays, the word is integral to navigating porn sites and erotic services.[11]
Although used more often by men, "tits" is on the upswing among
women. It is deployed by sex workers in an effort to claim ownership
of their top half in the jargon of their trade.[12] It is also fashionable
among teenage girls fond of rap music, who also talk about "titties" and

"yitties."[13] Although I initially found it awkward to utter "tits" in polite company, I now love the odd sense of empowerment I experience when I use the word. It thwarts puritanical taboos and embraces sexual freedoms. When women proud of their own tits say it aloud, it is not demeaning. It's a symbolic strategy that insists on repossessing a body part.

Sex work looms large in RedBone's life. At sixteen, she worked as a receptionist at Private Pleasures, a phone-sex business owned and operated by her mother. When she turned eighteen, she began taking the calls, keeping notecards on customers' desires and fetishes. She used a separate landline installed in her basement bedroom to play the role of a busty blonde named April for four formative years. "I was whoever I needed to be to make money," she explains, as if it were the most ordinary initiation into adulthood. "It was the era of *Baywatch*; Pamela Anderson was *the* sex symbol."

Having worked in various topless clubs in Minneapolis, Reno, Las Vegas, and San Francisco, RedBone jokes that she was "the best worst stripper." She loved her stage sets but found lap-dance sales—not the lap dances themselves—to be draining. "It was unpredictable and emotionally jostling," she explains, "because I never developed my armor for rejection, and found it hard to keep my spirits up."

o o

Patrons continue to trickle into the Condor. In a large booth, a white guy sits with four young women sporting turtlenecks and ponytails. They look like they just came from a casting call for the-nice-gal-at-the-office, except they are senselessly stoned. A Black couple canoodle in the dark while a pair of queer Latinas sit in brighter light. Four drunk men sit at a round table near the stage. One staggers up to tuck some bills into the dancer's thong, then dismisses her with a gentle spank.

In a digital world where human interaction is increasingly mediated by screens, the Condor engages our eight main senses. Friendly slaps on bare buttocks are not allowed but not uncommon. However, touching a dancer's tits on stage can cause great offense. Last week, I saw a customer cop a quick feel of a dancer's breasts. She made him pay by forcefully pushing him back into his chair with one hand and snatching his stack of cash with the other.[14]

The audience at the Condor contains more women than most strip clubs around here because the go-go-ing Carol Doda made the venue a tourist destination. Both the crowd and the dancers are also more racially diverse. Barbie is the only non-Latinx white girl working tonight, although she is not the only blonde. Melonie, a Pacific Islander, has blond highlights, while Nadia, a Black woman with three kids, wears a blond wig. Body types are also varied. Some have thick thighs, flat asses with cellulite, or less-than-perky breasts. Extra-large fake tits are notably scarce.

I ask RedBone if she saw that Jo "Boobs" Weldon is celebrating the thirtieth anniversary of her breast augmentation on Instagram. Weldon is a burlesque dancer and sex-worker-rights activist, the author of *The Burlesque Handbook*, and a scholar in residence at the New York Public Library exploring the history of sex worker clothing. In 1992, for her thirtieth birthday, she gifted herself double-Ds and she has loved them ever since. A former stripper and prostitute, Weldon lived through attacks from anti-pornography, anti-prostitute feminists and still feels wounded by the way that segment of the women's movement "infantilized" sex workers and stripped them of their agency. Indeed, well-meaning feminists still confuse consensual *sex work*, where adults willingly sell sex to make money, with *sex trafficking*, where people are prostituted against their will through abduction, threats, and other forms of coercion. As one activist put it, "Sex trafficking is to sex work what domestic violence is to marriage . . . not all wives are victims, and neither are all sex workers."[15]

"Doctor Boobs Weldon—I've always wanted to call her that," says RedBone. "I'm in awe of her tenacity. The way she pulls the whole history of sex work into her performances is cool as fuck."

Jo Weldon celebrates the thirtieth anniversary of her implants.

Weldon is a wellspring of fake boob stories. Back in the 1990s, when she worked at the Cheetah in Atlanta, Georgia, they used to do "boob smashes" or "stripper high-fives," wherein the dancers would jump and bounce off each other's inflated chests. Weldon relished the extra attention she received with bigger tits. Occasionally men would stare at her breasts and then inquire, "Are those real?" to which Weldon would reply, "Well, they're not imaginary!"

When working as a call girl, Weldon would wear athleisure outfits and tell hotel security she was a personal trainer. Having made it upstairs, she was once turned away from a hotel room by a john who was angry that she had implants. "Men who prefer natural breasts like to think that they are superior," Weldon told me. "They believe that their taste in women is a reflection of their intellect. When they declare, 'I'm a leg man,' what they're really saying is, 'I'm not a brainless moron.' But I'm like, 'Dude, you're no different, you're focusing on a body part instead of a whole human being.'"

In the 1990s, Weldon's creativity as a stripper led her to embrace burlesque and help revive the genre. "Burlesque" derives from the Italian word for mockery; after migrating through French, the term came to designate the sexy, tongue-in-cheek performances included in vaudeville shows and traveling circuses. These dance routines were characterized by elaborate costumes and mischievous undressing narratives that climaxed in "the big reveal" of the breasts. When many strip clubs went all-nude, featuring little or no disrobing, a "neo-burlesque" circuit arose, touring alternative theaters, comedy clubs, and queer bars.[16]

As the "headmistress" of the New York School of Burlesque, Weldon is adept at labeling and analyzing the impact of different tit-related dance moves. The "strap tease," as she calls it, uses the bra or bikini strap to build excitement. "If you're standing still, and only one part of your body is moving, that's where people will look. If you shrug, they look at your shoulder. If you stomp, they notice your foot," explained Weldon. Cupping your breasts with your hands is another way to acknowledge the gaze and give permission for people to savor your body. Consequently, Weldon sees pasties, the adhesive covers meant to censor nipples, as "boob jewelry that actually accentuates them."

The soundtrack at the Condor switches abruptly from hip-hop to Mötley Crüe's 1987 heavy-metal stripper anthem "Girls, Girls, Girls," redirecting our attention to the stage. The nine working women line up, then parade across the platform while the DJ announces a discount on lap dances—"Three songs for the price of two!" Even though I've seen the procession on many other occasions, it's a shocking sight that smacks of flesh on the auction block. As an ethnographer, I love immersive, experiential learning. Lame ethnographers come into a new environment with opinions that they stick to, whereas decent ethnographers are altered by the communities they study. Sometimes it takes all my willpower to stay curious and resist judgment. At this moment, I'm struggling. I abhor this dehumanizing spectacle.

∘ ∘

Neo-burlesque is a significant counterpoint to stripping. A witty form in which tits reign supreme, neo-burlesque often spoofs submission and features empowered women who have a range of older, larger, queerer, less conventionally sexy bodies. Last month, I attended a Dita Von Teese Burlesque Gala at the Orpheum Theater in downtown Los Angeles. The theater held some fifteen hundred people—at least two-thirds of whom were female or femme-presenting, many in cleavage-showcasing vintage dresses. The population conspicuous by their absence was the one that dominates strip clubs—individual and roving packs of heterosexual men.

Performing that night was a voluptuous dancer, famed for her talented tits. At five foot four and 195 pounds, Dirty Martini was introduced as "Miss 44 and a whole lot more."[17] The dancer went on to demonstrate "the world's most dangerous tassel-twirling tricks" to the high-speed surf-guitar of Dick Dale's "Misirlou." She whipped the long fringes of her pasties clockwise, then counterclockwise She twirled one titty while the other stood still. She bounced with her arms above her head, then wagged her tits in a vigorous shimmy. The whirling spectacle was nothing like strip club routines, where it is rare to see breasts move more actively than other body parts. In straight-male-dominated venues, sexiness and funniness are generally opposed. When women predominate, eroticism and satire go hand in hand.

Dirty, as her friends call her, is a sex symbol whose triumph has been hard-won. In the beginning, she struggled to make it through her BFA at the Conservatory of Dance in Purchase, New York, because she was repeatedly put on "weight probation." Worried she'd get kicked out of school, she told her teachers, "Forget it. This is my body. I might lose five pounds; I might gain ten; it's none of your business." Dirty's resistance to her profession's body norms was a powerful moment in her self-definition as a dancer. "A long-ass time ago," as she put it, Dirty also considered working in strip clubs but rejected it because she wanted to "keep a healthy eye" on her emotional state. She couldn't face the intimate interaction and so opted for burlesque. "I don't give lap dances and I suppose that's where the line gets drawn," she explained. "Instead, I recreate the sex work of the nostalgic past."

Burlesque appealed to Dirty because it honored her curves and her dance training, which started with childhood ballet. She had done naked dance productions, so nudity wasn't a concern. "What did Gypsy Rose Lee say?" asked Dirty, before answering, "I wasn't naked. I was completely covered by a blue spotlight." Dirty often works in gay clubs, and her big blond wigs and over-the-top makeup reflect drag's aesthetic sensibility. Indeed, Amanda Lepore, a Marilyn Monroe–inspired doyenne of New York nightlife, taught her how to apply pasties with tassels. "I've always gotten glamour tips from drag queens and thought their humor was in line with my own," she told me. "Some cross the line into misogyny, but the queens who are my friends inspire me to be a better woman."

Dirty sees her breasts as "a gateway drug to body positivity." As a plus-sized woman, she has relied on them as a "safe haven" when the rest of her body was seen as "controversial or naughty." When people work up a burlesque routine, they have to grapple with themselves as gendered, sexual beings. "Much of that is centered around your breasts," Dirty told me. "Or your solar plexus—the chest plate that reflects sunlight onto your face. That's the beauty of showing your breasts to the world."

o o

Back at the Condor, RedBone picks an unsmoked joint off the floor. "Look what I found," she says. Although now sober, RedBone spent many years as a "party girl." Liquid courage and brain-numbing drugs are integral to the ecologies of strip clubs. RedBone signals a passing waitress and places the legal weed on her tray. The waitress startles, then grins broadly, revealing her braces. Although patrons have to be twenty-one years old to enter the club, strippers and servers need only be eighteen—a gendered disparity that boggles my mind.

RedBone and I have been studying the moves of Paradise, a skinny but shapely young Black woman, now on stage with her booty bopping in the direction of a trio of recently arrived tech bros.

Would "titty bars" be more accurately called "butt clubs"? I wonder. If we clocked the time dancers spend flaunting their tits versus their asses, I'm certain buttocks would win. The reasons offered for the shift of focus from boobs to buttocks include the popularity of Kim Kardashian, the celebration of Black booties in rap music, the veneration of strong glutes by gay men, and the influence of athleticism on visions of feminine beauty and sex appeal. However, I ask RedBone the question that most interests me: Is the focus on butts more objectifying? When you fixate on a woman's tits, you can still see her face. Her subjectivity is harder to ignore.[18]

RedBone looks at me pensively. "Don't know, but my posture changed when you asked that. I felt, like, it's time to open up," she says. "The chest is where our heart is. Consciously or subconsciously, presenting the breasts, it's saying 'I'm ready. I'm listening. I'm allowing vulnerability.' Posture is important because it changes the way we feel, then strikes all sorts of feelings within the viewer. It communicates."

I'm an inveterate sloucher, I confess as I straighten up, cup Bert and Ernie, and recall an interview I did with a sex coach who gives workshops on "schlumpy versus sexy" body language.[19]

"I slump when no one is watching," admits RedBone. "When a voyeur gazes upon me, I carry myself differently." About her 36C bust, she declares, "I never knock the knockers! I love these bad boys. Got 'em from my Mama."

Strip clubs offer the promise of being more than just a voyeur. A few months ago, I unexpectedly "motorboated" a dancer at Larry Flynt's Hustler Club around the corner. It was fantastic, I tell RedBone with an embarrassed grin. In that club, you can sit right up at the dance floor as if it were a table. One of my straight male friends, a strip club aficionado, threw some money down and said, "Give it to her!" The dancer grabbed my chair, drew it toward her, then pulled my head between her tits and shook them. I did not make the lip-vibrating sound of a motorboat (the origin of the maneuver's name), but I got the gist of it. When you're so close to someone, you instinctively close your eyes, and the encounter shifts. What had been a detached, visual experience became a corporeal, sensual one. I enjoyed the warmth of her bosom on my cheeks and the fresh, powdery scent of her perfume. It didn't feel dirty or sexual, but human and funny. It was pleasantly bewildering.

Then, at the Garden of Eden, another strip club nearby, my friend once again threw down some money and said, "Give it to her." This time, the dancer grabbed my hands, pulled them to her breasts, and held them there. Her nipples pressed into the palms of my hands, which I found stressful. With the motorboating, I was rendered passive by a dancer who assumed playful control, but with this move I felt forced into a predatory position in which I was supposed to act.

In both instances, the dancers were violating official club policy, but as I am a woman, the rules around touching in public areas did not apply. Creative circumventions of local alcohol licensing laws are found in clubs all over the world to the degree that peculiar titty entertainment genres develop. In some cities, for example, strip clubs have a "body shot" waitress, who climbs onto the customer's lap and then places a long glass or test tube between her tits to deliver liquor into the patron's mouth. In private rooms, another popular diversion is the "titty bump," wherein people snort cocaine off a sex worker's bosom.

One of my interviewees, whose job consisted entirely of offering body shots and titty bumps, told me that her work was primarily about compassion for lonely men.

While I mull over the role of tits in a dizzying array of sexual services and erotic party tricks, RedBone offers a delayed response to my query about titty bars. "I think breasts come into play in more intimate settings, like during lap dances in the private rooms."

I confess that I've never had a lap dance.

RedBone looks at me incredulously. "You can't understand this," she says, raising her palm toward the stage and then wafting it over the crowd, "without having had one. A lap dance is a situationship. It's a relationship in a few songs. You have moments of awkwardness and connectivity, and then you break up."

o o

Tits are central to Annie Sprinkle's oeuvre as a prostitute, porn star, photographer, and performance artist. When she was a full-service sex worker, between the ages of eighteen and forty, she understood that her "big naturals" were "sex toys or objects of worship and healing." In addition to offering the classic "titty fuck" (wherein ejaculation results from cleavage frottage), she would dangle her nipples on her clients' eyes, over their faces, and in their ears. "Smothering was also a thing, smothering people with boobage," she told me. "Breasts are the heart to me. I was a whore with a heart of gold. I didn't go for the young jocks. I went for wounded war vets, elders, people who needed love."

When I visited the sixty-seven-year-old Sprinkle at home one afternoon before an evening foray to the Condor, her dyed auburn hair was crowned with an ostrich-feather hairpiece called a fascinator. She wore bright blue eyeshadow and presented a generous helping of cleavage. "Boobs make people smile," she explained. "Whenever I cover up, people's faces drop. They're so disappointed!" Satire is never far away from Sprinkle's sincerity. A self-declared "multimedia whore," she lives to entertain in all senses of the word: to amuse, receive guests, and mull over ideas.

Shortly after my arrival, as a mark of her hospitality, Sprinkle suggested that we take a "Tits on the Head" photo. Back in the 1990s, when she was touring her one-woman show *Post-Porn Modernist*, she made extra money during intermissions by placing her bare boobs on top of audience members' heads.[20] Hundreds, if not thousands, of Polaroids later, this series records thirty years of madcap human interaction. While I was seated at the kitchen table, Sprinkle stood up and pulled her large breasts out of her leopard-print blouse.

"Old naked tits are way more radical than young tits," said Sprinkle with a mischievous grin before walking behind me and placing one, then the other knocker on my head. They weighed a ton. The word "gravitas" sprang to mind.

"Annie has the friendliest boobs in the world," said Sprinkle's wife and artistic partner, Beth Stephens, as she took a dozen snapshots with my iPhone. "They're renowned, but they're sensitive. They have to be in the right mood for fun."

My tits-on-head experience was dizzying and oddly monumental, like engaging with a Rubens painting brought to life or one of de Kooning's women in 3D. After studying other people's photos, I realized I was not alone. The array of glee, bewilderment, mirth, and disorientation displayed on participants' faces was remarkable. The unexpected power of the work stems from the insight that, as Sprinkle explained, "Laughter and orgasm both relieve tension."

Sprinkle's wife, a cuddly butch-dyke professor, contrasts with one of the artist's first boyfriends, Gerard Damiano, the director of *Deep Throat*. The 1972 movie broke porn box-office records and was the subject of obscenity trials all over America. That year, when she was just eighteen, Sprinkle and Damiano made a trip to San Francisco, where they saw Carol Doda dance topless at the Condor. Sprinkle was mesmerized by Doda's hybrid performance style. "She blew my mind," said

Sprinkle. "I was like, wow, you can dance, and be funny, and have these huge knockers, and get arrested. Doda was an important person to me—an inspiration for sure." Shortly after this, Sprinkle abandoned her original name, Ellen Steinberg, a "nice Jewish girl" with left-wing parents, to become Annie Sprinkle, a liberated woman who is "sexy and fearless."

Sprinkle has devoted her life to the exploration of sexuality. "My body is my research laboratory," she explained. "Being in our culture, you grow up sex-negative, but I saw sex as a great mystery. I wanted to learn everything about it. It was like, oh, this would be fun. Let's try this. Let's experiment."

After a decade of in-person and cinematic sex work, Sprinkle shifted her primary activities into the vanguard art world. The transition was easy. As Sprinkle explained, "Prostitution is a performance in private . . . and sometimes even performance art." One of her most celebrated pieces, *Bosom Ballet*, started out as a performance in the 1970s and was translated into a series of photographs for a class assignment at New York's School of Visual Arts in the 1980s. Wearing long black gloves, Sprinkle moved, pinched, squeezed, and twisted her breasts in time to Johann Strauss's "Blue Danube" waltz.[21] Captured in video and black-and-white photographs, the witty choreography transforms her tits into dancers in a way that speaks to surrealists such as Man Ray and feminists like Eleanor Antin. Compared with other live performances, such as Sprinkle's infamous *Public Cervix Announcement*, the piece is tastefully PG-13. "For over twenty years, I performed *Bosom Ballet* as the climax to my visiting lecture at art colleges," said Sprinkle. "Now I wouldn't dream of it, because I don't want the drama. These days bare boobs on campus might trigger trauma. I love drama, but not with students!"

A fan of "boobacious" performance, Sprinkle also created burlesque-inspired *Strip Speak* routines in which she portrayed characters such as Nurse Sprinkle, a well-intentioned sex educator whose lesson was rather too explicit.[22] "As a porn star, I could go on the road as a headliner and

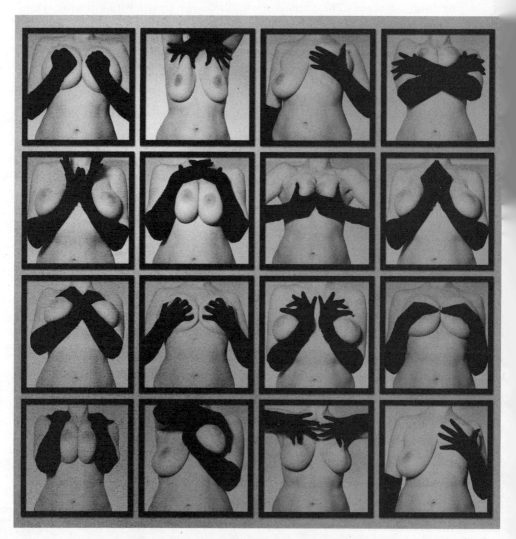

Sprinkle performs *Bosom Ballet* to the "Blue Danube" waltz.

tour strip clubs, even though I couldn't dance," explained Sprinkle. "I'd strut on stage and then do a demonstration using my own body. 'These are the tits, and this is a nipple,' I'd say. 'Who here wants to suck my nipple? A nipple can bring lots of pleasure to both the sucker and suckee.' And then someone would come up from the audience."

Strip Speak was a hybrid genre: part storytelling, part live sex show, part performance art.[23] The title of the piece exposes a social rule: those who strip do not speak. Indeed, nude stage performers are mimes, who must transgress convention if they want to make their voices heard.

A "wannabe painter," Sprinkle delighted in using her breasts as brushes to make *Tit Prints*. Body prints are a hallowed modern art tradition. Sprinkle's prints respond to Yves Klein's 1960s *Anthropometries*, wherein the artist dipped women into his "International Klein Blue" paint, and Ana Mendieta's 1970s *Glass on Body Imprint* self-portraits. "I saw my *Tit Prints* as an extension of my sex work and made hundreds of them," Sprinkle told me. By these means, her prints shift the meaning of promiscuity, making it a synonym for productivity and munificence.

Sprinkle has campaigned for years for the decriminalization of sex work. "Some sex workers think I'm bad for the movement, because I admitted to having orgasms with my clients," she said. "That's a very unpopular thing to say nowadays." Sprinkle was part of the "happy hooker" generation, who wanted it known that most sex professionals were not sad victims. "I was enormously privileged—a white fool-child in a supportive family. Some of us were in it for the money or drugs, or to heal our sexual abuse, but I was into sex work for the creativity."[24]

Sprinkle sees herself as a "pleasure activist." She first heard the term in the 1980s from a friend whose drag alter ego was Peggy L'Eggs, and assumed the idea emerged from gay male subculture because it had "the hottest porn, the kinkiest clubs, and the hanky codes."[25] Sprinkle popularized the expression in various stage appearances, then used it for her *Pleasure Activist Playing Cards*, published in 1995. The deck consists of fifty-four photographic pinup portraits that Sprinkle made of sex workers, lauded variously as "lap dancing luminary," "cybersex pioneer," and "Zen Buddhist nudist." In the booklet that accompanies the deck, Sprinkle asserts: "Pleasure activists represent an important, often under-appreciated, faction of the feminist movement. They're on the frontlines, committed to making a safer, more satisfying world for women . . . They dare to pioneer erotic frontiers . . . giving love and pleasure, evoking ecstasy and orgasm."[26]

After years of titty-centric sex work and art, Sprinkle's breasts are so famously sex-positive that a witch with her own apothecary made a special tincture for "magic breast wishes" from water in which Sprinkle's bosom had been ritually immersed.[27] The elixir evokes one of the artist's favorite adages: "It's not the size of your tits that counts, it's how you use them."

○ ○

As my investigation into hardworking tits progressed, it became evident that emancipating breasts would require progress on a body autonomy issue avoided by most reproductive rights campaigners—the decriminalization of sex work. So, a few afternoons after visiting Sprinkle, I sought out Carol Leigh, aka Scarlot Harlot, the prostitute and poet who coined the term "sex work."[28] When I visited Leigh at home, she had wispy, post-chemo hair, dyed orangey red. She had battled endometrial and ovarian cancer for six years, and the interview may have been the last before her death.[29] Boxes of old papers, which had been acquired by Harvard University's Schlesinger Library, punctuated several rooms, awaiting shipment to the East Coast. Over dark chocolates, we discussed the politics of language and how breasts featured in her art and activism.

From the 1970s to the 1990s, Leigh's main income came from prostitution. She never worked out of the Condor (although she knew women who did), preferring to be part of an unofficial network of "call girls" who set up appointments via the telephone. Her sizable breasts were an asset—a key reason why clients picked her. "They were pretty—saggy or not. In those days, perky wasn't the most important thing, because prostitutes weren't yet having boob jobs," she said with a tired sigh.

Like Sprinkle, Leigh was the daughter of Jewish socialists who prized nonconformity. But her route into the sex business was less sensual and more literary. She was captivated by the "sacred whores" mentioned in the Old Testament, who worked in the pagan temples before the arrival of monotheism. (These biblical references are the reason why prostitution is often proclaimed the "oldest profession in the world."[30]) She was also attracted to a strain of libertine feminism that celebrated "working girls" as brave forerunners of women's independence.[31] Before the introduction of the spinning wheel in the thirteenth century, which provided the opportunity to be a "spinster," European women had three main routes to economic survival: becoming a wife, nun, or prostitute.[32] While sex work is as old as the written word, the prevalence of prostitution rose dramatically alongside industrialization, urbanization, and migration.[33] When Leigh left graduate school in 1975, wondering what to do with an MA in poetry, she encountered a growth industry with surging demand that paid well and gave her something to write about.

As Leigh explored harlotry, she thought deeply about its stigmas. Like her gay and lesbian friends, she wanted to be free of shame, perhaps even out and proud, or at least "proud that I'm not ashamed."[34] Influenced by Robin Lakoff's 1975 book *Language and Woman's Place*, she also believed in the power of words to win political battles. She first came up with the term "sex work" while attending a workshop about the "sex use industry." She complained that the word "use" deprived women of their agency and recommended substituting "sex work industry." The shrewd linguistic tactic is not a euphemism. It helps detach prostitution from promiscuity, sin, and crime. Sex work can then be seen as a form of labor, which requires basic human rights protections like occupational safety and nondiscrimination.[35]

The new label was adopted by the world's first activist organization dedicated to decriminalizing prostitution—COYOTE, an acronym for "Call Off Your Old Tired Ethics." Its codirector, Priscilla Alexander, was instrumental in popularizing the term by publishing an anthology titled *Sex Work* and by taking the concept to her positions at the National Task Force on Prostitution and the World Health Organization (WHO).[36] Alexander had never been a sex worker but experienced slut-shaming after attending a women's college whose coed dorms led to media speculation about promiscuity.[37] Her mission was clear: "Women are stigmatized for being sexual. So long as women can be denounced as whores, there will be no equality."[38]

The decriminalization movement has grown substantially from its birth in San Francisco to victories in New Zealand and Belgium.[39] Recommended by WHO, Amnesty International, and Human Rights Watch, "decrim," as activists call it, should not be confused with legalization. In certain counties in Nevada, for example, legalization resembles state-regulated pimping, creating an environment where organized crime persists. Few female sex workers can afford the brothel licenses that cost $100,000 to $200,000 a year, and 90 percent of the prostitution in Nevada is still illicit. (Contrary to popular belief, prostitution is *not* legal in Las Vegas.) In Britain and many other European countries, prostitution itself is legal, but surrounded by a web of crimes including soliciting in public, pimping, and managing a brothel.

Decriminalization also contrasts with the "End Demand" model, adopted in Sweden and Canada, which punishes only the clients of sex workers. Unfortunately, when buying sex is illegal, the sellers of sex are driven underground into positions that compromise their health and safety. The other flaw in "End Demand" is the delusion that it can eradicate the oldest profession in the world. In a hyper-capitalist world in which we can watch paid actors having intercourse in porn movies, where we can buy sperm and outsource pregnancies to surrogates, it is perverse to outlaw prostitution.

Like most second-wave feminists, Leigh did not reflect upon or write much about her breasts. "I must have used 'tits' when I was talking dirty," she told me. "But it never became a push-button word like pussy, cunt, vulva, snatch, or twat." Keen for the perspective of a pioneering wordsmith, I explained my take on "tits" as a male-dominated, sexualized, and often monetized version of breasts. When women use it, one can sometimes hear the quotation marks. With consistent use, I hope we can reclaim some ownership of our sexy top halves. Whatever the case, I'm tired of the way "boobs" implies that breasts are fatuous and trivial. At least, tits are titillating.

"We need all the words," agreed Leigh with a nod, "and 'tits' is an important one."

Vintage photographs reveal that Leigh was an early champion of topless protests.[40] When performing "the prostitute" before the camera, she regularly posed with bare breasts. At street demonstrations and feminist conferences, performing as Scarlot Harlot, she also exposed her torso, framing it with a feather boa and placards bearing slogans such as "Keep Your Laws Off My Body," "Be Nice to Prostitutes," and "Sluts Unite."

As it happens, exposed breasts are integral to the history of sex work. Brandishing the bosom has long been both a form of solicitation and a reassuring advertisement for other anatomy-based services. The Latin root of the word "prostitute" means "exposed publicly, offered for sale," a meaning that commemorates the gender-authenticating significance of tits. In the sixteenth century, for instance, a bridge in Venice acquired the name Ponte delle Tette, or "Bridge of the Tits." The doge, also known as His Serenity, an aristocrat elected for life to act as the city-state's chief magistrate, encouraged "ladies of the night" to exhibit and even illuminate their bare breasts on and near the bridge to attract business.[41] Why? To answer complaints that cross-dressing men were moving in on Venice's sex business.

Leigh was also an advocate of "breast freedom"—now known as

"free the nipple"—which fights for the right of women to go shirtless
in places where men do. Due to activists of her generation, women in
some places, including New York City and Los Angeles, have the legal
right to bare breasts in public based on the First Amendment right to
freedom of speech. Technically, they shouldn't just be sunbathing, but
protesting, dancing, or expressing themselves in some way.[42] In other
jurisdictions, such as Colorado and New Mexico, women may be topless in public under the Fourth Amendment, which protects citizens
against gender discrimination.[43] To confuse matters further, in state
laws and city ordinances, breasts are variously called "sex organs," "private parts" or "intimate parts," and even "genitals."

During our meeting, I was impressed that Leigh had stayed on top
of debates, recommending, for example, that I read thotscholar's "pro-
heaux" invectives.[44] However, she still felt deeply aggrieved by the lay-
ered exclusions of the feminist establishment, which had tended to
position sex workers as duped prey, pariahs unworthy of basic human
rights, or sellouts to the big swinging dicks of patriarchy. "I really feel
that the women's movement needs to step up and acknowledge the
harm that it has done to sex workers," she told me mournfully. "I hope
younger feminists will come forward with some kind of pledge that people can sign to make the decriminalization of prostitution a real part of
their program for change."

∘ ∘

To flesh out the story about tits in sex work that I'd gathered from Sprinkle and Leigh, I met with Nova Dove, an entrepreneur with several sex
businesses. Dove is in her mid-thirties, a 34B, with a wash-and-go Afro.
"I'm very comfortable in my body," she told me when we met at a fabled
hotel on Sunset Boulevard. "My father is Jamaican. Growing up, we'd
have naked days at home, especially on Sundays after church. We'd do
chores while we aired out the pum-pum." When Dove was eighteen, she

pierced her nipples, a symbolic emancipation from a mother with serious mental illness. "My numb nipples became supersensitive," she told me. "It was an act of rebirth."

One of Dove's job titles is booker, wherein she matches men from her annotated Rolodex of carefully vetted clients with high-end escorts, some of whom she knows personally, others recruited through word of mouth, social media, and sex worker channels on KakaoTalk (an encrypted Korean communication tool similar to WhatsApp). Dove resists the label "digital madam," because madams are romanticized and exploitative. She also disdains the word "prostitute," because it implies abusive pimps and illegal activity. She uses "escort" because her "girls" have the privilege of working indoors, and "high-end" as sales shorthand for a vague set of qualifications that include being able to pass through a hotel lobby undetected.[45] "My preferred term is 'sex worker,' because it is all-encompassing," she told me. "It retains some discretion, so you don't out anyone for the exact type of service they provide."

For the first twenty years of its life, the term "sex worker" referred exclusively to prostitutes. As the expression spread, it became an umbrella term that includes strippers, sensual masseuses, porn performers, online and phone workers, sexual surrogates, professional sugar babies, dominatrices, "domis"—the late-night hostesses who entertain men in karaoke bars—and even the waitresses at Hooters and other "breastaurants." Acquainted with several escorts who began as cheerleaders, Dove thinks cheering can also be seen as sex work.[46] Faced with an ever-broadening category, we now talk about "full-service sex workers," such as Dove's escorts, who earn a minimum of $100 an hour when they meet for drinks and $1,000 in a hotel room when the customer has "the intention to fuck." As Dove advises these girls, "The less transactional it feels, the better for you in the long run. If you can keep the same twenty clients, there's less margin for hurt and harm."

When men order an escort, their requirements often start with race followed by tit size or tit type. "34DD, no Asians," she said, reading texts from clients. "Brunette, all natural, nothing more than a handful, $3,000 if she can be here by 11 pm," she continued, reciting another. Dove told me Black men in Los Angeles rarely request Black escorts, and the only sex workers on her roster who promote themselves as "exotic" are Blasian, meaning Black and Asian. "Exotic" is derived from the Greek word for foreign. In California, where everyone except Indigenous Americans is an immigrant, the term "exotic" denotes ethnic ambiguity.

Exoticism has an age-old relationship to sex work. Buying sex has long been an occasion for men to experience intimacy with women outside their racial, ethnic, and religious communities. Moreover, selling sex is often adopted by new immigrants without access to legitimate work. Before World War II, "exotic dancing" referred to most dance forms other than ballet and particularly belly dancing, where performers wore beaded bras over exposed midriffs.[47] From the mid-1950s onward, exotic dancing, a convenient sound-alike for "erotic dancing," became synonymous with striptease. Exoticizing foreign women is a global phenomenon. In Japan, where full-service sex workers are predominantly Filipina, a stripper from the Czech Republic told me that she and other European women were called "white horses." Japanese men would joke, "Did you ride the white horse?"[48]

After race, men request women on the basis of breast style. Fake or natural, voluminous or restrained, breasts are not just about physical presence but one's position on a spectrum of femininity. "Sex buyers are not just seeking standard 36Cs; they'll pay for giant mommy milkers or flat chests," explained Dove. "Flat is generally an age play. Guys use the code word 'nubile,' which I interpret as 'just old enough.' " As long as the women are over eighteen, Dove passes no judgment. One of her codes of conduct is: "Never yuck someone else's yum."[49]

One of many dangers for sex workers is incarceration. " 'I'm your bail call,' I tell my girls," said Dove. Back in her hometown of Chicago, when she was making appointments for "rub 'n' tug" massages with "happy endings," Dove got a call from a sex worker in tears. "She had used a different booker, who hadn't done his due diligence. It was a sting. The police officer booked the appointment, got his happy ending, then arrested her. He didn't pay her and took all the money she had."

Policemen exploit, harass, and entrap sex workers all too often.[50] As it was the masseuse's first offense, she was allowed to expunge it from her record by attending three days of a state-sponsored diversion program colloquially called Prostitute School. Dove went with her to this all-female class of "pissed-off sex workers" to watch a police officer show placards featuring photos of "dead hookers." Dove recounted, "He'd point and say, 'This one got her head cut off; we found it in the toilet.' It was terrible, but during the breaks, we went out to the schoolyard and traded notes and contacts," she laughed. "That was the real schooling!"[51]

Dove believes in ethical sex work. Just because you have sex with many people and the government criminalizes one or more of your income streams doesn't mean you lack a moral backbone. Whether it is monetized or not, ethical sexual behavior—some might even say "good sex"—depends on deep appreciation of all the nuances of consent.[52] Dove sees herself as discerningly polyamorous rather than promiscuous. Her relationships are often "sugared" or monetized in some way through gifts, dinners, and travel. "I have no interest in being anyone's arm candy or behaving like a traditional sugar baby, who is paid per date. My relationship style is that I like to better myself and learn from people I admire."

Many people express their love through money. Some say that housewives are sex workers, won over by the promise of "being taken care of." They even receive jewelry or other "push presents" whenever they deliver a baby. Romantic myths prevent us from seeing contemporary sex as highly transactional. However, when one considers all the wining, dining, and gifting, it is hard to understand love without referring to what anthropologist Heidi Hoefinger describes as the "general materiality of everyday sex."[53]

Among Dove's tit-related enterprises was a Japanese Nuru spa, where the massage therapist covered her body with a slippery, tasteless, colorless gel made from seaweed. She would then slowly slide her naked body over the client's, first rubbing her tits on his back or chest. Tits are often the starter, or the savory *amuse bouche*, that whets the appetite for a broader range of sexual services.

More recently, Dove set up a cam modeling agency, a completely legal sex business that takes the old peep show format online. "It may not be in-person, but it is live and highly interactive," said Dove. Her agency represents about seventy-five full-time and a hundred part-time erotic performers with high-definition digital cameras and good Internet connections. These women earn money through tokens spent by their fans on sites like Chaturbate and Stripchat. The most popular "tip menu" items include "flash tits," "flash feet," "twerk," and "Do you like me?" Dove's company builds their character profiles, writes their bios, and curates their photos. It also scrambles their VPNs (virtual private networks) to hide their locations, so they can't be stalked. Some breast-related moneymakers are: "lactation, a niche fetish," as Dove put it, where the women squirt breast milk at the screen and sometimes ship it to their viewers; shibari, a form of Japanese bondage in which tits, among other body parts, are tied up in ropes; and "nipple torture" with wooden clothespins, metal clamps, or electronic wands (vibrators controlled via WiFi and Bluetooth). Noting my wince, Dove exclaimed, "Don't worry, these kinks are no more popular than small penis humiliation!"

It is remarkable that these forms of live interactive porn are legal, whereas old-fashioned skin-to-skin sex work is not. An ongoing technological revolution distances us from the warmth of the breast and other forms of human intimacy. First, the printing press supplanted word of mouth, then photography and cinema displaced seeing things with our own eyes. Audio recording and radio meant that sound no longer had to be within earshot. Then, with the arrival of the World Wide Web and the availability of smartphones with cameras and videoconferencing abilities, the physical distance between our so-called contacts grew exponentially. One wonders whether doctors should start prescribing an hour of hand-holding or ten minutes of motorboating to alleviate the anxiety and depression engendered by sensual deprivation.

o o

Waiting for her turn on stage at the Condor is Valentina, another of my stripper spies. With shiny dark hair that extends to her waist, she is dressed in a red lacy bra, old-school garters, and fishnets. A Mexican "anchor baby" whose mother crossed the border to give birth so she could be an American citizen, Valentina went on to obtain a BA from Columbia University and an MA from Stanford.

Valentina is conservative about "extras," as strippers call the illicit physical activities of the private lap-dancing rooms. She has let men suck her nipples for extra cash, but she never gives a hand job. "I do *not* want to see a penis at work, even if its owner is super cute," she says. About Condor dancers who offer a broader range of sexual services, she says, "I'm glad they're doing it in a safe place rather than a back alley." Well-read in sociology, Valentina resists the "whorearchy" that ranks sex workers according to their location, pay, and level of service.[54] She has slept with men she has met at the club but never charged them. "I want a fun sexual experience and, ideally, a genuine connection," she says. "In the back of my mind, I'm always hoping we could date."

Women draw distinct "go" and "no-go" boundary lines on their bodies. Many have deep visceral reactions to the timing and style of breast handling that are hard to suppress. Catherine Healy, the activist who spearheaded the decriminalization of prostitution in New Zealand (the country with the most enlightened sex work legislation in the world), told me that when she worked as a prostitute in a massage parlor, she had many tactics to make sure clients couldn't touch her breasts. "I didn't want them grabbing my tits," she explained. "I always tell new sex workers that, if you're sensitive to your breasts being touched or think it's too much to give, sit south of their knees where they can't reach you."[55]

Valentina's route into stripping started with ballet. She began lessons at four years old in Tijuana and kept it up through high school. The form's aesthetic conventions contributed to a prolonged and severe eating disorder. "Ballet was everything to me. I wanted to be skinny, light, and graceful," she explains. "I didn't understand that my thick Latina body would never conform to the European ideal." Strangely, almost every stripper I've interviewed has done a lot of ballet. I have come to see the dance style as an insidious form of compulsory femininity, which idealizes virginal appearances and celebrates white girls as fainty, dainty, timid creatures.

Valentina's anorexia peaked at age fifteen, evolved into bulimia, and then escalated into more intense binging and purging when she was in grad school. The ex-ballerina mastered out of her doctoral program, took a dull desk job, and started pole dancing classes with a group of women, variously seeking to work through bodily traumas, improve their self-esteem, or find their libido.[56] Healing was located in a dance form rooted in sex work.[57] "The way you talk about bodies, beauty, and strength is different in pole," explains Valentina. "Curves are suddenly things that you want. It was validating."

DJ Bling calls out "Valentina" over the opening beats of "Up" by Cardi

B, an ex-stripper and one of the few female rappers whose music is played here. Valentina grabs the pole with both hands and flings herself up into the air, scissoring and windmilling her legs with great speed. She settles into a handstand, with one hand on the floor, pausing in upside-down splits. She grabs her heel and touches it to her head, then threads her legs through and around each other. During the flow, Valentina wears a "ballet smile," which brightens into something more flirtatious when she catches an appreciative eye. At the beginning of the third song, she lies back in an "inverted crucifix" position 6 feet in the air. She stretches her arms behind her back to pull the ties of her bikini, which she dangles and drops. Hanging upside down on the strength of her thighs, her bare breasts fall up a couple of inches toward her head, "lifted" by gravity.

Most of the dancers at the Condor don't have pole dance training, so this spectacular sequence of tricks is such that even Joey, the floor manager, gives Valentina a standing ovation at the end of her set. Joey looks like he just walked off the set of *The Sopranos*. A few months ago, he asked me if I was a reporter. When I told him I was a sociologist writing a book about breasts, he recited his script: "We sell fantasy here. My girls know how to make a guy feel like a million bucks." Since then, he has either ignored me or pretended to write on his palm, a gesture to which I raise my notebook. Occasionally, as I am leaving, he'll say, "Hope the boobs were good for you!"

"A tip for the tits?" jokes Valentina, as she leans over the table that RedBone and I have made our headquarters for the night. Valentina is keen to catch her breath before she starts soliciting lap dances. "It's not easy money. I don't have the patience to cultivate regulars. I'm a lap-hopper," she says. "Barbie likes identifying the whales, who will spend big money on her in the VIP room. Then, she'll text them the next day and get them to come back for more."

Stage names are a form of creative self-invention and a way sex workers shield themselves from stigma, harassment, and stalking. They also protect their families from knowing about their work and feeling shame. Valentina's mother thinks her daughter waits tables at an Italian restaurant. Her father knows nothing because when she was thirteen years old, he committed suicide. "It's a cliché that strippers have daddy issues," says Valentina. "But I find lap dances with the older dudes easier. I've always thought I'd make a good second wife."

o o

Crocodile Lightning, a trans feminine dancer and child therapist whom I met through RedBone's burlesque network, learned to speak fluent English while working as a "ladyboy" in Thailand. During the Vietnam War, when American soldiers were given "rest and recuperation" (R & R) breaks, they were shipped to Bangkok, where they focused on "intoxication and intercourse" (I & I).[58] When the long war ended in 1975, the country had become a destination for sex tourism.[59]

Lightning's memories of her sex-working days are primarily positive. "My parents *loved* me, but my trans sisters *understood* me," she explained over Zoom. Her feminine flamboyance found a home in the sex worker community. "It's like you're in the trenches together. You know that if you scream, they will come." The teenagers worked as members of a family business, overseen by a maternal madam whom Lightning likened to Blanca Evangelista, the trans housemother in the TV series *Pose*.

Thailand's recognition of a third gender goes back to the fourteenth century, when *kathoey*, or "ladyboy," arose as a label for children assigned male at birth who exhibited varying degrees of femininity. "The word 'ladyboy' got imprinted upon me when I was so little, like a stamp on my body, which determined how I was treated by doctors, teachers, and peers," explained Lightning.

While Buddhist nations have a reputation for being more tolerant of nonbinary gender identities, Lightning saw the downside. "Tolerance is oppressive. It's not the same as acceptance," she declared. "Also, my

Thai passport insists on calling me Mister, whereas, in America, my Illinois driver's license registers my feminine gender. I cried with joy when I received my ID in the mail."

Due partly to its large trans community and recognition of a third gender, Thailand has well-developed medical tourism for cheap, reliable sex change operations, or what in America is now called gender-affirming healthcare. At nineteen, Lightning started taking hormones, and at twenty she had surgery. Her breast implants came as both a relief and an anticlimax. Her primary motive for top surgery

Crocodile Lightning: breasts are part of her "validity."

was survival—to avoid being targeted for violence. "My boobs were not for sexual pleasure. They served a utilitarian function," she confessed. But she also harbored a fantasy about her breasts. "I expected a magical transformation," she told me. "They were supposed to make me feel more feminine, but they didn't." Lightning appreciates the advantages of passing as a woman because "no one questions [her] existence or validity."

Thailand has no burlesque tradition; the closest performance styles are drag or on-stage sex acts. After immigrating to America, Lightning went to what she thought was a Zumba class, but the workout turned out to be burlesque. She relished the prospect of expressing her sexuality and her "fluctuating, yin-and-yang femininity." She also had the opportunity to choose an artful stage name. "Crocodile" captures the castrating fear that some societies feel toward trans women, while "Lightning"—a bolt of light in a stormy sky—suggests an epiphany. This dramatic persona serves as a liberated alter ego to her gentle demeanor off-stage. For Lightning, one of the many "wins" of dancing in front of an audience is that her tits are now "at home" in her body.

Lightning sees her burlesque routines as a "process of humanization," where it is important to expose "the real vulnerability of your flesh." At the Stockholm Burlesque Festival in 2018, she moved with precision to Sidney Bechet's 1952 jazz clarinet classic "Petite Fleur." She wore a cloak with two giant red fabric roses in the location of her bosom while her hands sported the 6-inch-long brass fingernails traditionally associated with Siamese royalty. "That costume was a nod to matriarchs of the past who walked around topless," said Lightning. In tropical Asia, men and women were often top-free until they encountered Muslim conquest or European occupation. While Thailand has never been colonized, it has adopted the sartorial rules of the Abrahamic religions in the course of its internationalization.

"Burlesque stripping is a form of storytelling in which you can shed layers of societal scripts," advised Lightning. One social script recently subverted by a trans woman was the requirement in Chicago (Lightning's adopted hometown) for women to cover their nipples with pasties in strip clubs and other venues with liquor licenses. In 2020, Bea Cordelia sued the city for violating her First Amendment right to freedom of expression by forcing her to wear pasties. Issues arose about whether authorities could fairly apply laws based on binary gender to nonconforming people. Would police enforce the ordinance against a transgender woman who is legally female but whose chest is flat? Or a transgender man who is legally male but whose breasts have not been reduced or removed? The law was found to be discriminatory, Cordelia won the case, and Chicago removed its nipple prohibition.[60] "Nipples should be free to be adorned and honored in whatever way we want," declared Lightning. "Nipples are a virtuous part of our bodies, our temples."

o o

On their way to the Condor is another informant, a gender-fluid friend of Barbie and an acquaintance of RedBone, who just texted me to meet them outside. Once on the street, I loiter next to the bouncer. He's overseeing a chaotic scene of smokers, including the Condor's "housemother." She usually lurks in the strippers' locker room, acting as an agony aunt and ensuring their "vag" isn't exposed, as she once told me. The house mom is gossiping with a loquacious woman whose newly augmented cleavage shines out of a black latex V-neck. When this gal offers her hand to introduce herself, an unusually formal move in this context, we shake, and I ask if she is dancing tonight. She tells me they don't let her in the club because she steals their business. Disarmed by her frankness, I'm initially unsure if she is joking or making clear that she is a prostitute working this corner. Seconds later, I realize that she's telling the truth.

A tired police officer, with a backpack thrown over his shoulder, strides past. The bouncer hollers warmly, "Hey, sarge!" The older man looks back to acknowledge the greeting. When the officer is further down the block, the wisecracking streetwalker announces to the group, "That's my Pops!" and then starts calling after him, "Hey Dad!"

Kitty KaPowww arrives with Bex, a drag king performer. They both identify as nonbinary and use they/them pronouns. The pair are popping in to the club between parties. Barbie is in the VIP room, I announce as we enter the venue. After hugs, RedBone settles into a conversation with Bex while KaPowww tells me they once danced at the Condor. "I had the most financially successful night of my life here!" they declare. The event was an LGBTQ+ night featuring dancers rarely hired due to their gender presentation. KaPowww made $600 in four songs, explaining, "The community is thirsty for queer stripping."

Japanese American, KaPowww has a short haircut with a side parting. Tonight, they're looking butch in a white T-shirt and jean jacket. Last week, at a burlesque event exploring the joys of gender-fluid bodily expression, KaPowww wore a shimmering orange evening dress, while Bex sported a tuxedo, a mustache drawn on with eyeliner, and a comical chest-hair wig.

"Genderful" is one of KaPowww's favorite words. "Spelled with one L, like beautiful. That is language from a perfume company called Boy Smells." When I came of age, the only nonbinary gender expression was androgyny, a stripping away of gender, a neutral or neutered gray area on a linear continuum between the blues and the pinks. I find it conceptually invigorating to conceive of gender in an effusive, nonlinear way, as a sphere where extremes meet. "I am not either-or," declares KaPowww. "I am both gender identities. I feel like both and beyond. I am very genderful."

At twenty-six years old, KaPowww has started making peace with their breasts. "I've grown past a lot of negative feelings that I had as a teen during the height of Victoria's Secret," they explain. Curvier

Kitty KaPowww: "In a geometric world, organic
shapes come across as silly."

than their peers, KaPowww struggled against "Asian fat-phobia" and
Western expectations that Japanese women should be petite. They also
felt intense pressure to be "hypersexual." Nowadays, KaPowww sometimes feels "gorgeous" when flaunting an ample bosom; other times,
they wear a compressive sports bra to minimize and flatten. "I don't
resonate with the idea of top surgery because I swing along this wonderful pendulum of experience," they confess. "The more I build the
right wardrobe, the easier it is to be in my body." KaPowww has tattoos
of large pink peonies beneath their neck, which both frame and symbolize their breasts. "For people who are gender creative, adorning
and altering the body is sacred," they explain. "We reclaim our bodies
through art."

KaPowww describes the move from "she" to "they" as a slow progression of "testing the waters" and moving through a series of identities "from woman to femme to queer-femme to nonbinary." KaPowww doesn't describe themself as trans, although they are happy if others do. "Gender is a journey," they declare.

Even for a middle-aged woman like me who's never been mistaken for anything else, gender is a trip. My gender may be less adventurous, but it is not static. It has shifted with age, puberty, and menopause, male and female spouses, and rites of passage like birthing children and having a mastectomy. Now my wife is pregnant and I feel another challenge. I'm the mother of two and the expectant "father" of one; what will it be like to watch someone else give birth and breastfeed? The anticipation alone might drive me to a drag king workshop in which I learn how to perfect an eyeliner mustache.

Words are significant to KaPowww, who cherishes the frothy physicality and onomatopoeia of their chosen surname. When it comes to chests, they feel that popular expressions for boobs are more accurate than medical terms. They enjoy the cultural nuances. "The mouthfeel alone is so different," they explain. "Boobs feels inane and juvenile, while tits are raunchy and slutty in a positive way." KaPowww tells me that Bex uses slang terms for their breasts such as "tibbies" and "tiddies." In written form, they also discuss "bewbs" and "bobs." "I love the intentionally silly typos," says KaPowww with a giggle.

Distracted by a dancer who has just taken off her top, KaPowww declares, "She has a cute little boob job!" KaPowww pulls out a stack of one-dollar bills. "I love tipping. I wish I had more cash," they say, heading toward the stage, where they fling the bills in small clusters as if scattering seeds to beloved birds in the park. While the money tossing is literally patronizing, the dancers perceive it as praise.

According to KaPowww, bodies are inherently comical because "we exist in a highly geometric world where organic shapes come across as silly." In a world where the human-made dominates nature, many people are alienated from and embarrassed by their physical selves. "I saw a stand-up comedian whose opening joke was about how laughing is just a response to surprise," says KaPowww. "He then immediately screamed at the audience and everyone laughed. I think a good part of the humor in burlesque—and in life—is about surprising reveals."

Regarding sex work, KaPowww's experience is primarily online. They are vigilant about the emotional fatigue that sets in when their body, including their tits, is monetized. But they also believe that some sex work is creative in ways that foster growth. Bex taps KaPowww on the shoulder as it is time to head to their next event. As they leave, KaPowww hugs me and says, "My tits go places where civilian tits have not traveled!"

o o

Civilian tits. Indeed, my breasts have no idea what it's like to perform in public or go into combat as a member of a squad of body parts in a strip club. Having fed two babies and been sexually harassed, biopsied, amputated, and replaced by prostheses, I had thought my breasts had been through it all. I now realize that my mammary glands have led a sheltered life, as they've never been minted as performative "tits."

DJ Bling announces, "The one and only Tessla!" A catchy hip-hop track that uses the *Godfather* theme fills the Condor. Tessla, a leggy brunette with a dollar sign on each triangle of her black bikini top, strides onto the stage. The energy in the room surges. The three ponytailed gals in turtlenecks spring up and start dancing between the tables, waving dollar bills.

Tessla is a smooth dancer, oozing confidence in her own body. I've heard that she is "off the books." In other words, she does not officially work for the Condor and doesn't have to share her take with the house. She's been "grandfathered in" because she used to strip here, but now works in Las Vegas. A conspicuously handsome Black guy showers her with a wad of one-dollar bills. The trio of tech bros throw money, then an Asian dude gets her to stop and receive cash under the bikini strap between her breasts. It's the biggest round of tipping we've seen tonight—a bull-market spectacle.

"Are they tipping her or tipping the song?" asks RedBone. She uses Shazam to identify the music, discovering it's by a local gangster rapper, a "playboy, from the Bay, boy" called Mac Dre, who was born and buried in Oakland after being shot dead in 2004. The track, titled "Mafioso," deploys standard rhymes like "rich" and "bitch," but also unpredictable ones like "linguini" and "Houdini." It pays homage to the Mafia, the original gangsters, or OGs. Like the subculture of the Condor, the song celebrates crime. Strip club owners and operators are known for tax evasion, drug trafficking, money laundering, and racketeering.[61] In this scenario, tits are a decoy—a visual distraction from the cash and crypto businesses that pay for luxury compounds in the tropics.

When I set out to study the erotic performance of women's tits, I didn't expect it would lead me to prioritize the decriminalization of sex work as a political issue. Many strippers do their work between a rock and a hard place—law enforcement and organized crime.[62] Vitally, the liberation of women's breasts requires fully decriminalized tits. Indeed, I think the most fundamental issue inhibiting women's autonomy—our right to choose what we do with our bodies—is the state's policing of sex work. If some women can't sell their bodies, then none of us actually own our bodies.

Valentina slides onto the cushioned bench next to RedBone and me. Tessla is finishing her third song, lying on her back in a bridge position doing jiggly pelvic thrusts. The stripper move is common, so I wonder if it has a name.

"Presenting pussy? Giving birth?" volunteers RedBone.

"I call that vagina monster," declares Valentina.

Barbie comes over to say hello. She's been in the VIP room for an hour with the guy in the yellow baseball cap, a climate change scientist.

"What did you do in there for an hour?" I ask.

"Oh my God, I had so much fun," she says. "He was super normal at first, but then he became a kinky sub. So, I slapped him around, mostly on the face, and twisted his nipples through his shirt. Then I made him massage my feet while I drank champagne."

"Wow," I exclaim, dutifully taking notes. "How much money have you made tonight?"

"Hmmm . . . let me work it out," says Barbie. "I've done two single-song lap dances at $40 apiece and an hour in the VIP for $600. But the club subtracts $80 for the room rental and they take the first $150. So that's $450, of which I get 60 percent, so about $270, give or take some gouging. I'll also make $16 an hour and roughly a hundred in tips."[63]

"No wonder you keep a spreadsheet of your income," I remark.

"Yeah, my spreadsheet has twelve columns for every shift. They make it intentionally complicated," replies Barbie, who enjoys most clients but can't say the same for the management. "Whenever I get to be a domme at work, it's a good night."

Valentina has been leaning in to ensure she doesn't miss any mutterings under the loud music. She taps the back of my hand, then looks out of the corner of her eye toward a dark booth next to the DJ. "We have a pimp in the house tonight," she says. A bottle of Hennessy sits on his table. One of the club's strippers is draped over him. In many parts of the world, brothels are located behind strip clubs.

Barbie leaves to hustle lap dances. "Back to sales," says Valentina as she rises from her seat. "When I go to Trader Joe's, no one has to convince me to buy milk or apples. Here, men like us to work for the money!"

RedBone looks at me pointedly. "Is it time for *you* to get your lap dance?" she challenges.

With the aim of becoming a boob expert (or at least augmenting my "titspertise"), I consent, but insist that she accompanies me. We discuss the dancer options. It can't be Barbie or Valentina; that would be weird.

I suggest Paradise, who is standing on the other side of the room, look-ing forlorn. RedBone counters with Sativa, a nimble pole dancer with strong abs and small breasts. I defer to her authority in this environment.

Unusually for a Mexican American, Sativa is 6 feet tall, more in her heels. She grew up in the Mission, a historic Latinx neighborhood. Naming herself after an energizing type of marijuana, Sativa is "chill" in all senses of the word. She has worked in strip bars since she was eighteen, first at the Gold Club, a Déjà Vu strip joint in a techier part of town, and, for the past four years, at the Condor.

We find Sativa at the bar. RedBone asks her for a dance, then the three of us stand awkwardly in line so I can pay for two songs. Mike, who I later learn is her boyfriend, takes $60 from me and waves us through. Sativa chooses the third cubicle on the left. This part of the club has an old saloon feel with patterned carpet, burgundy flocked wallpaper, and historic photographs of Carol Doda and other chesty pinups. RedBone and I sit on the bench, while Sativa perches on a small round table cov-ered in a white tablecloth. We are all bathed in red light. Sativa assesses us impassively. RedBone's earlier reference to a "situationship" is apt.

In the hallway outside our cubby, two firemen stride by in suspend-ers and rubber pants.

"Their nightly fire inspection," says Sativa wryly.

Between Sativa's B cup breasts is an elaborate tattoo of a sacred heart, a Catholic symbol of Christ's sacrifice for human sin. The lifelike heart is pierced by a knife and crowned with a ring of thorns. On her right thigh is a giant tattoo of Our Lady of Guadalupe, a miraculous apparition of the Virgin Mary that took place in Mexico in 1531. "She is the only woman worshipped in my community," explains the statu-esque dancer.

Sativa leans in, her tits only an inch away from RedBone's nose. I sit up stiffly, watching their progress, unsure how to behave. I lament the no-alcohol rule I observe on nights of participant observation. I take a deep breath as Sativa approaches me, slowly and carefully passing her breasts inches away from my mouth. She is probably the same age as my daughter, I think, followed by a wave of shame. I bat the feeling away and wonder: Does she have a day job? What do her parents do? Sativa turns around and gives us her butt. This is not the object of my study, I muse. Next, she asks us to move down the bench so she can get into a different position and rub her breasts on our thighs. I have the bizarrely obvious epiphany: my lap is a stage for her dance, mammary glands suspended, nipples prancing. I can see how an erect penis might participate in this gambol, leaping and cavorting under clothing. This intimate commercial service did not evolve with a pair of women in mind. Suddenly, the second song is over. Sativa stands, towering over us, and we are done.

As RedBone and I wind our way out of the club, she describes the lap dance as "lackluster." It was useful for me, I declare. It helped me grasp the potential of the service, even if I'm still formulating my thoughts on the erotic business of breasts. Tits are warm, complex, and deep. They're an advertisement for and an appetizer to other services as well as a malleable tool in sex work. Tits are wholehearted and droll. Even tiny ones are generous. If they resort to violence, they can only smother.

On the threshold of cool, fresh air, the bouncer tells me that I may be in my fifties, but I'm as sexy as a bottle of Hennessy Paradis Extra Rare. He likes older women who read books. He gives me an implant-smooshing hug and says, "Come back soon."

2

Lifesaving Jugs

Vivien Lee's white schnauzer lies by her feet, protecting her while she pumps milk in her bedroom in San Jose, California. She would normally watch anime or YouTube on her iPad, but today she is talking to me on Zoom. "My husband and I, we love children," explains Lee, a thirty-six-year-old chemical engineer who grew up in Hong Kong, then went to community college in Southern California before transferring to UC Berkeley. For the past eleven years, she has worked on the complexities of manufacturing iPhones and other Apple products for an electronics company called Foxconn.

Lee is what human milk banks call a "bereaved donor," a phrase that confused me when I was beginning my research into the raison d'être of breasts. Contrary to modern myths, women do not have mammary glands to attract men; we have them to feed offspring in the event that we give birth. "Charles arrived by emergency C-section," Lee tells me, her voice cracking. "His nose and mouth didn't connect to his lungs, so he only lived for a few minutes. He just went. Peacefully." Lee lost not only her child but the fantasy of who she and her husband might be as parents. "Before I got pregnant, we decided on our name for a baby boy," she continues. "In our culture, we like fun nicknames for the munchkins. We chose Charles because in Cantonese, if you don't pronounce it quite correctly, it sounds like 'stinky poop.' "

A slim woman under 5 feet tall, Lee was astonished by the force of her milk supply. On the third day after the birth, her breasts became engorged. "They went up two cup sizes and started leaking everywhere," she recounts. "They felt like volcanoes—the lava flowed, very hot, very determined." A nurse came to her aid with a hospital breast pump, which offered immediate relief. After a conversation with a lactation consultant the following day, Lee decided to donate milk in memory of her son. "I thought maybe Charles could help the other kids," explains Lee, "and that it might be a way to grieve."

Lee's breasts wept; her milk became a river of tears. She has been giving about 350 ounces (over 10 liters) a week to the Mothers' Milk Bank of San Jose, the oldest continuously operating milk bank in America, which pasteurizes this "liquid gold" and then delivers it to more than a hundred newborn intensive care units (NICUs) and many outpatient babies in California, Nevada, Hawaii, and Washington State.

When Lee started pumping and became an unpaid milk donor, she knew she'd contribute to the health of fragile infants, but she didn't realize that she would experience improvements in her own wellness. By doing what her body had prepared to do, she helped her caesarean wounds heal and her womb shrink to its pre-pregnancy size. Given her loss, Lee was also fortunate to benefit from the flow of hormones that accompany lactation, particularly the so-called love drug oxytocin. Clinical research shows that oxytocin is released in a lactator's bloodstream as many as fourteen times during a single breast pumping session.[1] In addition, other studies find that women who do not breastfeed are more likely to have postpartum mood disorders.[2]

Although it was the last thing on her mind, Lee's milk donations also reduced her risk of obesity, diabetes, osteoporosis, cardiovascular disease, and cancers of the breast, ovaries, and uterus.[3] Most of the "breast is best" conversation has focused on the benefits of breastfeeding for infants, as if the health of mothers were irrelevant—a phenomenon that a militant might dub medical misogyny but that I prefer to call patriarchal obliviousness.

Having just reached three months postpartum, Lee has slowed down her pumping to once a day. "I am keen for my breasts to deflate," she says, "so I can start jogging again." She has been taking Chinese herbs to help reduce her flow and plans to give her remaining milk to a friend of the family, her "god-sister," whose daughter is two months old. "I am keen to give her little girl all my immunities," she explains brightly.[4]

Lee is grateful to have experienced milk flow. "It was a gift," says Lee. "An intense, funny feeling that I will never forget, like an alarm clock that says, oh-oh, it's time to feed the baby." Having had trouble conceiving, Lee is unsure whether she will ever succeed in having a child, so she has relished this physical sensation of motherhood. She feels privileged to have had this deeply mammalian experience. "Not all moms have strong lactation reactions," she explains. "Many people do not understand it, but nothing compares to this feeling so far in my life."

While Lee describes her milk ejection reflex, as doctors and lactation consultants call it, I think about how mammary glands are central to the sociality of our species. To an infant's ravenous cry or even the expectation of need, the maternal breast responds. It listens. It lavishes. I remember that weird itchy feeling, experienced by others as a sharp pain or a tingling sensation, that happens when the ducts contract and squeeze to deliver milk. Perhaps the rickety digestive systems of the children I birthed (my son's colic and my daughter's reflux) distracted me from the unique intimacy and biological beauty of breastfeeding. Certainly, the medical phrase "milk ejection reflex" didn't help.

Words frame experiences and set up expectations.[5] The notion that breast milk is "ejected" from a woman's body like a waste product or an old DVD disavows its nutritious function. It fails to capture the way breast milk delivers bliss to nurslings. It suggests disgust with women's porous bodies and erases lactation's role in the evolution of the human community. Couldn't this reflex be framed more positively—as a flow, uprising, or liberation?

The colloquial expression "milk letdown" is not much better, because when you let someone down, you fail or disappoint them. In Chinese, Lee tells me, it's called *shang nai*, which translates directly as "up milk." In Latinate languages, breast milk also ascends. They say *montée de lait* in French and *montata lattea* in Italian, both of which mean the rising of milk. In German, they talk about *Milcheinschuss*, which Google translates as "milk bullet" but is more accurately understood as the shooting in of milk.[6] Further etymological investigation of the English expression suggests that "letdown" originates with cows, whose udders spurt downward.[7]

o o

Kelly Adams is a high-capacity donor who also happens to be a thirty-six-year-old engineer. An observant Catholic, she has six children. "Girl, boy, girl, boy, girl, girl," she recites. "It's a challenge to keep their birthdays straight." Sitting on a sofa glider on her front porch in Montclair, California, Adams tells me that shortly after she delivered her second child, a friend of the family developed a blood clot and went into a coma only a few hours after a C-section. Adams, who already had a freezer full of milk in preparation for returning to full-time work at an aerospace and defense company, stepped in, feeding her own infant and that of her comatose friend. With baby number three, she had so much extra milk that they bought a second freezer. After calling around, her husband discovered the Mothers' Milk Bank and Adams started donating. With baby number four, Adams gave her milk to a single mother with a child adopted from overseas. Then, with babies five and six, she donated to the milk bank again.

Self-effacing and matter-of-fact, Adams resists the idea that her donations are altruistic or motivated primarily by concern for others. "I'm not a hero. It's selfish really. If I produce as much milk as possible, I lose weight," she says, as a blond, green-eyed four-year-old climbs onto her lap. "Also, we practice natural family planning. The more I keep up my milk supply and feed around the clock, the easier it is to space out the kids."

For Adams, breastfeeding has two downsides. First, she initially found it unnerving to nurse in public. "People stare at breastfeeding moms like they're a car accident," she explains. Now she feels comfortable and even nurses, discreetly, during mass at church. Second, over the course of bearing six children, her chest has inflated and deflated more times than she can count. "I have worn almost every bra size," she admits. But these inconveniences are overshadowed by the deep bonds fostered by breastfeeding. "It's the sweetest experience I've had in my lifetime," declares Adams. "I'm not the best mother in all areas, but somehow this closeness feels integral to raising morally strong human beings."

Luckily, emotional bonds can be established at any time. Indeed, in cases of adoption, the love between parent and child is no less intense than the affection between blood relations. However, the time frame to cut maternal ties is brief. In her book on how maternal instincts have shaped the human species, Sarah Blaffer Hrdy writes, "The window for relatively painless (or tolerably painful) termination of investment is . . . usually in the first seventy-two hours."[8] In other words, when women abandoned their babies at the orphanage, they did so before their breasts became engorged with milk.

o o

I see human milk donors as twenty-first-century allomothers. Rarely discussed outside of anthropology departments, allomothers are "other mothers," or people who perform some or all of the functions of the biological mother, including breastfeeding. Found in many mammals, including monkeys, elephants, dolphins, and wild dogs, allomothering is a practice wherein cooperation supersedes competition, and the axiom "survival of the fittest" refers to the group rather than the individual. Human allo-nursing is found in around 90 percent of documented Indigenous cultures.[9] I initially assumed that sisters, cousins, or other women in the bio-mother's generational cohort would step in to breastfeed an infant in the event of her death or illness, but statistically the most likely allo-nurser is a grandmother. Remarkably, when the life of a grandchild is endangered, the reestablishment of lacta-

Unlike wet nurses, allomothers gift their milk out of a sense of kinship.

tion is not uncommon, even among postmenopausal women. When anthropologists asked grandmothers in their fifties whether they were really feeding or simply pacifying a child, the women answered with an unequivocal spurt of milk.[10]

Allomaternal nursing is a nonurgent feature of infant life in only a few surviving cultures, such as the Aka, people of Pygmy ethnicity, who live in the Congo's rainforests in egalitarian groups. Allomothers breastfeed infants while their mothers are at work—hunting and gathering.[11] These communities give us a glimpse into how women spent most of their thirty thousand years on earth. "Working mothers are not new," writes Hrdy. "For most of human existence, and for millions of years before that, primate mothers have combined productive lives with reproduction. This combination of work and motherhood has always entailed tradeoffs. Mothers either . . . lost efficiency by toting babies everywhere . . . or else located an alloparent to take on the task."[12]

Allomothers should not be confused with wet nurses. Wet-nursing is a one-way commercial transaction in which a subordinate breast-feeds the offspring of a more affluent member of society, either for wages or involuntarily as part of their enslaved status. Allomothering, by contrast, is precapitalist and relatively egalitarian. It is a nonprofit exchange wherein both donor and recipient are perceived as peers with different relationships to luck or opportunity. Here, human milk is not a commodity but a personal gift, political gesture, or community offering.

While listening to Adams's story about nourishing her own six children and countless others, the meme "I make milk. What's your super-power?" floats through my head. Although I'm generally resistant to American hyperbole, having lived most of my life in the more cynical United Kingdom, I am actually leaning into the word "hero" since I discovered that the California Cryobank, the largest sperm bank in the United States, entices donors with the all-caps headline "BE A HERO." Men would appear to respond well to this solicitation, as the Cryobank boasts "semen standards" so high that the bank is "more exclusive than an Ivy League college."[13]

Heroes are often characterized by their self-sacrifice. When it comes to mothers, however, a selfless focus on others is expected and often goes unnoticed. If paid sperm donors can be positioned as heroes, then these valiant allomothers deserve the label too. When I mentioned this to a friend, she complained: ideologies of the good mother are oppressive enough; why put pressure on us to perform to an even higher standard? My reply was: let's not confuse praise with prescription. When we appreciate firefighters or paramedics as heroes, are we trying to make accountants and editors feel bad? No. By championing these allomothers, we can complicate and deepen the meaning of women's top halves. In these donor stories, breasts are not passive objects or sexy ornaments, but essential workers improving community health.

o o

Roughly a thousand women are on the books as active donors to the Mothers' Milk Bank in San Jose. Unlike many American milk banks where the donor base is almost entirely white,[14] donors here are a diverse range of Asian, Caucasian, and Latinx women, a reflection of both California's demographics and this bank's concerted outreach program. Most donors work full- or part-time. Although they skew toward higher incomes, a number of working-class women are major milk donors. Lily Pham, for example, lives in a house in San Bernardino with her husband's extended family. She has worked at an office supply chain store for eleven years. With her first child, she had to walk to a nearby Target to pump milk while on the job. Her boss, a father of four, understood the occasional urgency. He'd say, "I got you, girl. Go!" She now works at a different location that, fortunately, has a spare office in which she can comfortably pump. With the exception of one "asshole," everyone at her company has been "super supportive."

I speak with Pham as she drives to work in her 2004 Honda Civic. It's back-to-school season, so she's been at the store sixty hours a week. When I ask her how old she is, she says, "Thirty-eight. No wait! I am almost thirty-six," then laughs. Pham's husband is unemployed and her father-in-law has serious health problems. A Buddhist, Pham likes going to temple but never has the time. A "good Vietnamese mother," she explains, "puts her kids first. She needs to protect them, provide for them, like a bear with cubs."

Pham tells me that she enjoys pumping for two reasons. First, she wants her children to be as healthy as possible; pumping has enabled them to drink her milk and her milk only in their first year. Second, the babies in the NICU "melt her heart." Pham has gone to great lengths to donate. It took her two weeks to fill out the paperwork about her health and lifestyle, then she stood in line for an hour to obtain the blood test required by the milk bank to ensure that donors don't have HIV, hepatitis, or any other blood-borne viruses.[15] In her eyes, it was worth the hassle. When she sends off a cooler packed with bags of breast milk, she feels useful. "Even when I am having a bad day, I brighten up," she says. "I think, don't be so hard on yourself. You're doing some good."

○ ○

High-capacity donors, or "platinum pumpers," as I enjoy calling them, are reliant on a relatively recent consumer technology. Throughout the twentieth century, breast pumps basically came in two forms: heavy contraptions meant for hospital use or lightweight plastic suction cups that required squeezing by hand.[16] In 1991, a Swiss manufacturer called Medela introduced an electric-powered, vacuum-operated breast pump for home use. When I used this device in 1996, I had no idea that the freedom it engendered was so new. These handheld pumps made it much easier to stockpile milk in the freezer and go back to work or out for dinner. Since the Affordable Care Act became law in 2010, American health insurance companies have been required to pay for electric breast pumps. Then, with the PUMP Act of 2021, it became mandatory for employers to provide time and space for nursing mothers to express their milk at work.[17]

As a feminist with a strong desire to feel liberated, I struggled with the confinement and toil of breastfeeding two children, twenty-two months apart, back in the 1990s. It's one of the reasons that I nursed for only nine months, well short of the World Health Organization recommendation of two years.[18] I realize now that I would have appreciated the intimacy and bonding much more if I hadn't been threatened by succumbing to an identity that I found terrifying—the selfless mother. For me, pumping and freezing milk provided just enough freedom to make breastfeeding manageable. It also afforded the reassurance of measurable outcomes.

Breastfeeding requires trust in the opaque mysteries of the body.

How many ounces did the baby drink? If you pump, you know precisely. If you breastfeed directly, it's an educated guess. Being a mother can be tough on a high achiever's self-esteem. No matter how hard you work, you never obtain an A+ or a 10 percent pay raise. In a culture obsessed with quantification, to the extent that we compute our popularity in "likes" and no longer go for walks but count our steps, pumping offers a sense of accomplishment. However, these gadgets, if used too frequently immediately after birth, can contribute to hyperlactation. Moreover, switching back and forth between nursing and pumping requires shrewd management if you're going to avoid clogged ducts and infections. (I learned this the hard way when my inept juggling of the two modes of milk delivery led to mastitis.) True to California's combination of health consciousness and trust in technology, there are an astonishing number of "exclusive pumpers."

o o

Elysia Ramirez, a former IT professional based in Sacramento, California, keeps a Google spreadsheet of her donations. "Okay, I'm dorky. It gives me a sense of control to graph things," she explains. "I've made an infographic for Diego's baby book." Ramirez is nearing her donation goal of 10,000 ounces—almost 80 gallons. She gives to the Milk Bank in memory of her sister, who was premature and severely disabled.

Ramirez, a survivor of sexual abuse, decided well before her son arrived that she would not breastfeed in order to avoid triggering past traumas. As it happened, her body went a little berserk. When she was only twenty-six weeks pregnant, her breasts became engorged with colostrum, the bioactive pre-milk that kickstarts a newborn's immune system. By the time her baby was born, she had sixty ounces in the freezer. Then, when her milk came in postpartum, it was excruciating. "Worse than childbirth!" she declares. Ramirez has "elastic boobs," as she puts it, with huge storage capacity. "My nipples become heavy and I have this feeling of impending doom—but the milk doesn't release. It's trapped until I use a high-suction pump, and then it gushes out like a pressure washer." To manage her unusual situation, Ramirez assembled what she calls a Frankenpump, which combines parts from three different pump brands: Spectra, Medela, and PumpinPal. Now that Diego is over a year old and she is starting to wean him, she refers to herself as "a well-oiled machine, running a milk business."

Nourishing a baby has changed Ramirez's relationship to her breasts. "I see my milk as a product of love," she says. "I can't hate my body anymore. It's done something really cool. I am much happier in my body now, even if it is less objectively attractive."

o o

This windowless room in the heart of the Mother's Milk Bank (MMB) is dominated by a cityscape of stacked picnic coolers. Fifteen of them, containing 4,550 ounces of bagged frozen raw milk, were received yesterday. A few donors who live nearby in San Jose, such as the bereaved Lee, drop off their donations themselves, but most ship via prepaid FedEx.[19] The equal mix of red and blue coolers makes me think of the nonpartisan beauty of breast milk. In a country divided by hostile party politics, diverse allomothers bestow their milk for infants in need.[20]

I walk through a warren of narrow corridors, past multiple walk-in freezers and a bumper sticker that says "Keep calm and latch on." I discover a vitrine through which I can see the pasteurization lab. Three men in white coats, wearing hairnets, masks, and gloves, move through this spotless, stainless-steel environment. In here, the milk of up to five donors is pooled, bottled, and then pasteurized using the Holder method, a "low-temp, long-time" process that knocks out bacteria and viruses.[21] It's a slower process, but it cooks out fewer bionutrients than the "high-temp, short-time" pasteurization technique used by the dairy industry and for-profit milk banks.

The MMB charges a processing fee to hospitals and outpatients of

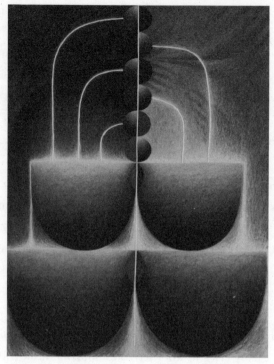

Nonprofit banks pool human milk donated by lactating heroes.

less than $4 an ounce, the cheapest in the nation. Their fee covers all their operational costs, including vetting, testing, pasteurizing, bottling, shipping, lactation consultation, and insurance outreach. Generally, nonprofit milk banks across North America have processing fees of about $5 an ounce, while the for-profits charge three to ten times that, depending on the product. While I observe the MMB's pasteurization process and reflect on money, it occurs to me that a nonprofit bank is an oxymoron. Wouldn't these human milk banks more accurately be called breast milk reservoirs?

o o

Nonprofit and for-profit milk banks offer divergent donor experiences.

Jessica Rivers, a mother who has given thousands of ounces to the
MMB, told me about her experience selling milk for $1 an ounce to
Prolacta Bioscience, a business that makes "specialty nutritional for-
mulations." Her husband had just switched jobs and taken a significant
pay cut. "We were really hurting," the stay-at-home mom recounted.
"They paid me $4,700. A real paycheck!" But she felt she was being
treated with distrust and disrespect. Then, when she discovered the
high prices that Prolacta charged hospitals for their human milk products, she became distressed. "It made me sick that it cost so much," she
said. She is currently nursing her own baby and giving raw milk directly
to a cancer survivor who had a double mastectomy before giving birth.
"I feel that God has given me a blessing," explained Rivers, who attends
an evangelical church. "And I can share that blessing by taking care of
His newest and smallest creations."

Selling and gifting feel different almost all the time, particularly
when it comes to our bodies. Human milk is an emotional, relational
substance. A baby cries in another room and the milk rolls in, sometimes annoyingly if the infant isn't ours. Mothers who pump at work
find it helpful to focus on a photo of their nursling; it accelerates the
gush. Whatever the case, selling breast milk for infant nutrition is
not the same as selling it to grown men. When researching chapter 1,
"Hardworking Tits," I interviewed a cam model, or sex worker with her
own online peep show, who sold her breast milk to fans.[22] Suffice to say,
the destination, purpose, and price of human milk impact its meaning.

o o

As I wander the halls of the milk bank, I pass an employee wearing a
"Milk Warrior" T-shirt, then enter the facility's only room with windows to the outside world. The MMB bottles three kinds of human
milk: "hospital grade," which has more protein and other nutrients
for premature infants; "mature grade," mostly for outpatients; and
"low dairy," which is donated by mothers who avoid cow's milk and

is prescribed for dairy-intolerant babies. The room is stacked with white cardboard boxes labeled "Mothers' Milk Bank. EXPEDITE—FRAGILE—PERISHABLE." If the order is placed today, the frozen milk is packed with dry ice, picked up by FedEx, and arrives at the NICU or outpatient's home tomorrow.

Having seen every room of the milk reservoir, I retrace my steps, this time noticing a T-shirt pinned to the wall asserting, "Breast milk, the original fast food!" The slogan stops me in my tracks, overwhelming me with a cascade of slightly contradictory thoughts. Yes, nursing is faster than formula insofar as it requires no mixing, boiling, or sterilizing, but it is not always easy.

My wife has had great difficulty nursing. She had a breast reduction when she was eighteen, then conceived through IVF and delivered via caesarean section at the age of thirty-nine,[23] all of which reduced and delayed her milk-making capacity. What's more, her status as a business owner meant that she couldn't forget about work and relax into maternity leave. During the first six weeks of baby Echo's life, we were lucky enough to receive breast milk from a kind friend whose freezer was full of it and a mother we met through a midwife network.[24] While milk bankers are uncomfortable with the lack of regulation and medical testing involved in peer-to-peer sharing, the benefit of milk from healthy friends and acquaintances is that it is frozen raw rather than pasteurized, so it nourishes the baby's microbiome. After many weeks of dedicated nursing and pumping, my wife's milk supply finally caught up with Echo's demand. But then she had to travel for work, which disrupted her supply and confused Echo's nipple-versus-bottle habits. It was educational for me, who was enjoying the luxurious role of the "father" on this occasion, to watch a new mother suffer and persevere. Altogether, it took four months for the dyad to settle into a cozy nursing routine.

In the middle of the milk bank, in an office that could be mistaken for a walk-in closet, I find my interviewee, Pauline Sakamoto. The energetic seventy-year-old is the retired former director of the MMB, who continues to work two days a week as a resource nurse and consultant. Sakamoto is the past president of the Human Milk Banking Association of North America (HMBANA) and a past board member of the US Breastfeeding Committee. A third-generation Japanese American, she was born a few years after her parents were released from a World War II internment camp. Sakamoto helped set up the first human milk bank in Japan, which she describes as "one of the highlights of my life."[25]

Sakamoto started as a milk donor, hand-expressing into a bottle, in the mid-1980s, then she became a volunteer, working bake sales and washing bottles. When she took over as director in 1998, the MMB had one full-time and one part-time employee; now there are more than twenty. In California, the milk banks were grass-roots initiatives, spearheaded by nurses and social workers. "Back in the 1970s and 1980s, most doctors were no help. They didn't want to deal with that icky stuff. They wanted a label, listing fats and proteins," explains Sakamoto. "Thankfully, we now have great relations with neonatologists at Stanford, who are convinced of the positive impact of human donor milk, including increased rates of breastfeeding at NICU discharge."[26]

The San Jose MMB is unusual insofar as it sends 40 percent of its pasteurized milk to outpatient babies on prescription. In Europe and many parts of North America, the banks only have enough milk to cater to hospitalized infants. The MMB prioritizes hospital orders, but once they've been filled, they send milk to infants who are being fostered or adopted, babies whose mothers have no mammary tissue (usually due to mastectomies), and mothers whose milk is dangerous for their children, such as those undergoing chemotherapy or those with HIV.

Why do premature babies need donor milk? Mammary glands typically develop the ability to lactate in the third trimester of pregnancy, so if a first-time mother delivers at twenty-six weeks, she may not be able to express more than a few drops. Add to this the shock and stress of having a baby without the strength to suckle who fits in the palm of her hand, and lactation is an even greater challenge. The mother of an early arrival can sometimes pump to create a good milk supply, but her baby usually still needs what they call "bridging milk."

One of the life-threatening illnesses that befalls preemies is a gastrointestinal problem called necrotizing enterocolitis (NEC), or "gangrene of the gut," as Sakamoto put it. "It's a horrific disease that results in expensive surgeries and long hospital stays. By the time they get out of the NICU, they're million-dollar babies." Cow-based formulas greatly increase the incidence of NEC, so milk banks worldwide collect human milk for these most vulnerable infants.[27]

Premature infants also need breast milk to ensure that their brains develop properly. During their last trimester in the womb and their first two years postpartum, babies undergo extensive neurological development. Studies show that low-birth-weight infants fed exclusively on human milk have higher cognitive development—an average of eight IQ points higher—than those fed breast milk substitutes. Skeptics have suggested that maternal IQ or household education might explain the gap, but recent MRI scans have revealed a human milk "dose-response" in brain morphology. In other words, low-birth-weight infants who received human milk have more of the white matter associated with brain processing speed than those who received formula.[28]

Lactivists have long complained that the term "formula" is misleading, as it is more accurately described as a recipe, processed food, or powdered drink. Since the nineteenth century, however, formula makers have used math and science as their primary marketing strategies.[29] Indeed, many alterations are required to transform bovine milk, a substance customized for animals with large bodies and small brains, into something appropriate for humans whose intelligence, dexterity, and longevity far exceed those of cows. No manufacturer has yet replicated all the bioactive compounds to create a human milk substitute anywhere near as good as the real thing. Even those innovators who are developing "engineered breast milk," or the production of liquids derived from lab-grown mammary cells, admit that their product will be static and uniform compared with the nutritional biodiversity of mother's milk.[30]

The shortcomings of formula include supply chain issues and product recalls. In 2022, for example, an Abbott Nutrition manufacturing plant in Michigan was found to be the source of a bacterial outbreak linked to the hospitalization of four infants and the death of two. The US Food and Drug Administration urged Abbott to recall Similac and two other powdered breast milk substitutes, and the plant shut down. In January 2023, the Justice Department began an investigation into the "egregiously unsanitary" conditions in which the formula had been made.[31]

o o

Unlike the Mothers Milk Bank in San Jose, most of the 32 breast milk reservoirs in North America call themselves *human* milk banks. "Americans are talking about a birthing person who chest-feeds," muses Sakamoto. "We don't want to offend anyone. Heck, back in the early 2000s, I got a lot of grief because I provided milk to gay couples who had adopted little ones. I just stuck to my conscience and was enamored by how their babies thrived."

We mull over the politics of the term "mother." It would be tragic, and possibly misogynistic, to erase the word from the conversation about human milk, I say. I respect a birthing person's refusal of the label for themselves, but we need to retain the term "mother" for those who find it fulfilling. In any event, the social role and energy of mothering transcend binaries. In the United Kingdom, "Shall I be mother?" means "Shall I pour the tea?" And in drag queen circles, the leader–mentors are heralded as "mothers."[32]

And "chest-feeding"? Technically, both men and women have breasts. However, many trans men (who were assigned female at birth but identify as male) bind their breasts or have top surgery to remove this stigma of femininity. Again, I'm happy for trans men to chest-feed, but the expression obfuscates the highly gendered history of this maternal labor.[33] Breastfeeding has already been marginalized by formula manufacturers, shooed out of public places, and censored from film, television, and social media. The erasure of breastfeeding is integral to the oversexualization of breasts, which many trans men say contributes to their gender dysphoria.

"Motherhood, breastfeeding, milk banking . . . they're feminist issues, social justice issues," says Sakamoto. "In California, the number one reason women go into poverty is because they have a child. Also, the majority of premature infants in the NICU are babies of color. Their parents don't have access to high-quality prenatal care. America's preemie rates are 10 percent. That's godawful high for an industrial country. If you rank us globally, we fit in between Myanmar and Thailand."[34]

Sakamoto tells me that the Black community has the lowest rates of breastfeeding in the United States. They also have the highest rates of obesity, diabetes, and cardiovascular conditions. "You gotta talk to my sister in Oakland, Brandi Gates-Burgess. She's dynamite," says Sakamoto. "She is very successful. Boots on the ground. She is what I believe this country needs to improve African American breastfeeding rates."

Until recently, it had never occurred to me that the majority of the world's women become mothers. It hasn't been reflected in the American women's movement, which has singled out abortion, or the right not to give birth, as its linchpin issue. As a result, activists who focus on issues like maternal mortality and infant nutrition tend to rally behind the phrase "birth justice" rather than "reproductive justice." Feminism has tended to focus on how women can be more like men, ignoring the power of what women can uniquely do—namely, give birth and breastfeed.[35]

Sakamoto raises her eyebrows. "That's probably one reason why breast pumps and pumping at work are mandated, but we have not had paid parental leave, federally," she says. In America, the priority is work, and the dominant perspective tends to be corporate. The United States is notorious for having the worst maternity-leave legislation in the developed world. For many years, only half of the female workforce was eligible to leave work for twelve weeks without pay and not lose their job.[36] Only when the Family and Medical Leave Act (FMLA) came into force in 2023 have *certain* employees enjoyed twelve weeks of job-protected leave, unpaid but with health benefits.

The consensus among milk bankers is that donor milk is not the best way to feed babies. The optimal delivery system is directly from nipple to mouth. The mother's body is the baby's natural habitat; their mutual well-being intensifies with increased skin-to-skin contact.[37] When babies latch on to their mother's breast, they ingest all the good bacteria and antibodies of the raw milk as well as the microflora on the nipple. Second best is a combination of breastfeeding and pumped milk delivered via bottles or cups. Third best is a situation of exclusively pumping, where a mother delivers her own raw milk to a baby with whom she is in close proximity. Fourth best is pasteurized donor milk. Last and least come all the cow and soy milk replacement beverages.

Sakamoto is therefore ambivalent about breast pumps. "The problem with pumps is, yes, they support lactation, but they don't entirely support breastfeeding," she explains. "When hospitals send a new mother home with an electric pump, it's like giving a crutch to someone who hasn't yet broken their leg. We need to enable moms to breastfeed, like they do in Norway." In the lactation world, Norway is not famous for fjords or salmon gravlax, but for its high breastfeeding rates.

o o

Anne Grøvslien runs Norway's largest human milk bank, which is housed in Oslo University Hospital. She is also the secretary of the European Milk Bank Association, which represents almost three hundred reservoirs. Grøvslien likens formula to smoking. "We must speak the truth," says the blond grandmother from her office overlooking a lush forest. "We can't say nothing just because we're afraid of insulting the smokers. Formula introduces health risks for mother and child."

Norway has the highest breastfeeding rates in the developed world, with 98 percent of women initiating breastfeeding and 78 percent still nursing at six months. Almost all Norwegian hospitals are "baby friendly," a World Health Organization category. They educate parents about nursing, put newborns to the breast immediately after delivery, help the pair establish a good latch, maximize skin-to-skin contact, and keep mother and child together at all times. Hospital staff also instruct mothers on "hunger cues" so they can appreciate when their babies need nursing well before they get agitated and cry. Most importantly, they never promote or supply breast milk substitutes.

Hospital policy is essential to high breastfeeding rates, because the dynamics of infant demand and maternal supply are established in those first days after birth. The length of maternity leave with full pay is also a significant factor.[38] "In Norway, we have the luxury of staying home with our baby for a year if we want," explains Grøvslien. "You can take 100 percent of your usual salary and stay home for less time, or you can have 80 percent of your salary for a longer period."

The near universal breastfeeding rate in affluent Norway rivals that of poor countries that never made the shift from nursing to human milk substitutes. I ask Grøvslien: Does Norway's breastfeeding rate arise in a conformist culture where those who use formula are disgraced?

"No one bullies a mother who is not breastfeeding," she says. "We don't have breastfeeding police." As a good lactation counselor, Grøvslien has helped women *stop* nursing. "When they are struggling, pumping 5 milliliters a day for weeks, because they gave birth in the twenty-third week. . . . Can you have peace in your soul, even if you don't breastfeed? It's part of my job as a counselor to help them quit without being devastated."

Norway is the only nation in the world that banks *raw* breast milk.[39]

When pasteurization was adopted across Europe during the first wave of the AIDS pandemic in the 1980s, the Norwegians began testing each and every 6-ounce box of donor milk. If they find a colony of staphylococcus or *E. coli*, the two most common pathogens, they discard the milk. If they find normal skin flora on the higher side of a standard bacterial load, they heat it up and purify it. With regard to intoxicants, Grøvslien explains, "You cannot collect milk when you're under the influence of alcohol—which means pump, then have your glass of wine. That's fine with me."[40]

For the past decade, Grøvslien has been part of a task force that has set up milk banks in Delhi, Jaipur, and Kolkata, with the aim of improving mother and child health in India. "I love Kolkata. It is hell on earth, but it's my favorite place. It is an exceedingly difficult place to work because you meet a lot of myths," says Grøvslien. One belief detrimental to infant wellness is the "colostrum taboo," a superstition that leads mothers to throw away their highly nutritious "pre-milk." Although the Norwegian team focuses on training staff, they need to understand local cultural dynamics. "Even if the patient knows that breastfeeding is the healthiest option, the Indian mother-in-law has her opinion, and she's the boss," explains Grøvslien. In many countries outside ageist North America, grandmothers are mighty influencers.

In Europe, Protestant countries have higher rates of breastfeeding initiation than Catholic ones.[41] With a Lutheran Protestant heritage, Norway is now predominantly secular. "I have no idea of the religion of our donors or recipients. It's rarely up for discussion," says Grøvslien. One exception involves observant Muslims, who believe in "milk kinship," a familial system wherein an allomother and all of the children who have ever received her milk are regarded as full-fledged family members. Just as incest taboos prevent blood relatives from marrying, so milk relatives are barred from matrimony. Muslim parents are resistant to donor milk because it could create an unrecognizable clan of "milk siblings" with whom their

child, once grown, could unknowingly commit incest. In these circumstances, Grøvslien has a solution. She promises the family that,
let's say, their infant daughter will only receive milk from a donor
who has birthed girls. "Two of the same sex will not have an Islamic
wedding," she explains. "In any case, Muslim women usually work
very hard to bring on their milk supply, as the Quran says that they
should breastfeed for two years."[42]

Grøvslien's passion for cultural diversity may be a reaction to the historical origins of her Oslo milk bank, which was founded by the Nazis
in 1941. "They occupied our country for five years and left one positive
thing," says Grøvslien. The first European human milk bank opened in
Vienna in 1909. The Third Reich adopted milk-banking as part of their
mission to foster optimal conditions for the creation of a superior race.

After several historical digressions, Grøvslien tells me that until fifteen years ago, the word for nipple in Norwegian, directly translated,
was the debased "breast wart."

"We sought a more positive word and launched a campaign to
rename them. Nipples are now called 'buds,'" says Grøvslien. "In Norwegian, we also have the equivalent of titties, big racks, and mugs." In
America, we talk about "jugs" rather than "mugs"—a reflection of our
higher-capacity busts? Apparently not. The average bra size in both the
United States and Norway is a 36D or 34DD, while most of the world's
women are an A cup.[43] In any event, there is no correlation between
breast size and milk supply.

Jugs and mugs: I savor these linguistic nods to the nourishing function of breasts. Yes, melons are also edible, but that expression points
primarily to a shapely appearance. "Jugs" is not a visual metaphor; it
is about the work breasts do. If gays are proud to be "queer" and feminists can celebrate "bitches," then I have hope for "jugs." If we can see
breasts as vehicles of altruism, capable of acts of generosity, then we are
all one step closer to draining "jugs" of its negative connotations and
filling the expression with body-positive power. "Jugs" could be part of

the small but significant perceptual revolution in which we reimagine our top halves.

○ ○

Looks matter in all societies, but perhaps nowhere more than in France, a country known for its fashion designers, perfumeries, and beauty products. "French women are held to very high standards of appearance," explains Mathilde Cohen, a legal scholar whose research focuses on milk. "They are expected to lose their baby weight and get back into shape as soon as possible."

The French public health system is famous for providing vaginal occupational therapy to postpartum mothers. Women are given a pre-scription for a dildo-like device and ten free "perineal re-education" sessions with a midwife to strengthen their pelvic floor. By contrast, the

Jayne Mansfield's generous jugs.

French public system provides no formal time with lactation consultants, most of whom are in private practice. As one medical student on rotation in the maternity and pediatric wards of a top teaching hospital in Paris told me, "We were not given any instruction in breast health or breast pumps, but we did have a course in which we taste-tested four different brands of formula."[44] I know several Californians who import artificial breast milk beverages from Europe in order to avoid the corn syrup in US formula, but I had no idea that Parisian doctors were positioned as sommeliers.[45]

Is it any wonder that France has the lowest breastfeeding rates in the world?[46] A mother in the process of weaning her second child, Cohen considers the roots of this situation. "France is the country that pushed wet-nursing into a full-blown regulated industry, starting in the fourteenth century with the aristocracy who hired nurses to live in, then continuing with the bourgeoisie who, when they had enough status or cash, would send their babies to wet nurses in the countryside."[47] Cohen is speaking to me from her parents' home in a small town in Normandy, whose historical association with the wet-nursing business is commemorated by road names like Rue des Poupardières, which means "Street of the Breastfeeders" or "Street of the Nurseries." The translations remind me that both the nursing profession and nursery schools find their origins in suckling.

French women have high employment rates and are guaranteed sixteen weeks of full-pay maternity leave. Upon their return to work, they enjoy high-quality subsidized day care in the form of neighborhood crèches. However, the day care system is generally resistant to the extra bother of breast milk, and few have lactation rooms where mothers can feed their babies before drop-off and after pickup. "Many consider breastfeeding for over three months to be heroic or slightly weird," says Cohen. When her firstborn was eight months, a prominent woman doctor affiliated with the best children's hospital in Paris told Cohen that it was time to stop. Why? "Because your breasts belong to your husband," recounts Cohen with an incredulous chuckle. "I was floored!"

France is one of the few countries to witness high-profile anti-breastfeeding polemics, such as that contained in Elisabeth Badinter's *The Conflict: How Modern Motherhood Undermines the Status of Women.* The outspoken billionaire feminist makes the important arguments that motherhood is not "the beginning and end of being a woman" and that nursing is "not the epitome of womanliness." Then she goes on an oddly nationalistic rant, defending "the failure" of French women to nurse because pumping is "repulsive" and they should be free of "the despotism of an insatiable child."[48]

"French feminists, don't get me started," says Cohen. "They have a long tradition of associating breastfeeding with patriarchy. But thankfully, there's a new generation of more eco-minded, hippie-ish people." Cohen turns to her seven-year-old daughter, who is missing her two front milk teeth, then says to me, "She likes looking like a vampire!" Cohen breastfed her daughter for two years. "It is a privilege to stay connected with a child through milk," she explains. "That is the beauty of it. It's a relational fluid, produced by one body for another."

Cohen sees breast milk as a form of "corporeal communication" in which the mother's physical condition is expressed, in all senses of the word, via her milk, while the nursling's nutritional and immunological needs are conveyed back through the baby's saliva, body temperature, and general disposition.[49] In customizing milk to the infant's needs, a mother's nipples are sentient. In a reversal of the presumptions of Enlightenment rationality, the breast perceives what the intellect can barely fathom.

"Breastfeeding is also an example of affective communication in which love, frustration, anger, a whole range of emotions are enacted," says Cohen. It also has important symbolic dimensions, conveying multiple meanings in different cultures, including gender identity, kinship, and/or privilege. "Breastfeeding is a form of social positioning in which you convey ideas about what a parent should be," she adds. "While you communicate with your baby, you're also communicating to those around you."

Corporeal, affective, and symbolic. I ask Cohen how milk banks and peer-to-peer milk sharing affect these three kinds of messaging.

"To me, they only extend, but I have an aspirational vision. Milk banks facilitate a broader form of communication," says Cohen, who goes on to cite a British study titled *Banking on Milk*. "The authors see milk banks as 'building liquid bridges.' That's a beautiful metaphor."[50]

Cohen's three-year-old son comes into view, whining in baby French. "*Demandes à Papa*," says Cohen, sending her son to his father.

"Weaning is an underdiscussed aspect of the breast's life, like menopause," she announces as she turns back to me, looking forlorn. "Apparently, in Chinese medicine, menopause is conceptualized as the season of spring, because it's a new life in which a woman keeps her energy to herself instead of constantly ovulating, shedding blood, making milk. It is not other-oriented, but self-oriented. I'd like to think of weaning in the same way, but I'm not there yet. I'm still in mourning, thinking about the connection I'm losing."

Weaning also brings on the pressure of reentering social worlds where appearances matter. In societies obsessed with youth and disdainful of aging, the wilting emptiness of dry breasts can feel sad even to feminists armed with intellectual resistance to the male gaze. We all need to remember that saggy breasts are wise; they are veterans of the mammalian miracle. Since the mastectomy, I miss my sagacious breasts. They nursed two kids. They had a story.

Changing the subject, I ask Cohen, "'Women and Cows in France and the United States'—how did you come to write this article?"

"The industrialization of dairying is a nineteenth-century phenomenon. Before that, maybe you had a sheep or a goat or, if you were rich, a cow or an ox, but bovine milk was not part of the average European's

daily diet," says Cohen, who avoids eating dairy except for the occasional butter-infused croissant.[51] Cohen dares to explore what women
and cows have in common. "They occupy parallel social positions," she
explains. "European men want to control their reproductive systems.
They're often exploited." According to France's bioethics policies, it is
against the law for women to share their breast milk, and until 2021,
single women and lesbians were barred from fertility treatment.[52] Cows,
by comparison, are forcibly artificially inseminated on a "rape rack,"
separated from their calves within twenty-four hours of birth, and
slaughtered for ground beef when they are just five years old—a quarter of their life expectancy.

Cohen's description of the dairy industry reminds me of Julie Smith's
eye-opening research into the carbon footprint of powdered breast
milk substitutes, which produce more greenhouse gas than regular
cow's milk. Formula is dehydrated, combined with additives, canned,
and shipped, often over long distances; upon arrival, it requires rehy-
dration with sterile water in glass or plastic bottles with latex or silicone
nipples. Smith provides overwhelming evidence that formula feeding is
not just a health disadvantage but an environmental disaster.[53]

Cohen rocks her head in despair. "In every supermarket, we see hundreds of dairy products. We have normalized cow's milk, this hypervisi-
ble product that's affordable because it's subsidized by the government.
Then women produce this tremendous resource, against all odds in
societies that give them little help," says the food lawyer. "Human milk
is the only food we produce with our own bodies and it has been completely marginalized."

o o

"When mothers ask me, which formula should I use? I'm like, honey,
the milk that's formulated in them titties!" says Brandi Gates-Burgess,
an international board-certified lactation consultant. As a medical professional, Gates-Burgess prefers the term "breasts," but she sometimes

slips into the vernacular of her clients in West Oakland, a neighborhood where most women live below the poverty line. The original home
of the Black Panthers, West Oakland is still mostly African American,
with a recent influx of people of color from other parts of the world.
Gates-Burgess works for Women, Infants, and Children (WIC), a US
government health program. When she transferred to their West Oakland clinic seven years ago, the breastfeeding rate was 7 percent. Now
it is over 30 percent.[54] "The norm in my Breast Friends group"—a personal initiative that Gates-Burgess runs parallel to her WIC duties—"is
to breastfeed for over a year," she explains, as she pulls up in front of
her apartment block and turns off the car. "People forget that duration
is key."

Gates-Burgess's phone, from which she Zooms, is affixed to her dash-
board, left of the steering wheel. A child knocks on the outside of the
car window. "I'm doing an interview," says Gates-Burgess to one of her
three daughters. "When I get done, I'll come in the house. If you need
to bring me Shaun Junior, you can."

"Exclusive breastfeeding is like life to me," says Gates-Burgess without skipping a beat. "Statistics show us that if Black women breastfeed
for at least six months, their child's and their own health changes.
Racial disparities are reduced. When breastfeeding becomes the norm
in your family, it can change everyone's life prospects for generations
to come." Gates-Burgess became pregnant at twenty-one, when she was
a sociology major. Having seen her mother nurse her little brother, she
found breastfeeding easy. "It was an amazing journey that I wanted to
share," says Gates-Burgess. "It is important for Black people to have
providers that look like them. I offer a safe space where they can share
their concerns without judgment. I can hear them and they are more
likely to hear me."

Another daughter arrives and carefully hands a hefty ten-month-old
to Gates-Burgess through the car window. "Hello, Shaun Junior. Say hi
to Miss Sarah," says Gates-Burgess to her son with a glance at me on the

screen. "As soon as I come home, he's ready for his milk," she says as she puts him on her left breast.

"What about breastfeeding is most relevant to your WIC mothers?" I ask.

"Breast milk is free. That's number one on my list," declares Gates-Burgess. "If you can't figure out how you're gonna pay your rent or put gas in your car, why would you want to add another expense? WIC provides formula, but it doesn't provide enough formula." Black women have high rates of being single parents, so it helps to understand the benefits of breastfeeding for themselves. "Breastfeeding reduces stress. It decreases your cortisol levels. It elevates your oxytocin, which helps you to be calm," says Gates-Burgess. "Kids do better in school when they're breastfed. Black kids are often labeled with ADHD, trouble focusing, and behavior problems. When they're six or seven years old, you do not want the school calling you all the time because your kid is acting up or having an asthma attack." Gates-Burgess addresses the positive health impacts on mother and child in practical and concrete terms because medical statistics can feel abstract and distant to parents who are struggling to make ends meet.[55]

"People always think they want to pump until they do and then they find out it's the devil," says Gates-Burgess with a hearty cackle. "It's a lot more work than breastfeeding, but we help them. We create pumping schedules for their return to work. We draft letters to give to their bosses about lactation accommodation law. We make sure they know their rights." A while ago, Gates-Burgess donated about 500 ounces to the Mothers' Milk Bank in San Jose, after which she met Pauline Sakamoto at a Kellogg Foundation workshop about strategies for helping children thrive. Since then, the two women have worked together on Oakland donor drives and California state policy.

"We need Black women to donate their chocolate milk to do their part for the many Black babies in the NICU," says Gates-Burgess, who currently gives about 150 ounces a month to a coworker who has insufficient glandular tissue, or IGT, a very rare condition where the mammary glands do not develop properly during adolescence. Nowadays, breast reductions are the main cause of insufficient glandular tissue for women of all races and a leading reason why otherwise healthy women have serious trouble breastfeeding.

When asked why they didn't breastfeed at all or for long, women most commonly answer that they didn't have enough milk. What lactation consultants know is that the problem of "not enough" is usually about a lack of support at home and in hospitals. If "lactastrophes" were a common biological occurrence, they would have wiped out the human race long ago.[56] However, we no longer live in a world where nature rules. We inhabit a complex Anthropocene of rigid timetables and hard surfaces where we are estranged from bodily rhythms in general and the feminine virtuosities of birthing and breastfeeding in particular.

When I was born in 1965, I was taken away from my mother and put in a separate room full of infants where parents gazed at their offspring through a vitrine. Given this doctor-prescribed disruption in the natural flow of supply and demand, not to mention the fact that my mother was under a general anesthetic when I was pulled out of her with metal forceps, it is a tribute to natural resilience that her milk flowed in full force. By the time I was six weeks old, however, my mother's weight had dropped to ninety pounds and she was advised to quit breastfeeding.

Shaun Junior makes a whimpering sound. "Okay, let's go to the other side," says Gates-Burgess, whose comfort nursing on Zoom in her car-cum-office suggests that she does it all the time.

"If you could change anything to improve breastfeeding rates, what would you do?" I ask.

"I would stop WIC from giving out free formula," Gates-Burgess says without hesitation. "It's a Catch-22. WIC provides breastfeeding education, lactation support, free breast pumps, peer counseling, and healthy foods for families who breastfeed, but then it's all undermined by free formula and this surface idea about freedom of choice."

The infant milk beverage business has appropriated the feminist rhetoric around a woman's basic human right to bodily self-determination.[57] "In my opinion, if you choose to have a baby, you should do the optimal thing to protect your child," says Gates-Burgess firmly. "I honestly believe that if we didn't provide free formula, more people would feel confident about and committed to breastfeeding."

The ubiquity of canned breast milk substitutes suggests that breasts are unreliable, difficult, uncooperative resources. According to Kimberly Seals Allers, author of *The Big Letdown*, the formula business generates profits through fear, uncertainty, and doubt. Their business model aims to create dependency.[58]

Although I believe that women have a right to choose what they do with their bodies, I've never loved the consumerist slogan "pro-choice," I admit. Abortion is often a decision of forced circumstances rather than an optimum solution in an ideal world. Similarly, the adoption of formula is also dependent on context, related to women's health and home life as well as their work and intimate personal history with their breasts. Although it is vexing that formula marketers use feminist slogans, I am compelled to agree with them. As a matter of principle, it is a woman's right to choose how she feeds her baby.

Real choice is a privilege that women who live below the poverty line don't have, explains Gates-Burgess. "Once her breasts are dry and she's used up her monthly allocation of formula, what does she do?" she asks. "Water it down to stretch it out? If she could afford formula, she wouldn't be in the WIC program in the first place."

The US government is the biggest buyer of breast milk substitutes in the world. The full name of WIC—the Special Supplemental Nutrition Program for Women, Infants, and Children—betrays its origins.

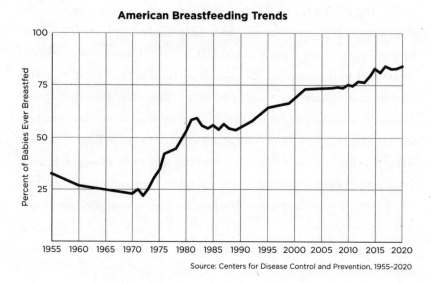

American Breastfeeding Trends

Source: Centers for Disease Control and Prevention, 1955–2020

Its precursor was the IFIF, or Iron-Fortified Infant Formula program. Intriguingly, the WIC program started when breastfeeding rates were creeping back up.

The year 1972 marks the nadir of maternal nursing in America. WIC opened its first clinic in January 1974. Weirder still, a program that targets low-income pregnant women, breastfeeding women, and children under the age of five is not administered by the Department of Health and Human Services but by the US Department of Agriculture (USDA), a government agency that knows more about udders than breasts.[59] "Why would the Women, Infants, and Children's program fall under the USDA?" asks Kim Updegrove, the director of the Mothers' Milk Bank in Austin, Texas. "Because WIC is a US dairy farmers' subsidization program. Do you think it's their mission to improve community public health by having more breastfed children? No, they say a whole lot of things, but their mission is to make sure that the bovine industry is alive and well in the USA."[60]

The logic of locating WIC under Agriculture also suggests that women and children are lesser mammals, ranked beneath wise *Homo sapiens*. Some scholars have linked WIC's distribution of free artificial breast milk to the legacy of slavery, seeing both as colonial disruptions to mother-infant relations and as forms of "food oppression."[61]

Gates-Burgess discusses slavery and wet nursing when she gives presentations on the history of African American breastfeeding. "If a mom brings up the legacy of trauma, I would engage her by asking: What is it about your chocolate milk that is so valuable? If we once fed other people's babies, how much more important is it to give that precious breast milk to our babies?"

Shaun Junior unclamps from her nipple. Gates-Burgess sits him up on her lap. She smiles with satisfaction. He is blissfully woozy.

o o

Some women cannot breastfeed. Cristina Jade Peña has been HIV-positive since 1984. There is a 50 percent chance that she caught the human immunodeficiency virus in the womb and a 99 percent chance that she was infected through maternal breast milk. Her mother was not aware she had HIV, nor that her husband had a secret life. In 1986, Peña's father developed full-blown AIDS, dying just before her third birthday.

The AIDS pandemic changed the face of public health all over the world. Most American human milk reservoirs closed, leaving the Mothers' Milk Bank of San Jose the oldest continuously operating institution of its kind.[62] Meanwhile, the European human milk banks all surrendered to pasteurization, leaving Norway the lone upholder of the raw milk tradition. And the French passed their bioethics laws, prohibiting both peer-to-peer sharing and the sale of human milk.

While growing up in Los Angeles, Peña was in and out of the hospital, the subject of many studies. "I've done my bit for medical research," she says. Through her teenage years, Peña's friends were "the eclectic world of the HIV community." She would often ask, "Can I be a mom?" Her mother always found ways to be positive, saying. "Of course, you can. You might not be able to have your own children, but you can adopt, you can be an aunt, you can be a mom in so many different ways."

Science eventually caught up with Peña's dream. She maintained a viral load of "undetectable" for several years before conception and stayed on antiretroviral drugs throughout her pregnancy.[63] With her HIV under control, she was even able to have a vaginal delivery. "It was the experience I wanted," says Peña, who brought a 7-pound boy into the world after seventy-two hours in labor. Tested immediately and repeatedly, her son is HIV-free.

Having known about the immune system from a young age, Peña worried about nursing. "Breastfeeding is framed as a choice. But for me and many women, due to illness or surgery, that choice is removed. I'm so grateful to be healthy in my thirties in a loving relationship and so very grateful to have a child, but knowing how beautiful breastfeeding is, there was . . ." She breaks off. "Breastfeeding is a hard topic for me," she says, regaining her composure. "There were tears." Peña and her husband investigated the options. Doctors told them, maybe you can breastfeed if you enter a study and put your baby on medication. "I didn't want my baby to be a guinea pig," confesses Peña. "I couldn't do that anymore."

The parents-to-be were delighted to find a solution that "aligned with our values," as Peña puts it—a prescription for human milk and the telephone number of the Mothers' Milk Bank. "The San Jose breast milk people, they were fantastic. They made sure we had frozen milk three weeks before my due date," says Peña with relief. Her ob-gyn and the UCLA BirthPlace staff were completely accommodating, taking safe custody of the bottles and allowing only one to defrost when the baby arrived. (Other mothers have told me that their hospital refused to receive donor milk. It was not refrigerated and left to spoil while they were in labor.)

Peña's delivery marks the first time that UCLA medical staff gave human donor milk to a full-term baby that wasn't in the NICU. "We worked out a whole new system with the hospital, which they hope to make a standard of care for other families in similar situations," says Peña. "I was able to feed our son warm breast milk, skin to skin, right after he was born. It was magical to make that happen."

Now that their baby is five months old, Peña and her husband have a problem. They have been paying $4,000 a month for donor milk, but their United Healthcare PPO insurance will not reimburse them. "The American Academy of Pediatrics advises breastfeeding exclusively for the first year and the CDC is clear that HIV-infected mothers should not breastfeed their infants," says Peña. "It's a real medical need, but it doesn't fit into the narrow categories of their claim forms."[64] The staff at the nonprofit Mothers' Milk Bank would love nothing more than to give the milk away for free, but their shipping, testing, and pasteurization costs mean that the best they can do is help recipients with their insurance. When the infant is premature or ill or even cow's-milk-intolerant, medical necessity is relatively easy to prove. However, when a mother cannot breastfeed a healthy baby, there is no vehicle for coverage.

One problem is that the American medical system does not recognize the symbiosis of mother and child, whose health is interdependent for many months postpartum. Obstetricians take care of the pregnant mother, while pediatricians oversee the delivered baby. The moment the umbilical cord is cut, legal responsibility for the baby's life transfers from one to the other. As a result, neither specialist is well educated about lactation. Ob-gyns are focused on the bottom half of women's bodies and are generally better trained in understanding breast cancer than breastfeeding, whereas pediatricians generally attend one lecture, if that, on the topic. One has to ask: Do these blind spots have anything to do with the many donations that formula manufacturers make to university medical departments and hospital wards?[65]

An expert in early childhood health policy and program design, Peña works at a nonprofit organization called First 5 LA, where she often deals with the Department of Health. "I love the health system and I thought I knew how to navigate it," she says. Her expertise in the lives of children under five fueled her conviction that her baby needed human milk to enjoy the resilient immunity that she didn't have as a child. Our immune system is a complex, mysterious network of cells and proteins that protects the body against infection. It keeps a record of every virus and bacterium it has vanquished so it can defeat those germs quickly if and when they return. "We all know breast is best," explains Peña. "My husband and I, we sometimes joke that we are crowdsourcing antibodies and nutrients for our little one through pooled donor milk."

Indeed, a virtual community of diverse allomothers has gathered around a nonprofit milk reservoir dedicated to the health of the next generation. In a capitalist society where women's breasts are commodified like no other body part, here their jugs are the key players in an economy that is not about money. This market may be about oxytocin and the satisfactions of great flow. It may involve weight loss, quantifiable achievement, and the aspiration to be a good mother. Whatever the case, most milk donors will tell you that this market, mediated by a machine called a breast pump and a network of FedEx delivery drivers, is about love.

3

Treasured Chests

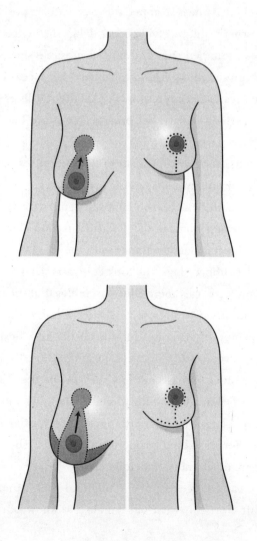

Her two oversized breasts shimmer with iodine under the bright lights of the operating room. Supine with her arms outstretched, Anne is strapped into a cruciform position, inhaling a general anesthetic and receiving other drugs through an intravenous drip. Her eyes are taped shut and blue disposable sheets, referred to as drapes, are pulled into position to conceal her face. Black markings delineate the arcs of her areolas as well as the midlines of both sides of her chest. Defying gravity, her breasts look more like architectural domes than body parts.

"Disco queens? Yacht rock? Hipster BBQ?" inquires the anesthesiologist about the plastic surgeon's music preferences.

"As long as it's inoffensive, you choose," replies Dr. Carolyn Chang. "I don't hear it unless I hate it." The plastic surgeon's long black hair is shoved into a blue hairnet. Combined with the surgical gown she wears over scrubs and rubber clogs, the look contrasts dramatically with the Chanel skirt suits and cashmere Dior ensembles that she sports around the office. Committed to precise aesthetics, Chang is a clothing connoisseur who enjoys wearing head-to-toe outfits from designer brands.

Chang has never worn a bra and, despite a 36AA bust, has never considered having a "breast aug," as they say in the trade. As a surgeon, she doesn't want big boobs to get in the way, and as a clotheshorse, she appreciates that high fashion is made for flat chests. "If you want designer clothes to hang properly on the body," she explains, "you don't want to be much more than a B cup."

"Time out," announces a nurse. "Bilateral breast implant removal with breast lift. Forty-one-year-old female. No known drug allergies."

Before the first incision, medical protocol requires a "time out," or pause, to confirm that the surgeon is about to perform the requested procedure on the correct parts of the right person.

"The implants are too big for her frame. Her pectoralis muscles ache. She wants them out," explains Chang as she scrutinizes the chest of her patient, Anne, a slim white mother of two who lives in a fancy neighborhood with views of the Bay. "After breastfeeding, many women just want a lift, but some surgeons will say, 'Oh, no, you won't look good without an implant.' It's a male-centric aesthetic and it's out of date," explains Chang. In women over forty, large breasts are often read as matronly.

A good lift is a custom surgery requiring sculptural and reconstructive skills on the part of the surgeon, whereas a mass-manufactured silicone implant delivers a fast and easy shape. Chang holds out her right palm. Her registered nurse first assistant (RNFA), Ryan Gourley, a tall rugged man wearing a navy scrub cap, hands her a scalpel. "Explantations are like spring cleaning," continues Chang with enthusiasm. "You throw out the old junk, clean out the breast, and reshape a loosey-goosey form into something beautiful. It's very satisfying."[1]

"Removing right implant first," announces Chang to the circulator, a nurse who is responsible for recording every medical action and material used during the procedure. Fleetwood Mac's "Go Your Own Way" mixes with the whooshing sound of the pneumatic compression stockings that are squeezing the patient's legs to prevent her blood from pooling, clotting, and forming dangerous embolisms.

"Plastic surgeons don't like to admit it, but breast sizes are subject to fashion," says Chang. "Implants, or at least large ones, are trending out. Women want athletic bodies." While the rate of breast augmentations peaked in 2007, they remained the most performed plastic surgery in America until 2021, when liposuction took over the top spot. If you add together all the aesthetic surgeries of the top half—including the growing business of implant removals and replacements—breasts

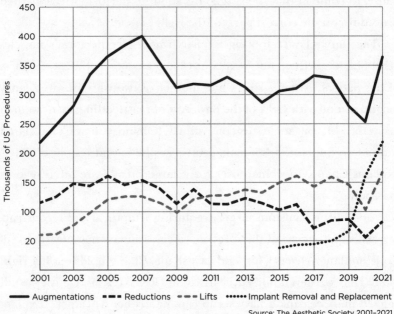

Breast Surgery Trends

Thousands of US Procedures

— Augmentations ▪—▪ Reductions ▪▪▪ Lifts •••••• Implant Removal and Replacement

Source: The Aesthetic Society 2001–2021

account for 40 percent of all plastic surgeries. In 2021, they generated a total of $3.8 billion in revenue in the United States alone.[2]

Internationally, the breast is the site of over a quarter of all plastic surgeries. In Europe and Latin America that figure rises to a third, and in Asia, it declines dramatically as people prefer to alter eyelids and noses. Notably, gynecomastia, the removal of "man-boobs" (or "moobs"), is one of the top three aesthetic surgeries for men worldwide. Chests, it would seem, are the primary battleground wherein nature and culture—or living shapes versus gender ideals—fight for supremacy.

Chang falls silent to draw a decisive slice through the skin of the inframammary fold, the crease under Anne's right breast. Her light touch draws little blood. After gently retracing her incision, Chang hands her scalpel to Gourley, who replaces it with a long thin Bovie cauterizing pencil. She starts burning a crevice through the underlying flesh to reach the capsule of scar tissue that surrounds the implant. A wisp of smoke spirals up from the patient's breast, accompanied by the smell of sizzling meat.

"It's like being at a yakitori grill," quips Gourley. The surgical assistant spins a clamp in his right hand as if he were a drummer twirling his sticks. Gourley served in Iraq as a paramedic and a surgical "scrub" tech, so he has encountered more traumatic injuries than most. After an honorable discharge, he went to night school to become a registered nurse, then took further certificates in suturing and first-assisting to become an RNFA. Gourley and Chang have been working together, performing six to eight surgeries a week, for a decade, so he generally anticipates her needs before she asks.

While Gourley grew up in an environment characterized by what he calls "disorganized crime," Chang was raised by her Chinese parents in the scientific community of Oak Ridge, Tennessee, famed for the National Laboratory that, in the 1940s, helped develop the atomic bomb. For her BA, MD, and residencies in general and plastic surgery, she attended her father's alma mater, Stanford University. This high-end education was followed by prestigious fellowships in hand reconstruction and facelifts.

I ask the team whether plastic surgeons are the artists of the medical world.

Focusing on her breast excavation, Chang doesn't answer. However, Gourley looks up and offers, "Orthopedic surgeons are like carpenters, dealing with joints and bones."

"They're the jocks," adds the anesthesiologist. "Talking about football and fast cars during their surgeries."

"Maybe dermatologists are like painters, working on the surface of the skin," says Chang, without shifting her gaze from her patient. "Plastics is a clean, controlled, predictable specialty. I could never be an ob-gyn, delivering babies—all the puke, poop, and uncertainty. Pregnancy is dangerous. Women hemorrhage, stroke, have seizures. When I was a resident, I was shocked by how earthy it was. I hung out in the fertility clinic because it was so tranquil."

"A crash C-section gets your heart pumping," admits Gourley.

"I come in here to relax," says the anesthesiologist. "Low-acuity surgeries on healthy patients are low-stress."

"What do you mean?" says Gourley with mock incredulity. "We have emergency breast augs. Code blue! Tits down!" he deadpans.

"Watching vitals during a breast aug is not the same as a liver transplant," replies the anesthesiologist. "Sick patients keep you on your toes."

Chang specializes in complex breast revisions and "natural aesthetics." Patients require redos when they no longer like the size or placement of their implants. Sometimes they seek a post-pregnancy makeover or have problems with capsular contracture (when scar tissue thickens and shrivels, creating discomfort and distortion to the shape of the breast). Surprisingly, implants have only ten-year warranties. Patients are advised to swap them out every fifteen years before they deteriorate or rupture.[3] Like car tires, these silicone hemispheres garner wear and tear that can result in a messy blowout. "Sometimes the implant just loses its integrity. It becomes a blob instead of a sphere," says Chang, as she pulls a silicone orb out of Anne's breast. She holds it up to the light to examine it. "Allergan. Looks good. It was only in there for four years," says Chang as she passes it to Gourley, who tosses it into a tray dedicated to surgical waste. Allergan is the market leader in breast implants and many other aesthetic treatments, including Botox, a neurotoxin used to relax facial muscles and reduce wrinkles, and Juvéderm, an injectable filler used to lift cheeks and plump lips.

I ask Chang how she defines a natural aesthetic.

"That's a tough question," says Chang. "People choose me because they don't want to appear like they've had anything done. They want to

look like themselves. They don't want to be judged as frivolous or vain."
Chang delves further into Anne's right breast with the Bovie cauter-
izer to remove the scar tissue around the implant. "Career women—
and even ladies who lunch—need to look good to be competitive. They
want to be taken seriously. They don't want to be caught cheating to
look better."

So, "natural" means inconspicuous and discreet, but also intelligent
and somehow honest, I summarize, marveling at the irony.

"Natural also means proportionate and appropriate," says Chang. "I
steer away from the anatomically abnormal. A lot of what I do for my
patients is restorative. I reconstruct their bodies after C-sections and
breastfeeding. I get them back to where they were before. My beauty
ideals are at the center of the bell curve. Some very popular surgeons
make breasts that I find distasteful."

"Distasteful?" I inquire.

"Cleavages that are too high on the chest, too round on the top, too
large for her body. Sometimes you can even see the implant. That big
round look is awful," says Chang. This style of surgery disrupts breast
dynamics, creating immovable objects without any organic sway.[4]

Allergan promotes their implants under the brand name Natrelle,
cleverly associating its version of beauty with both nature and French-
ness. Johnson and Johnson's implant brand is Mentor, an odd personification of expertise, while the other implant on the American market,
Sientra, sounds biotechy but feminine, like AI assistants Alexa and Siri.

Chang teases some gnarly flesh out of Anne's breast cavity. "It's thick,
calcified scar tissue," explains the surgeon. "It's a defense mechanism.
The body walls off the implant to protect itself."

"Scar tissue—it looks like a balloon and a squid had a baby," says
Gourley, noting my grimace. The circulator nurse puts the specimen in
a container and labels it for pathology.

"We always check for atypical cells," says Chang. "Last year, one
patient wanted a standard breast reduction. Her mammogram was nor-

mal. We sent the breast tissue we removed to pathology. Came back showing cancer. Then she had to have a mastectomy. She told me that she thought the reduction was a waste of $20,000 at first, but then she realized it was the best $20K she'd ever spent."

With the right implant and scar tissue removed, Chang lets me peek over her shoulder into the pocket where they were. The pectoralis muscle looks like rare steak, while the chest wall is pale pink with gentle ridges of ribs. I return to a spot a few feet away while Chang sutures Anne's pecs back where they belong. Most cosmetic augmentations position the implant below the muscle rather than on top of it, where the breast tissue naturally resides. It is less bloody and more efficient. However, many athletes insist on having their implants over the muscle so as not to compromise their pec strength and so their breasts don't "animate" and swing toward their armpits when they flex.

"Beautiful breasts, in my opinion, have a gentle slope and are rounded at the bottom with the nipples a tad above center," says Chang.

As a straight man who has seen many breast surgeries, Gourley must have a view, so I ask him for it.

"A good-looking breast?" says Gourley, buying himself time. "Ten years ago, I was like, 'Go big or go home.' Dr. Chang would roll her eyes and ignore me. I liked voluptuous women with a close cleavage. About five years ago, I got more subtle, understanding that an ideal breast is the one that makes the patient happy."

"What about when you're dating?" I probe, having heard that Gourley is divorced.

"You don't have to be any size or shape to be sexy," he replies. "She can have natural or augmented breasts, a reduction or a lift, but I am not keen on capsular contracture. I like two soft pillows, not hard cantaloupes. It's uncomfortable for her and me."

A placard on the wall of the operating room catches my eye. The Wi-Fi password at this surgery center is "newbeauty." I ask Chang if she has a definition of beauty.

"Inner beauty comes from outer beauty," jokes Chang, reversing the platitude.

Philosopher Kathleen Higgins argues that beauty is "an ideal of balance and health" whose truth, unity, and order incite love. She argues that the opposite of beauty is "kitsch . . . an aesthetic form of lying," characterized by flawlessness and glamour. Flawlessness, for Higgins, is an "empty achievement" characterized by inert features that lack unity.[5] Glamour is trapped in webs of fantasy that typically engage women "in a vicious circle."[6] Cosmetic surgery focuses on flaws and is greatly influenced by the glamour business. In short, the big boob jobs that Chang finds tasteless could be seen as kitsch.

"My beauty ideal is—or was when I was growing up—a tall, thin, European model," says Chang. "It's awful, because I'm Asian. My mother wanted me to have double eyelid surgery from the age of about twelve, but I resisted. I actually have some pride in my heritage." Chang notes that the dominance of European models in fashion campaigns has finally waned, with protests such as recent Black Lives Matter and Stop Asian American and Pacific Islander Hate. "But if you look at the models that the media claims as diverse," she adds, "they are usually mixed-race and pretty pale compared to the Asian or African population as a whole."

Beauty standards have long been determined by the ruling classes, I confirm.

"Cosmetic surgery is not democratic either," says Chang. "It is not an equal opportunity option." Chang has an upscale client base who tend to pay in full in advance. Unlike most plastic surgeons in private practice, she does not work with medical financing companies. She'd rather not have clients going into debt to bankroll their boob jobs. As one unlucky patient, who had trouble with infections and capsular contracture, told me, "I could have bought a Bentley for the price of all my breast surgeries."

o o

"They say that Washington DC is Hollywood for ugly people," quipped Dr. Kelly Bolden when I interviewed her in her fourth-floor office at Howard University Hospital. Passionate about breast surgeries, Bolden had not yet had one herself. She was still breastfeeding her baby and thinking about having a second child. "Once that's done," she admitted, "something has to happen to these girls." Born in Houston, Texas, the birthplace of the breast implant, Bolden studied chemistry at Spelman, a historically Black college, before attending medical school and obtaining plastic surgery training at the University of Texas, Southwestern, in Dallas.

"Dallas loves them bigger, better, higher, tighter. At dinner parties, people will ask, 'Who's your plastic surgeon?' They're not ashamed," explained Bolden, who was wearing turquoise scrubs with sizable diamond stud earrings "stolen" from her mother. Her office was dowdy but cheery, decorated with thank-you cards emblazoned with fun-font declarations, such as "I'd love to live in a world run by women like you." Bolden was working one day a week here, operating with university residents, and spending the rest of her time in private practice. "In DC, people just want to look less tired, a little younger, refreshed. They don't want to be the most glamorous person in the room and certainly don't want to stand out as enhanced."

Miami is the American city with the most plastic surgeons per capita.[7] "Florida does not require doctors to carry malpractice insurance. They can still be sued, but the cost savings reduce their overhead," explained Bolden, with a glance at a blue crate of well-fingered silicone implants on the floor. In the Sunshine State, one occasionally hears about "stacked implants," where the surgeon inserts more than one silicone bag to obtain more volume than condoned by the FDA.[8] Meanwhile, in Hollywood, rumors abound that actresses swap out implant sizes to reposition themselves for new movie roles—transitions that are noticeable to their fans but vehemently denied by their publicists.

Predictably, "Beverly Hills natural" looks nothing like "Berkeley natural" or "Baltimore natural." Indeed, "natural" is a word that Bolden tries to avoid. "Nothing we do is natural. We dye our hair, wear makeup and bras. Natural means letting nature run its course. Nobody comes into my office to do that."

Roughly 95 percent of Bolden's patients are women of color—mostly African American with a subset of Latinas. "They have similar aesthetic desires. They don't want large breasts as much as full breasts. They want an hourglass figure with a flat tummy, small waist, and curvy hips." As a consultant to Allergan's DREAM initiative (which stands for Driving Racial Equity in Aesthetic Medicine), Bolden is sensitive to the way class, ethnicity, and religion affect people's perceptions of the aesthetically pleasing. Her job as a body sculptor is to "create harmony," as she put it, "and resist monolithic versions of beauty where everyone is the same." White beauty, she notes, is no longer always dominant, citing the trend toward the fuller lips associated with the African diaspora.

Bolden is resistant to the idea of beauty universals. Playing devil's advocate, I suggested that human attraction to youthfulness could be cross-cultural because aging is ultimately associated with death. Bolden disagreed. "Some men find it very attractive when women look like they've had and breastfed children," she said. "They don't mind stretch marks or breasts that are a little deflated." When I mentioned the much-discussed love of symmetry, speculating that it could relate to primal fears about illness or amputation, she exclaimed, "But symmetry is not natural!" Indeed, the expectation of symmetry likely resulted from the invention of geometry, its resurgence during the Renaissance, and its dominance in the industrial age. We now measure ourselves against representations and machines.

People of color have more difficulty with scarring. Higher-melanin skins are associated with scars that mushroom and spread (called keloids) and thick raised welts (called hypertrophic scars). "I spend a lot of my time figuring out how to minimize and camouflage scarring," said Bolden, with a glance at the print above her desk depicting

an operating room full of tall, slim African American medical professionals. "I want to give my patients the most favorable scars possible by
using the right suture materials and applying negative pressure bandage systems that decrease swelling and promote blood flow. It's also
important to be atraumatic or gentle with their tissue."

Tissue. I asked her why doctors don't use the word "flesh."

"Tissue is a broad term, embracing all the body's material, including
bone," said Bolden. "Flesh makes me think of church." Indeed, bibli-
cally, the flesh is opposed to the soul. The word came into Old English
from *fleisch*, the German for "meat." "Tissue" is much more genteel. It
derives from the past participle of the French verb *tisser*, meaning to
weave. In other words, "tissue" was initially an analogy used to describe
a collection of cells woven together into an organ like a breast.

I'd also been ruminating on the designation "plastic" surgery. "It
comes from the Greek *plastikos*, meaning to mold and shape, which is
basically what we do with the body," said Bolden. For the record, silicone is not a plastic, developed primarily from fossil fuels, but a synthe-
sis of silica stone, water, and natural gas–derived methanol. Although I
usually savor the opportunity to talk about design materials, thinking
about the content of implants was refocusing my discontent with Bert
and Ernie.

Bolden performs both reconstructive surgeries covered by insurance and cosmetic surgeries for cash, so she has a clear understanding of the ideological and practical differences between the two
genres. "As a fully trained general surgeon, I went into plastics for
the reconstruction," she explained. "In my mind at that time, cosmetic surgeons were dabbling, doing the frou-frou stuff, while reconstructive surgeons did the big, important stuff. But, now, if I'm honest
and transparent about the breast surgeries I do, my most challenging
cases are cosmetic. When the sole reason for the surgery is aesthetics,
the patient is going to assess every millimeter of the contour and scar.
It can be stressful."

One of Bolden's specialties is the upper body lift in which she com-pletely reconstructs her patient's torso after massive weight loss brought about by gastric surgeries and other medical interventions. When a woman loses 200 pounds and goes from being morbidly obese—now labeled Class III obesity—down to "normal" or simply "overweight," her breasts can be hard to distinguish from other billowing curtains of skin.[9] Sometimes a patient's nipple is so misplaced that it is a serious business determining where the "nipple–areolar complex" should go. "When we're in training, we're taught all the averages, like 20 to 23 centimeters is the distance from the sternal notch to the nipple," said Bolden, rattling off more dimensions than I could absorb and reveal-ing her inner math nerd. "But it is also important to use a patient's own anatomy as landmarks to ensure you don't put anything where it is not supposed to be. Sometimes I'll align the nipple with the midpoint of the humerus in the upper arm."

The biggest challenge for breast reconstruction after major weight loss is skin laxity. "When someone is obese, the collagen fibers in their skin fracture and they have elastosis, evidenced by stretch marks," said Bolden. "When we operate, we take away as much skin as we can and everything looks great on the table—tight and lifted—but, as they heal, the skin stretches even more." To mitigate against postoperative breasts slipping out to the side or sagging further, Bolden will sometimes stitch the breast onto the chest wall or use bioengineered pigskin, known as Strattice, to improve the stability of her work. She prefers Strattice to Alloderm—skin harvested from human cadavers—because it is less stretchy.

Women who were obese and now have deflated, low-slung boobs often opt for implants as part of an upper body lift. "My patients don't just want their breasts lifted back onto their chest wall, they want them high and they want volume," explained Bolden. "They are sensitive about upper fullness, probably because they've never had it. Maybe 80 percent of my private post–weight loss patients seek augmentation."

When their breasts are back in place, these patients are elated to see their pubic mound. "Some of them haven't seen their FUPA [fatty upper pubic area] in years."

Less than 18 percent of active plastic surgeons in the United States are women, despite the fact that over 90 percent of the clientele is female. This contrasts with the most female of medical disciplines, pediatrics, which is 65 percent women. The most male-dominated and, not coincidentally, the most lucrative medical specialty is orthopedic surgery, which is 94 percent men. Meanwhile, people who identify as Black or African American account for just 3.4 percent of plastic surgeons, which compares poorly with obstetrics and gynecology, where Black doctors account for a more significant 11 percent of the profession.[10]

Bolden looks forward to the day when women plastic surgeons have a greater influence on the aesthetic standards of her industry. Some surgeons intentionally design breasts with nipples far above their normal location. "When I go to plastic surgery conferences, the majority of the experts on breasts are still men," she said. "When they talk about an aesthetically pleasing breast and show their before and afters, the female surgeons in the audience will cringe because it's obvious that these men find what we call 'pseudo ptosis' attractive." Ptosis means droop. Pseudo, or fake, ptosis is a confusing term; it describes a condition where the nipple is in the upper half of the breast, sometimes even pointing up, and the sag is in the lower half of the breast only. "Women don't like it," continued Bolden about this mannerist shape that reminds me of the cartoons in old *Playboy* magazines. "They find it disconcerting when their nipples pop out of their bras."

"The most social part of the breast—which has stood the test of time—is the cleavage," said Bolden. "So that's a primary goal—to give them the best appearance of their cleavage as possible. We see trends in certain age groups for showing under-boob and side-boob. But most of my patients are extraordinarily happy if they can show cleavage." Indeed, cleavages are friendly and outgoing. They can be a mark of hospitality and largesse. As Bolden put it, "Across the board, men and women, it doesn't matter, an attractive cleavage, it's the first place that your eyes go."

○ ○

Back in San Francisco, Dr. Chang is now on the other side of Anne, excavating her left breast with a fresh scalpel. The plastic surgeon's clientele consists primarily of slim white women who range from functionally anorexic to mildly overweight. For safety reasons, she rarely operates on patients with a body mass index over 29.

"Operating on obese people is physically exhausting," says the circulator nurse matter-of-factly.

"Many Asians have fat phobia," admits Chang. "As open-minded as I think I am—or want to be—it is hard to resist the idea that thinness is next to godliness. That's why menopause is hard for me. I've gained weight and I hate it." Chang's forties were not easy. After failing to get pregnant, she and her husband had a daughter through a surrogate. Tragically, their daughter died of cancer at the age of two. With two fertilized embryos in the freezer, they tried again. This time, two women gave birth within a few months of each other to their son and daughter, whom they call the twins.[11]

One of Chang's office assistants, Joey, has the overtly enhanced appearance of a character in a Japanese anime movie or video game. A young Asian American woman from California's Central Valley, she has built up her shoulders and glutes through intense daily workouts. Her naturally small waist is crowned with a DD bust, the result of 700 cc saline implants. With her pale pink hair and matte black eyeshadow, she comes across as a petite superhero.

"Joey has amazing style," says Chang. "She can get away with anything. Strength is the new skinny."

An international bounty of evidence suggests that the split in beauty ideals between a natural-looking bust and an overtly synthetic one relates to class background and disparate versions of authenticity. A segment of British working-class women, for example, seek fake tits as a "form of conspicuous consumption that gives them status" and signals that they are independent women in "control and command of the male gaze."[12] Similarly, a contingent of Brazilian women "who began their lives in poverty" want people to know they have implants as "a form of achievement and financial accomplishment."[13] In America, self-declared feminist rappers like Cardi B, whose augmented cleavage is neither a visual nor a verbal secret, imply analogous arguments when they talk about their success.

The godmother of the conspicuous boob job is Dolly Parton. The singer-songwriter is also a pioneer in publicly acknowledging her plastic surgery. Indeed, she strategically uses fakeness to enhance her realness. She jokes about her giant bosom as an emblem of her unsophisticated "white trash" roots and a badge of her honesty as a "diamond in a rhinestone world." When asked if she has been the real Dolly Parton, she has been known to reply, "Honey, there is no such thing as the real Dolly Parton."[14]

Having completed her "spring clean" of Anne's second breast, Chang proceeds to the lift portion of the surgery. With a sterile purple marker, she creates a perfect circle on the areola using a metal "cookie cutter" 42 millimeters in diameter. Then, with the help of Gourley, she starts pulling up and reshaping the breast using a surgical stapler.

"When a woman stops breastfeeding, the breast tissue involutes and shrinks. The areola can be really big and the nipple is usually low. It's a big baggy mess," says Chang. "My mission here is restorative—to give her back the breasts she had before she got pregnant. She wants her identity back." Along the bottom of Anne's left breast in the location we might associate with a bra underwire is a smile of metal clips. A short line connects this smile to her stapled areola, which resembles a sundial.

"This is the design stage," says Chang, who mocks up her newly con-

Dolly Parton, a self-made woman.

Cardi B: breasts as a sign of success.

structed breasts before removing skin or doing anything permanent.
"We're doing a lollipop lift, so-called for the shape of the scar. This
patient also has an anchor scar, but that's from her previous surgery."
Chang breaks off to concentrate on shaping an elegant breast.

o o

While various American surgeons have published papers claiming the
invention of breast lifts that look like the lollipop, Brazilians assume
that they were innovated by Dr. Ivo Pitanguy, a plastic surgeon and
philanthropist who became famous for proclaiming, "The poor have
a right to be beautiful." Dr. Barbara Machado, the head of Pitanguy's
medical team for sixteen years, spoke to me over Zoom from her office
in Rio de Janeiro. "Professor Pitanguy was doing breast reductions
before we were born," she acknowledged. Pitanguy started operating
on underprivileged people in the 1950s, often performing charity surgeries for asymmetrical and uncomfortably oversized breasts. Rejecting
what he saw as a false dichotomy between reconstructive and cosmetic
procedures, Pitanguy argued that aesthetic improvements were medical necessities where the "real object of healing was not the body, but
the mind."[15] Indeed, studies show that breast reductions improve confidence as much as they ameliorate backaches.[16] Needless to say, breast
lifts elevate self-esteem.

Brazilians undergo more cosmetic surgeries than people from any
other nation, likely due to the influence of Pitanguy's ideas. Machado, who did residencies in oncology, plastic surgery, and microsurgery in Brazil and a PhD in medical sciences in Britain, offered several
other reasons for her home country's enthusiasm for aesthetic surgery.
"First, we have a sunny, hot climate," she said, "with 8,000 kilometers
of beaches where the body is exposed. We can't use heavy coats to
hide our imperfections." Second, the Latin influence from Italian and
Portuguese migration means that Brazilians put a high premium on
romance and sex appeal.

"What do you want me to solve in your life with the knife?" Machado asks prospective clients. "Most patients come to be submitted to surgery because they do not love themselves as they are. They want the knife to make an inner change. The plastic surgeon must make sure the patient knows that we are not magicians. You get new breasts, but you have scars. You have to accept them to accept the new you." According to anthropologist Alexander Edmonds, many Brazilians believe that plastic surgery is an effective therapy, hence the joke: "What's the difference between a psychoanalyst and a plastic surgeon? The psychoanalyst knows everything but changes nothing. The plastic surgeon knows nothing but changes everything."[17]

In Brazil, women with breast implants are nicknamed *siliconadas*. However, breast augmentation is not the most frequently performed plastic surgery. Indeed, only 13 percent of Brazilian cosmetic procedures are breast augmentations, compared with an astonishing quarter of all aesthetic surgeries in the United States.[18] "In Brazil, we don't

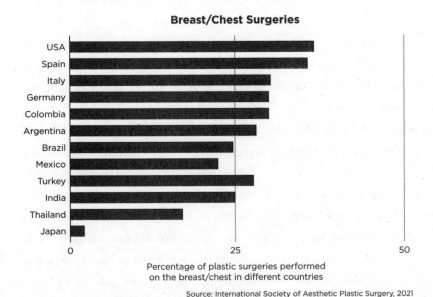

Breast/Chest Surgeries

Percentage of plastic surgeries performed
on the breast/chest in different countries

Source: International Society of Aesthetic Plastic Surgery, 2021

like big boobs. We like the gym. We like sinuous, sculpted bodies," explained Machado. "The miscegenation of many races means that we have a common sense of beauty that embraces diversity as a positive," added Machado, whose ancestry is predominantly Italian with an Indigenous grandmother to whom she attributes her straight black hair. Put another way, Brazilians aim to be aesthetic relativists, appreciating many versions of attractiveness. A consensus has nevertheless formed around a golden-brown mixed-race ideal that reflects Brazil's fantasy self-image as a place of racial harmony.

"Beauty is a sensation," Machado told me in conclusion. "When a child sees something that is beautiful, their eyes shine. When they see something that is not pleasing, they retreat. Beauty is comforting. This is how beauty and normality come together."

○ ○

Anne's chest rises and falls ever so subtly under the hands of Dr. Chang and her surgical first assistant Gourley. Having completed lifting their patient's left breast with staples, Chang and Gourley are now elevating and reshaping the right.

I ask everyone in the room if they think humans are hardwired to experience beauty as a source of pleasure.

Absorbed in her work, Chang doesn't seem to hear me. Gourley, however, raises his head. "We're hardwired to like salt and fat. Why not beauty?" he says. "But what's beautiful has gone from Olivia Newton-John to Cardi B. It's impossible to extricate beauty from social norms. Just like when people say, 'I want to look natural,' what they really mean is 'I want the look that is trending at the moment.' "

"When you're bombarded by images all day, every day," says Chang without shifting her gaze, "your version of natural beauty is hyper-real."

Low breast esteem may correlate with high levels of media consumption, possibly because representations amplify the role of cosmetic surgery in creating false norms. A recent survey of women from forty nations found that "breast size dissatisfaction" increased with Western media exposure. It also found that discontent with one's chest was higher among less financially secure women.[19] Various studies reveal that rates of cosmetic surgery do not correlate with those who can most afford it.[20] I wonder whether working-class women are more inclined to view their bodies as their main repository of value, whereas upper- and middle-class women see themselves as having diversified assets, which include educational capital, social networks, family-related financial security, and status-conferring professions and careers.

I recently interviewed a seventy-year-old woman who has had seven breast surgeries. First a lift, then implants, then larger implants, then smaller ones, and upon divorce, bigger ones again. After those five elective surgeries, she started having trouble healing and experienced skin death.[21] After two further surgeries and ongoing complications, she still clings to a pretty hefty pair of implants. She initially had no explanation for her relentless alteration of her bosom, then she told me two revealing anecdotes. First, she had never seen her mother's bare breasts and "had no idea what they looked like." Second, shortly after her parents divorced, she and her sister discovered their father's old *Playboy* magazines on top of a cupboard in the garage. "Those pictures of upturned, puffy boobs," she confessed, "made an impression so deep."

"In our culture, there is an undercurrent that breasts are empowering," says Chang, "so some women alter and exploit their bodies to further their own interests." She looks up at the anesthesiologist and says, "Okay, let's sit her up." The torso rises on the top half of the table, invoking a parody of *Dawn of the Dead*. Chang always considers the effect of gravity on her forms. The surgeon stands back, crosses her arms, and inspects how the breasts are hanging. "It's easy to make two independently good-looking breasts," she says. "The hard thing is getting them the same and my clients expect symmetry."

"Breasts are just sisters, but everybody wants identical twins," says Gourley, as he hands Chang a sterile measuring tape. "The nipples need to be level and center. We can't have east–west Chihuahua eyes."

Chang puts her thumb on the top of Anne's sternum and measures the distance between it and the right and then left nipples. "One and a half centimeters off," she declares. She walks a few steps back, contemplates her patient's chest, then steps forward and palpates the lower-hanging breast with one and then two cupped hands. "Ok, you can lie her back down," says Chang. Once the patient is prone, Gourley and Chang quickly extract all the staples from her right breast to start over.

I wander behind the drapes to chat with the anesthesiologist. When I ask if she has had any aesthetic surgeries, her facial expression makes it clear that she has not. "Breast surgeries are indulgent," she says under her breath as she monitors Anne's vitals. "Except reductions, which are mostly necessary. Tubular breasts—that's a real disfigurement. Extreme asymmetry—okay. But most cosmetic surgeries are taking aim at a moving target, which means you're always going to be insecure."

Moral judgments about breast surgeries are abundant. Based on the hundreds of interviews I've done on breasts, it is evident that augmentations are the most condemned—one reason why many women with implants are so secretive about them. Implant removals and exchanges are accompanied by a fair amount of patient shame and self-blame. Lifts receive less opprobrium perhaps because, without a silicone insert, they are not seen as fake or fraudulent. Also, lifts might be condoned because saggy breasts are widely perceived as an eyesore—even an infirmity—while small ones are not. Women with breasts big enough to want a reduction often have backaches, muscle strain, bra-strap grooving and bruising, skin irritation, exercise intolerance, and other health deficits that legitimize their surgeries. Indeed, over a third of reductions in the United States are considered reconstructive, if only because they tick enough boxes for health insurance companies to pay for them.[22]

Since 92 percent of American cosmetic surgeries are performed on women,[23] I ask Chang if she thinks plastic surgery is a feminist issue.

"I don't know," says Chang. "I've never identified as a feminist, although I'm the main breadwinner. My husband is an artist who does a lot of childcare. I believe in equal rights, but I'm not a militant or puritanical. I enjoy being a woman. I like being pretty. I appreciate positive male attention."

For many years, feminists viewed plastic surgery, especially aesthetic breast surgeries, as evidence of internalized misogyny. In her widely read book *The Beauty Myth*, Naomi Wolf decries breast surgeries as "socially approved self-injury."[24] Even nuanced philosophers of bodily experience like Iris Marion Young saw breast augmentation as a form of "phallocentric" compliance and disdained post-cancer breast reconstruction as "the ultimate in breast objectification."[25] Melissa Febos laments this history, admitting that she delayed a long-desired breast reduction because she associated the surgery with a "failure to be a real feminist."[26] The sanctimonious rejection of her profession did not exactly welcome Chang into the feminist movement.

"I don't see women who are making choices as victims," says Chang. "Women need to use the power they have. Cleopatra, Helen of Troy, Nefertiti—their beauty contributed to their influence. It's silly to turn your back on your allure. Destroying one of the few powers you have is not strategic." Indeed, in the 1990s, some businesswomen opted for big breasts as a "compensatory and de-threatening" strategy to enhance their womanliness and avoid being stigmatized as dykes in the masculine domains in which they had won success.[27]

While most feminists have seen beauty as a form of submission, others have argued that it is a means of resistance. For me, the binary logic of this "structure versus agency" debate is a dead end. The pursuit of beauty can be *both* a form of obedience *and* an effort to subvert or surmount. As Rita Felski writes, feminists need to craft thicker descriptions of aesthetic experience so we can balance the political costs of being beautiful with the emotional benefits. Only then can we do justice to the reasons why humans pursue and take solace in beauty.[28]

"Sounds healthy to me," says Chang.

The appeal of beauty is a deep-seated part of our humanity. It's a source of joy and wonder, whether it's a setting sun, a sensuous silk, a couple of kittens, or a balanced pair of buoyant breasts. "Our preoccupation with [beauty] cannot be wished away," writes Eleanor Heartney in *Beauty Matters*. "It knits the mind and body together at a time when they are too easily divided."[29]

"When people are stressed or depressed, they stop grooming," says Chang. "When you take pride in yourself, you take care of yourself. The better you look, the better you feel, and vice versa. Beautification can be a means of revering the value in yourself." Having finished rearranging and restapling the right breast, Chang requests that the patient be sat back up. Again, the top half of the table ascends and Anne rises zombie-like into the room.

"This is going to look so much better, more normal, less freaky," says the circulator nurse.

"She had cute little boobs before and now she has them again," says Chang. "She should be happy with this." Chang remeasures the distance between Anne's sternum and both of her nipples. "Perfect," she says. "We've optimized the shape and placement. Now we have to make it permanent." Chang strips off her stained gloves and gently smudged gown, swapping them for fresh ones.

o o

While most plastic surgeries of the breast are cosmetic, a significant number are deemed reconstructive, or medically necessary, due to deformities caused by genes, disease, or injury. Officially, reconstructive surgery repairs a function, such as the use of a finger, but reconstructive breast surgeries never restore lactation, the mammary gland's only biological purpose. Indeed, in the case of a breast reduction deemed essential to a woman's health, the surgery often disrupts her capacity to breastfeed.[30]

In the medical world, "functional" is a synonym for "normal." As one plastic surgeon explained, reconstruction tries to "restore the normal," whereas cosmetic surgeries want to "achieve the supernormal."[31] When breasts are lost to cancer, reconstructive surgery is often said to rebuild a sense of womanhood. For this reason, I sometimes see my own breast reconstruction as a gender re-affirmation surgery. It did not restore any real functionality; it reinstalled a graphic marker of my gender.

Dr. Elisabeth Potter has a broader and more nuanced view.[32] She's a leading surgeon in what is arguably the most advanced form of breast reconstruction, the DIEP (pronounced "deep") flap, which transfers a woman's own belly tissue, along with the blood vessels that sustain it, to her chest.[33] A tall, athletic woman, Potter comes from a family of male doctors and female nurses. Her brother is a urologist, specializing in "men down there, penises and bladders"—a striking contrast to Potter's resolute focus on the feminine top half. Like many surgeons, Potter wears a sports bra in the OR, citing favorites such as Lululemon's Free to Be bra and Outdoor Voice's Athena, whose name pays homage to the goddess of wisdom and warfare.

The surgeon and I spoke in a small windowless room with a sign on the door that read "Nourishment Closet"—a ridiculously appropriate location, as "nourish" comes from the breast-related Latin verb *nutrire*, meaning to suckle, feed, bring up, and look after. Alongside a small counter and stools, it featured a coffee machine and hot-water maker, boxes of saltines and peanut butter pouches, and a fridge where medical staff stored their lunches and leftovers. The cramped space was down the hall from the operating room in which I'd observed Potter perform a DIEP flap microsurgery on an anemic woman with no eyebrows who was fresh out of chemotherapy.[34]

Most of Potter's patients are breast cancer survivors.[35] A few have had prophylactic mastectomies because they have genetic mutations, such as BRCA. Medical necessity, along with a fear of recurring cancer and a dread of further mammograms, biopsies, and other invasive tests, contribute to women's choice to remove both breasts. A final reason is the availability of reconstructive plastic surgery services.[36] Certainly, the brutality of my decision to have a double mastectomy, which removed all my breast tissue, was softened by the promise of reconstruction. Still, only 40 percent of women who lose their breasts for cancer-related reasons go on to have reconstruction.[37]

According to Potter, breast reconstruction is not just about femininity, even if the "end goal is to feel beautiful again." Potter's interest in plastics was sparked during childhood by concern for her grandfather, a deputy sheriff who got by on one leg and a clunky prosthetic until an infection in his "good leg" led to a second amputation. A proud, strong man in his sixties, he became depressed. "Reconstruction helps women rebuild a little bit of what's been taken away. It's often the first time during their cancer journey that they're talking about the future. Planning for the future is healing," she explained between swigs of fruit punch with added electrolytes. "When you lose a body part, the way you see yourself changes. We know that women feel happier when they are given choices about reconstruction, especially in a society where the appearance of a woman's breasts is so charged. Just because you've had cancer doesn't mean that you can't participate in the conversation."

Potter sees the positive decision to "go flat" as an important reconstructive choice. "I love it when a woman comes in and says, 'I'm done with these. I just want to get on with my life. I want to get healthy,'" said Potter. "All sorts of women choose a flat closure. They are usually burnt out with surgery or psychologically strong in their skin, or both." In these circumstances, Potter will perform a "beautiful flat closure"—a smooth even smile of a scar with no wrinkly grimaces or lopsided scowls.[38] Once healed, some of her patients opt to beautify and reclaim their chests with tattoos.

A historic image of what I see as a "liberated rack" involves a tat-

Deena Metzger: the body as a book.

tooed flat closure. After her unilateral mastectomy in 1977, the eco-feminist poet Deena Metzger had foliage tattooed along the scar. She then posed for a photo—top-free with her arms outstretched and her face tilted toward the sun. Inscribed on the poster version of the work are Metzger's words: "I have the body of a warrior who does not kill or wound. On the book of my body, I have permanently inscribed a tree." The iconic portrait transforms what has been perceived as disfigurement into a new kind of beauty. It shifts a private loss into a public expression of glorious survival.

Potter admires the Metzger image and laments the sexism of some members of her profession. "During training, we were told that if a woman wanted to go flat, it was a sign of poor mental health. It was assumed that she didn't care about her body," said Potter. "No one ever talked about the result from the patient's perspective. The male faculty at UT Southwestern focused on what they found sexy and appealing. Natural breasts were criticized. Artificially inflated ones were glorified. They commended the surgeon who asked the husband about sizing up the implants while the wife was asleep."

With breast reconstruction, the plastic surgeon often steps into the OR just after the cancer surgeon has completed the mastectomy. Having had this surgery myself, it was stressful to observe another woman go through it—a forty-four-year-old Black woman from rural Texas brought to the hospital by her tearful mother and adult daughter. The inside of her whole left breast was placed on the scale, looking like a few pounds of uncooked ground lamb with a forlorn nipple in the middle. Later, the pathologist announced over the PA system that one of her sentinel lymph nodes, which I'd seen in a petri dish, had tested positive for cancer. When Potter came into the room to place a temporary "expander" inside her breast cavity, she explained that African American women are more likely to be diagnosed late with more advanced and aggressive cancers and have higher mortality rates. They also have a higher incidence of "triple-negative" breast cancer. "What a loaded term," she said with exasperation. "It means that their cancer is not responsive to the three treatments we've developed and use to classify breast cancer."[39]

Most breast reconstructions involve implants. Potter performs breast augs and recons with implants, but the procedures don't bring her much job satisfaction. "They're easy. They can be hard to finesse but, basically, you just take the implant out of the box and put it in," she said, pausing to bite into a peanut butter power bar. "I try to approach my job without biases. I don't think that my patients have the same feelings about their breasts that I have about mine." Recently, a woman drove 500 miles to see Potter because the plastic surgeon who'd installed her implants refused to remove them. He didn't like the appearance of breasts after implant removal, declaring, "My results are my calling card and I don't want my name on that." Potter was irate. "He disempowers the patient. He doesn't care about individualized results. He negates her body, her choice."

When Potter does a reconstruction using implants, she prefers to place them over the pectoral muscles rather than in the most common position, under it. "I have done both," she said, "but putting an implant under the pecs isn't the natural anatomic place of the breast. It throws your body out of alignment. It pulls your shoulders forward because your pecs are attached to your clavicle, sternum, and humerus." Prepectoral or over-the-muscle reconstructions are also less prone to developing the uncomfortable scar tissue called capsular contracture and have quicker recovery times.[40]

When I had reconstructive surgery after losing both breasts, I was not offered a choice. No one mentioned that it was possible to place implants over the pecs, despite my request for athletic "yoga boobs," and now I have "exercise intolerance" in the form of pain and stiffness after swimming and yoga. Having not had a doctor look at my breasts since my follow-up with the surgeon who did the work (described in the introduction), I asked Potter to give my tits a quick assessment. Within seconds of hoisting my top, she told me that the implant on my right side was flipped; the flat side looked out while the curved side faced my rib cage, which explained that breast's curiously dead appearance. On my left side, the implant was being strangled by the scar tissue around it, dragging it up and out toward my armpit. This common condition, known as capsular contracture, was also contributing to my pectoral soreness.

Potter's favorite surgery, the one for which she is gathering renown, reconstructs a breast from fatty flesh. She sees something "magical" in the fact that "you can use spare parts." Many women gain weight with menopause and chemotherapy. "That's one reason why DIEP flap reconstruction can be so nice for these ladies. The tummy tuck tissue is usually thrown away, but here we repurpose it to rebuild her breasts," said Potter. "With cancer, her body betrayed her. But with this form of reconstruction, her body gives back. It's a happy ending to a super shitty experience."

In the past, autologous breast reconstructions involved transplanting muscle from either the abdomen (TRAM flap) or the back (a latissimus flap). Potter sees these surgeries as archaic, if not barbaric. "They are deforming surgeries that deprive women of strength," she said. "They are more painful and prone to nasty complications, like hernias. They're substandard, if not debilitating."

DIEP flap surgery is particularly useful for women who've had complications. "We see a lot of radiated implants," said Potter. When I followed the surgeon on her preoperative rounds, we saw one woman whose radiated skin was so thin that her breast implant was visible and another patient who had crunchy doughnuts for breasts, the result of chronic postoperative infections. "The FDA warns against combining implants and radiation," explained Potter.[41] On our last visit, a younger woman, who had traveled from Nashville for her DIEP flap reconstruction, felt invaded by her hefty implants. "They don't feel like mine. I want these foreign objects out, but I hate surgery," she confessed. "And I'm really nervous."

"I'm not nervous at all," replied Potter. "I will treat you like my sister. I don't have kids; I have patients." Potter and her husband live with a motley gang of dogs, including eleven-year-old Judy, a rescued laboratory animal used for breast cancer research. She suffered through mastectomies, radiation, and lab-induced lymphedema, a common side effect of cancer treatment in which the body swells with undrained lymphatic fluid.

Compared with implant reconstructions, the downsides of DIEP flap surgeries are more scars and a longer recovery time. DIEP flap surgery is also more expensive in the short term. In the long term, implants need replacing. By contrast, natural-tissue reconstructions last forever. "Insurance companies don't usually care about the long term. Flaps fail fast. The complications usually happen within forty-eight hours, whereas implant recons tend to get worse with time," explained Potter. "Implant manufacturers support the entire machine of plastic surgery. Anything that threatens implants gets a lot of criticism because they generate work every ten to twelve years."

Potter and her microsurgical partner, Dr. Steven Henry, have performed well over a thousand DIEP flap breast reconstructions together. "Practice makes perfect," as she put it. Microsurgery, which uses high-magnification microscopes and superfine instruments, is physically intense. Potter is always concerned about "staying hyper-focused so we can deliver for these ladies." There are no guidelines about the appropriate time length of a DIEP flap surgery. "Our colleagues often take eight hours. We usually do it in four and have lower complication rates," said Potter with pride. "Dr. Henry and I have had only three flap failures in the past five years and no failures in the past two."[42]

Planning is essential to Potter's speed and accuracy. She studies detailed CAT scans of the patient's abdomen to determine exactly which artery and vein she will extract for the tissue transplant, then draws a map of mysterious lines and numbers that she takes with her into the OR. "Dr. Potter is a master," said Henry. "She has a 3D picture in her head of the vessels. We're efficient and our outcomes are reliable. It's a joy to work together."

Potter, in turn, praised Henry's "highly refined, calm perfectionism" at suturing blood vessels. To join a vein that used to reside in the belly with one that has long nourished the chest, he uses a romantic little instrument called a coupler. Arteries are too thick for the coupler, so Henry sutures them by hand, stitching and knotting black thread that is no wider than a human hair. He performs these feats using a microscopic camera that magnifies his activities to eight times actual size. The sight of blood flowing through two newly united vessels is wondrous. "I get a kick out of it every time," admitted Henry. The sound inspires even more awe. Through an ultrasound doppler, everyone in the OR can hear the pulse of blood enlivening a new breast. It echoes the thrill of a fetal heartbeat.

Breasts made from transplanted belly tissue are warm, soft, and enduring. They don't just look like real breasts, they *feel* like real breasts. "The theme of my career has been getting out from under the male gaze," said Potter as she polished off her power bar in anticipation of another four hours in the OR sculpting two more DIEP flap breasts. "My patients wake up to their body transformed," she said. "They feel more at home in their body—with no foreign invaders. They feel less betrayed, less dependent, more sovereign. It's the beginning of a process of taking back power."

o o

Dr. Chang is using a sterile purple marker to designate exactly which pieces of skin will be removed. Gourley extracts the staples and Chang starts cutting away the top layer of the epidermis with a "ten blade." Blood trickles down Anne's breast. Butchers were the first surgeons, cutting off cancers and gangrenous limbs in the back of their shops because they had the sharp tools and the experience of slicing up animals. No wonder it's an operating "table" with "drapes," rather than a "bed" with "sheets." Surgeons also wore "aprons" before they switched to sterile "gowns."

Chang liberates a final triangle of skin from Anne's right breast. Gourley places it on a tray for biohazards. It looks a bit like Canadian bacon.

"Make you think of *Silence of the Lambs*?" asks Gourley, referring to the classic horror movie.

With the skin removed, Chang trims some of the edges with fine scissors so they are perfectly formed and makes a few tacking stitches to pull together the skin that will surround the new site of the nipple. With a few more stitches, Chang and Gourley line up the black Sharpie lines of the right breast's midline and then pull the nipple under and through to its new home. It's a deft act of assemblage. The pair start suturing the underlying flesh of Anne's new breast using a strong, absorbable thread that looks like fishing wire, then switch to smaller curved needles and a finer thread called Monocryl. Sometimes Anne's skin resists the needle like leather hide.

"Suturing is the first thing you learn as a surgery resident," says Chang, who ties a knot with great dexterity four times really fast.

Aesthetic surgery is a form of haute couture—a custom-made breast, dependent on highly refined sewing skills, I venture.

"It's only haute couture in the sense that we are both tailoring," says Chang. "I'm not creating something from nothing, just taking their breast and remodeling it. I'm more of a renovator."

Changing the subject, I ask if she has many trans patients.

"I've done augmentations on trans women. They've been great patients. Successful, educated, committed in all aspects. The latest one was a Google engineer," replies Chang. Although it is a lucrative surgery in San Francisco right now, Chang hasn't performed a chest masculinization. "I love breasts and mastectomies are very permanent. I don't have the staff or the experience to handle that ethical responsibility."

Dr. Potter, who is best known for her DIEP flaps, prefers performing masculinizations over feminizations, I volunteer, because she identifies with her patients' feelings of relief. Her main concern is exactly when to schedule the top surgery in the timeline of the patient's transition. When they have not taken testosterone, they can have "feminine fat" that gives them an androgynous rather than a masculine look, "which is fine as long as that's what they want." Her main question is invariably: "How can we make your body resonate with how you feel?"

"I respect that," says Chang, as she sutures Anne's breast with exacting efficiency. "I deal with a range of body dysmorphias, but gender dysphoria is not my strength."

Nonexperts often confuse body dysmorphia with gender dysphoria, despite the fact that psychiatrists and therapists are trained to treat them as completely different conditions. In the latest edition of the

Diagnostic and Statistical Manual of Mental Disorders (DSM–V–TR), published in 2022, dysmorphia is classified as an obsessive-compulsive disorder wherein the patient is preoccupied with perceived flaws in their physical appearance to the degree that they are emotionally distressed and socially impaired.[43] This condition is associated with cisgender straight women. Gender dysphoria, by contrast, is a stand-alone category, defined as a "marked incongruence between one's experienced/expressed gender and assigned gender."[44] It used to be called "gender identity disorder" and, prior to 1994, "transsexualism." Some trans people object to the pathological label, which echoes the way homosexuality was treated as a mental illness back in the 1950s.[45] Others see it as a necessary means of obtaining gender-affirming healthcare on insurance. As one psychologist told me, the DSM is a "screenshot of scientific knowledge and the biases of the time. In future, gender dysphoria may be understood as a cognitive difference like autism rather than a psychiatric illness."[46]

While Chang and Gourley work in silence, I mull over the perspectives of my other interviewees. Dr. Machado, the Brazilian surgeon, told me she was concerned that mastectomies have become a rite of passage essential to acceptance as an authentic insider in the transmasculine community. "It's an inner desire, yes, but it's a social pressure as well," she said. "To belong to the gang, you must pass through the ritual."

Many breast surgeries are the result of social pressure, although the sociality of people's choices is often disavowed. Trading beauty secrets and sharing aesthetic experiences can create bonds between girlfriends. Breast augmentations and so-called "mommy makeovers" (a lift with a tummy tuck) can facilitate insider status in certain social circles. When I reflect on my own breast reconstruction, I realize that other people's expectations were a significant factor. The medical team and my closest confidantes assumed I would have it. I never thought seriously about the idea of going flat.

Cisgender people, like myself, sometimes get into a muddle around trans terminology. "Cis" is the Latin prefix for "on this side"; it suggests that the gender of your body and psyche are aligned. The "trans" prefix means "across." Trans women are people who were assigned male at birth (AMAB) but identify as female or femme. The destination of their transition is womanhood. Trans men, by contrast, were assigned female at birth (AFAB) and are moving toward manhood.

Some people welcome the indeterminacy of a transitional body and opt for they/them pronouns. If they were assigned female at birth, they make a variety of decisions about their breasts. Some reject surgical intervention, alternately minimizing and displaying their cleavage as part of their gender-fluid or "genderful" identity, as Kitty KaPowww put it in chapter 1. One of my interviewees, who would prefer to have "no gender at all," opted for a reduction, shrinking their bosom by half to honor their "genderqueer inner landscape." Meanwhile, another interviewee, who calls themselves trans rather than nonbinary because they want to "*be* something, rather than *not* something," sought a masculinizing mastectomy, which they felt best chimed in with their tomboyish androgyny.

In many cultures, gender ambiguity can be a difficult position to occupy, threatening one's physical safety and psychological security. In these instances, top surgery is "a choice to sacrifice nuance for legibility," as writer Cyrus Grace Dunham puts it.[47]

Trans masculine people are twice as likely as trans women to have top surgery.[48] A mastectomy is generally the first and often the only surgery a trans man undergoes.[49] One reason is that the male body is the generic body and the breasted female body is stigmatized by gender. As Jack Halberstam, a trans masculine professor at Columbia University who had top surgery at the age of fifty-four, recounts, the procedure was not about "building maleness" but "editing some part of the femaleness that defined me."[50]

Another reason for lower rates of top surgery among trans women is their comparative satisfaction with hormonally induced tits. While

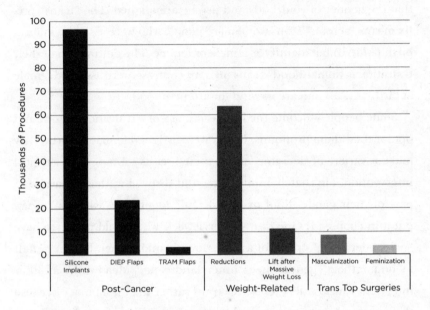

Reconstructive Top Surgeries

trans women can grow breasts on estrogen, no amount of testoster-one will remove boobs from the body of a trans man.[51] Wearing a padded bra is only a slight inconvenience for a trans woman, com-pared to the pain and discomfort of flattening one's chest by using a binder. Finally, trans women have greater difficulty obtaining top surgery on insurance.[52]

My friend Zackary Drucker, an artist and film director-producer, started taking testosterone blockers twenty years ago and estrogen shortly after that. Her left breast "popped" first and the right appeared a month later. Since then, she has been pleased with her breasts. "My prototypes are not big-breasted," she told me. "I wanted to look like Mia Farrow when I was young." Facing her fortieth birthday, however, she wondered whether a small implant boost might embolden her "cougar years." Keen to acquire a range of first and second opinions, she saw a couple of plastic surgeons in Los Angeles, and then flew up to San Francisco for back-to-back appointments with Dr. Chang and an older plastic surgeon, whom I'll call Dr. Moore, known for having a trans feminine clientele.[53] In accompanying Drucker, I witnessed two dramatically different approaches. Chang was happy to do the surgery using small 140 cc implants, a size often used to correct asymmetry rather than to enlarge breasts. Dr. Moore, however, insisted that 385 cc implants would be best because his ideal cleavage had a gap no wider than a pinky finger. The smallest implant he could imagine was 280 cc, I suspect because he'd established his surgical standards in the 1980s,

Zackary Drucker: budding affirmation.

when Pamela Anderson's bust was iconic. In the end, Drucker opted for a fat graft using liposuction, which extracted adipose tissue from four incision sites around the circumference of her midsection and then injected this liquified fat into her bosom. Drucker's breasts grew from a 36B to a 36C, which meant that she obtained, in her words, "exactly the subtle boob job" she wanted.

I found it strange that Dr. Moore was so concerned about a "gappy" cleavage, because Dr. Bolden, whom I saw in DC, told me that the greatest challenge of chest feminization was avoiding symmastia, otherwise known as uniboob. "You have to make sure not to violate the boundaries of the breast pocket," she explained. "Because the chest of someone born male doesn't necessarily have the same tissue attachments in the cleavage that prevents the implants from sliding into the center and becoming a monoboob."

With masculinization, Bolden identified the key challenges as scar style and nipple placement. Although male and female nipples are identical before puberty, they change shape and orientation after that. Male nipples tend to be smaller and have an elliptical shape brought about by the pectoral tension that pulls them toward the shoulders, whereas mature female nipples are round as a result of being pushed out by the volume of the breast. Shape, size, and location subtly register gender. As a 3D nipple tattoo artist explained to me, "nipples are really important because their absence or misplacement can cause unconscious alarm. Our brain goes into a loop searching for this fundamental marker of our humanity."

How will our unconscious expectations shift as more cis and trans people opt for surgically altered bodies? Writing thirty years ago, Susan Stryker, a historian and trans woman with augmented breasts, confessed a "deep affinity" with Frankenstein's monster. She described the trans form as "an unnatural body," "a technological construction," and "flesh torn apart and sewn together again in a shape other than that in which it was born."[54] Over tea in Stryker's garden, I noticed a tattoo on her right arm of the femme robot in Fritz Lang's 1927 film *Metropolis*. We ruminated inconclusively about why an android would need the spherical insignia of functionless breasts. Since then, I've mused further. All of the FDA-approved implants sold in America are made by robots, and several interviewees—cancer survivors who've had reconstruction—refer to their breasts as Frankenboobies. A few young women with cosmetic augmentations told me they felt their new busts were futuristic forms of body armor.[55] The confluence of these science fiction references suggests that *all* humans are increasingly unnatural creatures.

o o

Chang and Gourley have been working for three hours in this cool room, whose 68°F temperature is starting to give me a chill. The anesthesiologist is preparing for "wake up." The circulator nurse is stuffing used gauze into a hanging plastic container that manages her inventory to the sound of Elton John's "Goodbye Yellow Brick Road." Gourley injects a local anesthetic into the skin around the incisions on the completed breast, while Chang continues to suture the remaining one.

"What were the surprises of your research into breasts and sex work?" she asks me unexpectedly.

"It's still fresh in my head," I reply, racking my brain for a soundbite. "Breasts are essential to sex work. They're an advertisement and an appetizer. Without the presence of breasts, there's not much business. If an escort gets a mastectomy, she loses her clientele."

"I have one patient who is a very smart, motivated, professional escort," says Chang. "She came to me for breast augmentation to increase her business and it did. She has clients coast to coast, including Nobel Prize winners."

"At the high end of sex work, augmentation is common," I reply. "At the low end, the women can't afford it. The opportunity costs are too great."

"They can't take two weeks off work," concurs Chang. Gourley under-scores the conversation by humming the tune of the can-can dance.

Women spend billions on beautification in general and aesthetic breast surgeries in particular. When it comes to appearance, what are men spending on? The simple answer is cars. Women buy more cars than men, but they are interested in safety and reliability, whereas men buy the majority of new cars, fast cars, and luxury brands. A man's car is not just a symbol of his status, it is an extension of his body.[56]

"Men use cars like male peacocks use feathers," says Gourley, who drives a red BMW. "We do it to attract a mate."

The word "chest" has its origins in the ancient Greek word for box. The various containers we currently call chests hold things of great value, such as a heart and lungs or gold coins and precious gems. Human chests are rich repositories of meaning. Many women have invested a small fortune in their chests.

"My patients treasure their chests," says Chang dryly.

Remembering Chang's original question about sex work, I say that I was surprised by the sheer volume and array of boob moves. On the entertainment side, the repertoire of teases—tassel twirls, pastie styles, big reveals, nipple fondling, and lap dancing—is dizzying. Then, on the full-service side of sex work, I was gobsmacked to learn that men order women according to race and breast type.

When Chang makes her final stitch, she takes off her gloves and sits at a distance on a stool, rubbing her chin and reviewing her work. She watches while Gourley and the circulator wipe down the patient's chest, removing any remaining iodine. They apply a barrier of zinc antibiotic ointment and then a goopy dressing of mesh that won't adhere to the wound.

"Cleaning the crime scene," quips Gourley.

The anesthesiologist dismantles the drapes, then removes the res-pirator, revealing Anne's pale face. The circulator hands Gourley a

6-inch-wide Ace bandage that he wraps around the patient's chest to protect and compress her breasts.

Anyone who has spent time in the military has likely been to a load of strip clubs, I remark to Gourley, telling him that I did most of my participant observation at the Condor.

"I've been to a few strip joints, including the Condor," he admits. "There's nothing more magical than a good motorboat. But beware of the boob that is hardened by capsular contracture. You might get a black eye."

"Aah," says the patient woozily. Her brows furrow.

"You are still in the OR," says the anesthesiologist to Anne. "Everything went smoothly. You may have a sore throat. Nothing to worry about."

Gourley takes off his gown, revealing a muscular arm tattooed with Japanese waves and fish scales. "You are doing great. Just relax. We'll do all the work," he says reassuringly. He, the circulator nurse, and the anesthesiologist slide Anne onto a white plastic board to transfer her to a gurney, then cover her with white blankets. "We're gonna wheel you out now," he says.

"Wheel where?" says Anne, her eyes still closed and her words slurred. "To the strip club?"

4

Active Apexes

Eight women are staring critically at her bust. A fit model, upon whom clothing designers test their prototypes, Amanda Price describes herself as a human mannequin. With long blond hair tied in a messy bun, she wears a bra sample in an unbecoming greige, a shade characteristic of the undyed fabrics used to make factory samples. The thirty-four-year-old is standing in the center of a windowless room with gray walls, three vertical mirrors, a curtain behind which she can make quick garment changes, and benches for the participating design and merchandising staff. The fit room, as it's called, is a three-dimensional blank canvas for solving garment-on-body issues.

Amanda once aspired to be what she calls a "*model* model" until she discovered that she was too short and shapely for a career in front of the camera. After an unexpected booking as a fit model, she realized that she had "won the genetic lottery," as she puts it; she has ideal proportions for behind-the-scenes work in the apparel industry. Amanda is five foot seven with a 34C bosom. Her figure doesn't resemble a pear, an apple, or an hourglass. Her breasts do not hang low, high, east, or west. Her body is that great rarity—absolutely average. As a result, Amanda isn't just *a* medium; she is *the* medium for all clothes created by Old Navy for the top half of women's bodies. In the days before mass manufacturing, everyone was their own fit model. Nowadays, one woman's bust is a stand-in for millions.

Old Navy usually fits their women's clothing on two fit models standing side by side, but Reese Clayton, an extended-size model with a 42D bust, couldn't come in today as two of her children are home from school with the flu. It's rare for apparel brands to consistently fit clothes on two models at the same time, but Old Navy believes in what they call "bod equality." On the level of business practice, the brand is committed to delivering all their garments in all sizes at the same price, but on the plane of cultural and political allusion, "bod equality" implies that women, who comprise the majority of their customers, deserve dignity and appreciation whatever their ethnic or economic status.[1]

"Bod equality" is an evolution of their "democracy of style" mission. As a writer, I'm usually suspicious of catchphrases concocted by marketing consultants, but having interviewed over a dozen people who work at Old Navy, I am taken aback by the degree to which the brand mission is genuinely motivating.

"I had a nightmare about this bra last night," says Rachel Kraus, a technical designer on the intimates team, as she adjusts the slider on the back of Amanda's bra strap. Technical designers used to be called pattern makers, but Kraus describes herself as a bra engineer. She began her career in customer service at a brassiere start-up called ThirdLove, talking on the phone eight hours a day to women about their boob problems. Obsessed with the fit, feel, and function of bras, she now spends her spare moments analyzing "TikTok hauls," in which Old Navy customers try on their latest purchases and discuss them in short videos.

"This is style D4664, our smoothing full-coverage underwire bra, second fit sample," says Kraus, who acts as a kind of master of ceremonies, keeping the meeting on schedule and reminding those assembled of the bra's history and timeline to manufacture in Sri Lanka. "The original construction of the wings was too expensive, so we adopted a clean, seamless, free-cut solution with a thin layer of liquid silicone between two pieces of fabric," she continues, using the jargon of her trade and effectively demonstrating that bras are the most complex product made by the apparel industry. The bra engineer stands back to inspect Amanda's cleavage and side-boob, or "sleavage," to confirm that her breasts aren't spilling out, then she looks inquiringly at the group. Silicone, which I associate with breast implants, is often used as an alternative to elastic in bra manufacturing.

Laura Gordon, the design director who architected this bra, is standing with her head tilted to one side. Five foot two with a 32C bust, she was hired a year ago to grow Old Navy's intimate apparel business. Prior to her arrival, the company used "blocks," or blueprints, from the Gap brand to make its bras. However, this comfy-looking bra has been cooked up from scratch in answer to a consumer pain point—the bulging of underarm flesh. "We hope it will be the ultimate smoothing bra," says Gordon, pointing at an extra piece of thin, soft fabric that extends beyond the official bra to rein in surplus voluptuousness.

Amanda runs her hands along the wings at the side and then over the gore at the center between the two cups. Her pet peeve is a sweaty cleavage. "The fabric is so cool," she says, impressed.

"Our biggest cost lever is the fabric. When it looks and performs better than it costs, it's magical," says Lindsey Martin, Kraus's boss, the lead bra engineer. This fabric is 82 percent recycled nylon and 18 percent spandex. Spandex, an anagram of "expands," was invented in the late 1950s to improve the comfort of women's girdles and was redeployed in form-fitting aerobics wear in the 1970s. It's an important ingredient in most bras. Obsessed with the nuances of "fabric behavior," the design team would enjoy nothing more than talking about the temperature, weight, stability, durability, washability, stretch, and recovery of fabric all day if time allowed.

Designers at Old Navy are 90 percent female all the way up to the boss, Sarah Holme, the executive vice president of design and product development. Male designers are mostly sprinkled through the menswear, denim, and T-shirt graphics teams. Old Navy could adopt the ubiquitous tagline "designed by women for women" but, as one staffer explained, "most clothes are designed by women, so the slogan is bogus."

As an experienced fit model, Amanda is skilled at articulating the sensations that most of us ignore. She started her career at Levi Strauss, modeling jeans at sales meetings, then worked for eight years as the female medium at The North Face, a brand that specializes in mountain sports. Having modeled for Old Navy for six years, she has a longer history as a freelance consultant for the company than many of the employees in the room. "I'm outside the corporate hierarchy, so I can be honest," she tells me. Still, she avoids comments that might dispirit the designers. "If I have any concerns, I have to express them as early as possible, not after the trims and fabrics are booked." The trims include underwires, elastics, pads, hooks, and eyes.

Like most American women, Amanda rarely leaves home without a bra. "I prefer some sort of hold. I don't like the feeling of nothing," says Amanda, who has a bachelor's and a master's in economics. "Studying microeconomics made me better at my job," she says. "It expanded my understanding of the way consumers make decisions."

"How does the underwire feel?" asks Martin. The lead engineer has been standing at the back of the room and now approaches Amanda. "Is it digging in anywhere?" A single mother of two, Martin wears a maroon bralette under an open shirt. Formerly known as camisoles, bralettes are a relaxed alternative to bras that offer coverage but little support. As fashions have shifted away from "Victoria's Secret cup armor," as she puts it, "to more natural-looking solutions," Martin has slowly come to terms with the natural shape of her top half. "Dating after breastfeeding two kids, I went through a period of feeling very self-conscious, but now I'm comfortable with myself," she explains. "I'll even go braless. As a feminist, I want to be unapologetically myself." After working for ten years at Nike, a footwear company whose raison d'être is track and team sports, Martin relishes the female-led environment at Old Navy, where they would never take a menswear design and simply "shrink it and pink it" for their women customers.[2] She also loves the challenge of constructed bras. "With a lot of apparel, you're at the whim of your designer. They can do

whatever they want when the garment is primarily aesthetic," she tells
me. "But when it comes to bras, if they aren't fulfilling their function,
then they're unlikely to be successful. I love having a stronger voice."

"The wire . . . ummm," says Amanda pensively. "It's firm. It might
not be comfortable after a couple of hours. Could it be a little more
flexible?" Among younger and small-breasted women, underwires have
a bad reputation as torture devices. But older and well-endowed women
tend to appreciate the way a wire creates a standard round shape. Personally, I don't wear a bra around the house, but when I get dressed up
with any likelihood of being seen, I wear an underwire bra that cradles
my bosom in a reassuring way that shields me from the bogeyman of
social embarrassment. For someone with fake tits, underwire has little
function. It's a habit, a hug from an imaginary friend, and a talisman
of self-protection.

Amanda puts her hands on top of her head while Martin and Kraus
move in to inspect the relationship between the underwire and her
"breast root," the name these designers use for the crease under the
boob that plastic surgeons call the inframammary fold.

"Let's ask the vendor to experiment with reducing the gauge of the
wire, so it's less rigid," says Martin.

"Any other call-outs?" asks Kraus. "Straps? Hooks, eyes, sliders?"
Amanda turns around. The straps are slender; the back of the bra is
unexpectedly minimal for a full-coverage contraption.

"The back-on-body is straight and clean," says Gordon, evidently
pleased.

"All right, onward," says Kraus. The engineer hands Amanda
another bra with one hand while she draws the curtain of the changing
area with the other.

Amid the breakout chatter, I hear the term "bra math." While
Amanda changes, I ask, "What is bra math?"

"Oh my God, bra math drives me crazy," replies Kraus. "Wacoal,
Natori, Calvin Klein—every brand has its own formula for coming

up with bra sizes based on the relationship between your under-bust [the number] and your over-bust [the letter]. But bra math is super-dependent on breast shape, and as you go up in sizes, the formulas don't work."

"Sister-sizing is hilariously confusing," adds Martin. "Generally, a bra designated as a 32C will have the exact same cup size as a 34B *and* a 36A. The alphanumeric sizes have no bearing on the actual measurements of the body."

"Bras are an inventory nightmare," continues Martin. Old Navy will carry *forty-two* sizes of this underwire bra, ranging between a 32A and a 48DDD, whereas most of the brand's other garments come in just nine sizes, from an extra-small to a 4X.

Amanda emerges from behind the curtain in a younger, hipper-looking test sample.

"Next up, style D4665, the wireless version of our smoothing full coverage," declares Kraus, who once again waxes lyrical in arcane bra talk.

"Okay," says Martin pensively.

"Well, well," says Gordon.

"Amanda, could you point at your apexes please?" asks Martin.

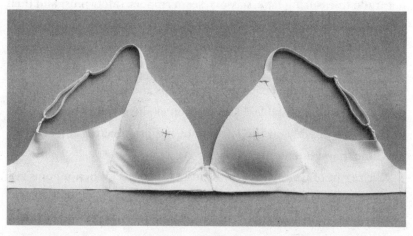

Old Navy prototype, marked with the location of the fit model's "apexes."

The fit model looks down at her bosom and pauses. "Where are they?" she quips, hovering her index fingers over her breasts before zeroing in on her nipples through the foam cups. "Apex" is clothing-industry jargon for the highest point of the cup, but it is also code for that unspeakable body part—the nipple. Synonymous with a high point or summit, the word "apex" conjures images of the Alps or the Rockies and reminds me that in some languages like Hebrew, the words for "breast" and "mountain" are one and the same.

"Apex" also begs the question: Why are there hundreds of slang English words for breasts, but so few for nipples? I mention that, in all of my research, the only interviewee to use slang for nipples was a male burlesque performer called Jonny Porkpie, who referred to his "nips."[3] For reasons that are not yet clear to me, nipples are more threatening and distasteful than boobs.

"To your point," says Kraus with a giggle, "On *Parks and Rec*, when Rob Lowe is talking to Rashida Jones about her sore nipples—their characters are a couple expecting a baby—she gets irritated and snaps at him, '*Stop* using the word nipple!' Then he's tongue-tied and after a long pause, he refers to her 'boob hats.'"

Kraus pulls a marker out of a fanny pack that contains the tools of her trade (measuring tape, scissors, seam rippers, safety pins) and then carefully delineates the vertical and horizontal axes of Amanda's left and right nipples with short lines on the bra sample. A plus sign now adorns each cup.

"What if we trimmed back the upper cups and lengthened the straps to make it more adjustable?" says Gordon as she sketches her proposal with marker directly on the left side of the bra, making it look more curvilinear and intentional.

"We're out of time," declares Kraus. "All good?" When no one says anything immediately, she announces, "Okay, time's up!"

The maternity team is already at the door, waiting to get in for their fit meeting. One designer carries an assortment of blouse samples while another holds a prosthetic pregnant belly labeled "7 months" for Amanda to strap on.

o o

"I feel more powerful when I have a bra on—ready to jump into action!" says Laura Gordon, the bra architect, as we exit the fit room. The wide hallway is full of headless dressmaker's dummies hanging from metal poles. This multi-sized throng of mannequins is custom-made by Alvanon, an international company that creates dress forms based on 3D scans and quantitative data about human anatomies in specific regions.[4] Their unbleached cotton bodies are firm to the touch with detachable arms and legs but fixed chests. The breast style of the femme dummies suggests that they're already wearing bras that "lift and separate," a phrase imprinted on my memory due to the heavy rotation of TV commercials for Playtex's Cross Your Heart bra during my childhood.

Gordon and I walk through the open-plan office toward the elevator. The bra designer has promised to give me a tour of the airy building that serves as the headquarters of Gap Inc., the largest specialty apparel company in America. Old Navy, the most lucrative brand in the firm's portfolio, occupies two floors. Banana Republic and Gap brand occupy another few. Athleta is due to move into the property soon.

Gordon describes herself as "a feminist but not a bra-burner." At the 1968 protest outside the Miss America pageant that brought the women's liberation movement to the attention of the general public, no one set their bras ablaze. The rally was initiated by a press release inviting "women of every political persuasion" to Atlantic City to oppose an event that degraded women as "Mindless-Boob-Girlies."[5] About a hundred women set up a "Freedom Trash Can" into which they threw bras, girdles, false eyelashes, curlers, wigs, high heels, issues of *Playboy* and *Ladies' Home Journal,* and other symbols of objectification and inequality. While no fires were lit on the wooden boardwalk that day, one of

The so-called "bra-burning" protest outside the 1968 Miss America pageant.

the organizers characterized the action as a "symbolic bra-burning."
Shortly after, the metaphor was reported as a historical fact, whipping
around the media like wildfire. Bra-burning became a "catchphrase to
trivialize feminist protest," suggesting that it was "merely concerned
with the discomfort caused by women's undergarments."[6] The event
also associated feminism with destruction, particularly "a form of violence against femininity" that was comically unsophisticated.[7]

In the 1970s, many women did abandon bras. My mother didn't wear
one for many years. She wasn't a radical but a small-chested hippie

ceramicist, and she didn't resume the habit until my sister insisted that she wear a bra to parent–teacher meetings. That brassiere, which was identical to my first bra, was a soft, unpadded garment that fastened in the front.[8] Called a Dici, it was marketed as a vehicle of liberation. In a 1974 TV commercial (which you can see on YouTube), the Dici bra breaks free of its packaging, flies upward, metamorphoses into a seagull, and soars into a blue sky. Sung by an ultrafeminine soprano, the jingle declares: "Let me be or let me fly."

"I'm pro-women, so I'm pro-supported breasts. I want women to feel uplifted, confident, and competent," says Gordon as she presses the elevator call button. "The history of fashion is about contorting the female form. I suspect the future of fashion will be about that too, conforming to the evolving patriarchy." Gordon grew up on a farm in Ohio. The middle child in a strict Catholic family, she was fascinated by the mysteries of the flesh. While studying apparel design, she focused on the functionality of clothes, writing her senior thesis on darts, an old-school way to accommodate the three dimensions of bodily curves. After her BA and a stint at Abercrombie and Fitch, she worked at Victoria's Secret for eight years, designing bras on 34B fit models, including the legendary Kathy Fichtel, the 34B of the New York bra world upon whom a huge number of businesses tailored their bra prototypes even though the average size of an American woman is now a 36C or more.

Upon exiting the elevator on the seventh floor, Gordon and I wander through the Gapeteria food court and then onto an outdoor terrace with spectacular views of the feat of suspension engineering that is the San Francisco–Oakland Bay Bridge. "When most women think of a bra, they imagine a 'constructed bra,' with a molded pad and underwire. She puts it on and her bust adopts the garment's shape," says Gordon, adding that sports bras and bralettes now hold significant positions in the undulating landscape of high-, medium-, and low-support garments. "My definition of a bra," she explains, "is anything that takes care of breast tissues."

"Take care?" I repeat. How exactly do bras *take care* of breasts?

"From the moment they emerge in puberty, breasts are something women need to manage, particularly in America, where we are taught to dislike our natural breast shape," explains Gordon. "Bras defend and uphold breasts in so many ways—socially, emotionally, and physically."

Since embarking on this research, I have pondered the question: Can fashion emancipate? The simplest argument for the liberating power of clothes comes from cross-dressing. The people assigned female at birth who bound their breasts and dressed as men in order to pursue professions closed to them, such as soldiers (Joan of Arc) and doctors (James Barry), broke out of the shackles of women's roles—at least for a while. In the late twentieth century, power dressing emerged, favoring pantsuits with broad, padded shoulders that camouflaged women's curves under boxier, masculine silhouettes. This light form of cross-dressing coincided with women's rise through the corporate world. In many circumstances, clothes talk louder than words. Their minimization of breasts can be a visual means of prioritizing professional equality.

Bralessness is a completely different emancipatory strategy. It puts a premium on physical freedom and the revelation of heterogeneous breasts with unrepressed nipples. The two modes represent different versions of women's advancement and likely appeal to different women based on their age, race, religion, region, gender orientation, sexuality, and line of work. Remarkably, a woman's breast size may also factor into her preferred route to empowerment. Why? Because flatter women are already less likely to wear bras than buxom women. Personally, I appreciate both paths. My daughter, a 34B now aged twenty-four, summed up the politics of breast coverage this way: "Bras are a useful shield to protect me from the male gaze, but I'd still like to have the bare chest privileges of a man."

"We've noticed that women sometimes bond over their breast size," says Gordon, referring to some recently conducted focus group interviews done by the brand. The research led to many size-related revelations. For example, women's definition of comfort shifted with their bra size. For women with D and DD cups, comfort was associated with the sensation of support, whereas for the A and B cups, it was linked to the feeling that nothing was there. Not surprisingly, large-breasted women bought more bras and were willing to pay more for each one than small-breasted women. "Bras are loyalty products; when the customer finds one that she loves, she generally comes back for more," explains Gordon.

I ask why we have double-Ds and even triple-Ds, but no double-Bs or Cs.

"When the alphabetized cups were invented back in the 1930s, D was the largest size," replies Gordon. "To this day, Es and Fs are not embedded in the consciousness of American women." I muse over the cultural connotations of the letter sizes. Double-D sounds sexy, voluptuous, and desirable, whereas E feels heavy and dumpy, and many associate F with failure. It is uncanny the way bra sizes have accrued meaning.

"Any discussion of bra size should acknowledge a woman's twenty-eight-day cycle," says Gordon. "If you get measured right before your period, when your boobs are swollen, your measurements are different than ten days later. That change is part of the beauty of being female. It's the life force that flows through us. From a very young age, we're told to ignore it, but really, we should celebrate it."

Gordon and I return to the second floor and weave our way to the intimates design zone, a pod demarcated by 8-foot-high canvas room dividers covered in thought clusters of bras and swimsuits. At Old Navy, bras and underwear are categorized as "intimates." "In America, 'lingerie' is perceived as sexy wear and associated with European labels. It's not much used in our vernacular," explains Gordon. Derived from the French word for linen at a time when undergarments were made from flax, "lingerie" was introduced into English as polite code for undergarments. Nowadays, the term extends to cotton and synthetics. "Intimates," an early twentieth-century euphemism, suggests garments that are closely acquainted with our bodies. "Intimates are next to the skin," says Gordon. "They're the first thing we put on in the morning and the last thing we take off at night."

I wonder aloud why women's undergarments are "intimate" while men's are not. Is it because our bodies are more sexualized? Mysterious? Or unmentionable?

"That's a tough one," says Gordon. "Let me think about it." She notices that I'm looking at a thin, clear orb of plastic on the table. Inscribed on it in neat hand-printed blue ink are a load of letters and numbers, including 42D. "That's a 3D pattern for a thermal-molded foam pad," she explains. "Pads are popular for modesty. The pads in our full-coverage bras will have just enough thickness to hide the nipple."

"What is so shameful or offensive about nipples?" I ask.

"I don't know," admits Gordon. "Perhaps it's because nipples are a functional part of the body that makes clear we're animals? Because they dispense liquids? Maybe men's nipples are acceptable because they're useless. I really don't know."

For centuries, physicians like Erasmus Darwin (Charles Darwin's grandfather) were obsessed with the mystery of the male nipple.[9] Now we understand that nipples are evident in human embryos before the male and female chromosomes start expressing themselves. In other words, nipples are so fundamental to our universal humanity that they precede sexual differentiation. When we are born and for the first eight years of our lives, male and female chests are virtually indistinguishable. Only when a girl is about eight years old, when she starts getting her breast buds, a stage of puberty called thelarche, do they start to look different.

"You're reminding me of something peculiar that I saw in Paris at the runway shows during Interfilière," says Gordon. Interfilière is the world's most important lingerie trade show. "The models were all wearing pasties under their bras," continues Gordon. "I was shocked. If we cannot free the nipple at a lingerie show in France, where can we?"

o o

"In lingerie, France is the mecca. For denim, the United States has a history of leadership. Every type of apparel has a market-leading country," says Ra'el Cohen, cofounder and chief creative officer (CCO) of the brassiere start-up ThirdLove. "My design director and I go to Paris twice a year for inspiration. We spend a small fortune on bras that come in only a handful of sizes, but they have this elevated European aesthetic."

We may be talking about Paris, but we're actually standing side by side in Los Angeles. I flew here this morning to observe a photo shoot at Smashbox Studios, where I plan to fathom the differences between the average bodies of fit models and the extraordinary appearances of lingerie models. I hope the contrast between backstage mammaries and camera-ready breasts will give me a perspective on the specifics of the real and the ideal.

When the CCO excuses herself to talk to the crew, who are setting up cameras, lights, and computer monitors, I peek my nose into the dressing room. A makeup artist and a hairstylist are deep in a discussion about pap smears while they groom two women, who are absorbed by their iPhones. The models sit in swivel chairs in an area that looks like a hair salon with mirrors encircled by light bulbs. Upon introducing myself, the two women look up and smile. I had heard that lingerie models were cast for their cleavage, but because these two women are cocooned in gray terrycloth dressing gowns, I am confronted by another casting criteria—spectacularly straight, bright white teeth.

Modeling is one of the few businesses where women are paid more than men. Moreover, having your photograph taken in a bra and underwear commands a surcharge, making lingerie one of the most lucrative products in commercial modeling. The day rates of the models hired for this shoot range between $5,000 and $10,000, depending on their

Sonnie Givens: "Lingerie is my bread and butter."

experience and the degree to which they're in demand.[10] "Lingerie is my bread and butter," confirms Sonnie Givens, a green-eyed blonde whose face is freshly familiar to me because she is all over Old Navy's website. "Lingerie rates are higher because you're more exposed. You have to be even more comfortable in your body." Twenty-six years old with a 36DD bust, Sonnie is a modest dresser who rarely wears anything low-cut. "It's ironic that I am all over the Internet in a bra," she admits. "A sparkling icon of body positivity."

Sonnie is categorized as a "curve model" because she wears a size 10 to 12. A varsity volleyball and softball player who loves to ski, she also works for athletic brands such as Lululemon, Nike, and Under Armour.

"My family would call me big-boned or say that I have 'more to love,' " she explains. "But I see myself as a normal, healthy-sized woman. I work out and care about nutrition."

The fashion industry classifies women's bodies as "straight," "street," "mid-size," "curve," and "plus." The traditional high-fashion model is an A or B cup and wears an extra-small (size 0 or 2). These women are called "straight" because they have few curves. In the early 2000s, the "plus" category developed to promote models who wear extra-large sizes, 12 and up. Only recently has an in-between classification emerged for women who wear sizes 4 through 8, which is sometimes called "street" because these models were never seen on the runway. "Street-sized" is a synonym for "mid-sized," which to me connotes a family sedan. "Curve" is a newer, more affirmative way to say "plus."

"Straight models are starved. That's why they so often look miserable," jokes Yvonne Simone Powless as the hairstylist brushes out her long black hair. "We're all on a spectrum between the starved and the eating. 'Straight' is a natural size for a minority of European women who are genetically stick figures."

Native American on her mother's side and African American on her father's, Yvonne acknowledges that her ethnic ambiguity contributes to her busy schedule. She started out representing the University of Texas, Austin, on *America's Next Top Model: The College Edition*, and since finishing her English degree has worked for several dozen brands, including Kim Kardashian's SKIMS. As a part-time yoga teacher, she particularly enjoys modeling for Athleta, a brand that she commends for accommodating her weight fluctuation—"a variant of 30 pounds"—and giving her the cover of one of their "Power of She" catalogs.

Between the ages of twenty-three and twenty-eight, Yvonne had breast implants. "Having bigger boobs directly impacted my income," she explains. "Size 0 models usually have no boobs, so they don't want plus girls with no boobs either." Yvonne never liked her augmented breasts. "They didn't feel like they were mine, even though I paid a shit-

Yvonne Powless: High-fashion brands prefer flat-chested
women because "thin signals their exclusivity."

ton of money for them," she says. In January 2020, she had an implant removal and breast lift, so now her bosom settles into a ThirdLove 38D.

I ask her why high-fashion designers prefer to model their clothes on the "starved."

Yvonne offers a pitchfork of smart answers. "Those girls look like hangers. They don't disrupt the clothing at all," she explains. "It's what the designers have always done. It's their legacy. Their staff probably don't know how to make clothes that look good on people with any shape." Yvonne pauses while the makeup artist applies a hint of gloss to her lips. "High-fashion brands don't want to be inclusive," she adds. "If everybody can wear it, then it's boring. Thin signals their exclusivity."

Yvonne rises from her chair, ascending to five-foot-ten. Sonnie joins her, ascending to almost six feet. The wardrobe stylist appears with two delicate gold chains in hand.[11] At five foot one, she requires the models to stoop so she can fasten the chains around their necks. The sight of these Amazons is a revelation. In the industry, photo-friendly lingerie models are roughly 5 inches taller than the fit models, who stay out of public view.

The stylist hands the models their first bra assignments and ushers them behind a few freestanding racks hung with samples. Sonnie returns in a 24/7 Classic Uplift Plunge Bra in a pale blue called "daydream" with matching lace bikini underwear, then Yvonne strolls out in a "perfect coverage" bra in a gleaming copper labeled "mocha." A glance at the models makes clear that much thought has gone into pairing garment hues with skin pigmentation. After the greige test samples, it's invigorating to see the ready-for-retail shades.

The makeup artist moves in to inspect their cleavages, then carefully applies moisturizer and her own mixture of "body-perfecting shimmer" with a brush. She evades my request for her recipe but reveals that her brief for this shoot is "glowy, 'no makeup' makeup." After finalizing their cleavages, she lightly sweeps the models' shoulders, abdomens, and thighs with the iridescent emulsion.

I venture out into the so-called black box studio, which is dominated by a white, edgeless, seemingly limitless space that plays tricks with your sense of distance. The photo crew have been fine-tuning their elaborate equipment for several hours. When I ask the senior lighting master what he's doing, he replies, "Preparing to turn normal people into goddesses."

A gaggle of ThirdLove staff, including the CCO, stand behind a bank of monitors that display the lighting tests as they are captured. I learn that ThirdLove doesn't photograph bras below a C cup because their

top-selling sizes are 36D and 36E (also known as DD). I also discover
that they do minimal editing of their models' bodies via Photoshop.
They keep moles and scars, editing only the occasional large tattoo.
Postproduction is mostly about color-correcting the images so they
accurately reflect the real bra dyes.

"Any boob insights for me?" I ask the women while we wait for the
shoot to start.

"Boobs are like fingerprints. Not even the right and the left are the
same," says one woman.

"You can inherit your breast size from either your mother or your
father," says another.

"Boobs are the source of our career sustenance!" says the CCO,
whose favorite party trick is accurately guessing a woman's bra size.

Shawn Merz, the photo art director of ThirdLove, is holding a large
Canon camera with a 70 mm lens. "It's a great workhorse, much punch-
ier than a 35 mm," he says. "It distorts the body less and has rapid-fire
settings." Merz also works with an analog Pentax and a video camera.
Smartphones have democratized photography up to a point. Only a
professional has the staff and the know-how to take eight thousand
photos in a single day and then select "a half-dozen bright genuine
moments for each look."

Noting that Merz wears Issey Miyake pleated pants and a Jacquemus
short-sleeved shirt with Birkenstock slippers, I ask him why high fashion appears to disdain breasts.

"They say fashion models are flat because gay male designers are
attracted to Twinkie boys," he says with a shrug that suggests he's not
entirely convinced. "Twink" is gay male slang for a slim, youthful man
likened to a Hostess Twinkie snack. A gay man himself, Merz "never
sees bras in the wild," as he puts it.

I tell Merz that I recently interviewed supermodel Christy Turlington, who signed a million-dollar deal back in 1988 with Calvin Klein,
the only high-fashion brand to enjoy a major underwear business with

multi-decade success. Turlington, who is five foot ten with a 34B bosom, told me that she and the brand were well paired. Through the 1990s, Calvin Klein bras and underwear riffed on androgyny, while Turlington had subtle and self-possessed sex appeal that she described as a "sister vibe." In those days, Calvin Klein's campaigns were the opposite of Victoria's Secret's, which featured more overtly salacious supermodels such as Stephanie Seymour after she'd augmented her bust to a 34D. Many of the photographers with whom Turlington worked for Calvin Klein ad campaigns were queer: Richard Avedon, Steven Meisel, Herb Ritts, Mario Testino. In their work, we see oblique evidence of the gay male gaze.

"Gay men were in hiding for so long," says Merz. "That generation had to be subversive to sneak their perspective into popular culture." Merz studied photography at UCLA and cites a large-format portrait class he took with Catherine Opie as an influence on his choice of career. One of Opie's most famous works is *Self-Portrait Nursing* (2004), which depicts the butch-dyke artist breastfeeding her son. The word "pervert" is etched into her skin above her bust. "Cathy is a pioneer," says Merz. "It's amazing that she can be as outspoken as she is. That's not what we do here."

As it happens, I recently caught up with Opie, whom I know through the art world. She believes in nipple equality and sees the double standard as farcical. "It's ridiculous that men with moobs don't have to wear shirts," she told me. "When I see a pair out on a hot day, I want to yell, 'Strap in your man-boobs!'"

Merz notices Sonnie stepping into his limelight, so he removes his slippers and walks onto the set in his socks to greet her. After a short chat, Merz hollers to his assistant, "Can we please have some ABBA for Sonnie?" He steps back from the model and takes one shot and then looks at his viewfinder. He takes another and looks again. "How's our focus?" he calls out. His assistant zooms in so closely on Sonnie's cleavage that we can see the fine weave of the fabric framing it. With the

Catherine Opie's *Self-Portrait Nursing*, an LGBTQ+ icon.

basics confirmed, Merz presses down on his first spray of photos to the lyrics "Mamma mia, here I go again."

Sonnie turns on instant shine, click-click-clicking through her inventory of poses. She raises her hands above her head, clasps them behind her back, and then gracefully relaxes them in front of her belly. She gazes into the soul of the camera, then looks away in three versions. She flashes a smile, a coy smirk, and then a pleasant open expression that says something like "hey." The model is not interacting with Merz as much as performing in her own world of expression—a silent actress with a friendly bust who downloads herself into a still image every few seconds. The one pose conspicuously absent from her repertoire is the arched back, tits-and-ass-out position that dominates Hooters calendars and strip club websites. She finishes off her segment by doing a side plank for a potential banner ad.

I follow Sonnie back into the dressing room to find Leonna Williams, whose lion's mane of curls is being delicately arranged with chopsticks by the hairstylist. A twenty-five-year-old art student concentrating on sculpture, Leonna is paying her way through college by modeling for the likes of Nike, Levi's, Apple, and a number of online makeup brands. "Modeling is like making sculpture," she says. "If I can see myself on the monitor, I can shape myself, carve out a position." Leonna's mother is a buxom Filipina with Chinese heritage; her father is a former karate champion who was raised as a Black man. "Not many Asian-ish girls have breasts like me," says Leonna, who is a 34D. "They're my key asset. My livelihood comes from the display of my face and my tits."

Leonna admits that she did not initially love her full bosom. As a competitive breaststroke swimmer, they got in the way. Bras gave her a headache and she preferred the boyish look of a white cotton bandeau. "I like my breasts now," she declares. "ThirdLove is a big part of that." Her first "mother agent" advised her to run 4 miles a day and get a breast reduction—advice that still makes her flinch.

"That makes me so angry," says the wardrobe stylist maternally.

"I was actually underweight then," adds Leonna.

Sonnie, who sports a new bra–panty combination under her robe, has taken a seat next to Leonna in order to have her hair and makeup refreshed. "Models are already too critical of their appearance," she says, joining the conversation. "Is she prettier than me? Does she have better boobs? We have a hard time with comparison."

People's body images are fragile, I remark. In a world where we are surrounded by zoom filters that remove wrinkles, Photoshopped selfies on social media, and e-commerce where superlative-looking

Leonna Williams: Modeling is like sculpture. You "carve out a position."

women have teams of professionals making them look even more sublime, models experience psychological stress as much as or more than mediocre-looking civilians. "Models," by definition, are supposed to be the epitome, the ultimate, the exemplar. Perfection has its price.

"Has anyone seen *Angels and Demons*?" asks the makeup artist as she highlights Leonna's collarbone with a few confident brushstrokes of emulsion. *Angels and Demons* is a Hulu docuseries about Victoria's

Secret, which focuses on the connections between its founder, Les Wexner, and convicted sex trafficker Jeffrey Epstein. Although Victoria's Secret still has the largest share of the American bra market, business has been declining since 2014, when the brand launched its obnoxious "Perfect Body" campaign featuring skinny models with augmented breasts. Their male leadership subsequently missed the profound change in women's attitudes after the election of a US president who bragged about grabbing women "by the pussy." With the rise of #MeToo campaigns against sexual assault and the resurgence of women's marches, Victoria's Secret appeared to have *Playboy* values. In 2022, the misogyny of the brand was the subject of an international hit single by Jax, which declared that Victoria's real secret was that she's "an old man who lives in Ohio" who got rich by exploiting girls' vulnerabilities and promoting ultra-thin bodies with overblown boobs. "I know Victoria's secret," went the refrain, "she was made up by a dude."

"I could never work for Victoria's Secret, even with a rebrand," says Leonna, who dislikes it when "trendy hot girls" appear frail and foolish. "They need to do some restorative justice by funding nonprofits for sex-trafficked and sexually abused women." As it happens, ThirdLove was founded as "the antithesis of Victoria's Secret" in part because Cohen and her colleague, Heidi Zak, were angry at the way the brand catered to straight male fantasies and espoused sexist gender roles. In an open letter to Victoria's Secret in the *New York Times*, Zak wrote: "It's time to stop telling women what makes them sexy—let us decide. . . . Let's listen to women. Let's respect their intelligence. . . . Let women define themselves. . . . To each, her own."[12]

○ ○

It's not every day that you meet the woman who designed your favorite bra. Born in Britain, Clare Karunawardhane has been in the bra business all her life, including nine years in Hong Kong developing patents for Clover, a company that manufactures brassieres for many major brands, and two years in Sri Lanka, an island with extensive lingerie manufacturing facilities, where the native Sinhalese word for nipple translates rather wonderfully as "nozzle."

Karunawardhane loathes a bad bra. "A poorly designed bra gives a woman the sense that there is something wrong with her breasts," she tells me in an interview at ThirdLove's San Francisco headquarters. "The fact is that different brands imagine different breasts." Karunawardhane is a Reiki healer who believes in energetic forces, so for her, beautiful apparel is soulful. "You can feel the emotion in a great bra," she says. "You can feel the care and attention to detail in your bones. That intentionality is part of the power of bras to transform, to pull you together, to help you stand up straight, to make you feel slimmer or younger."

I understand her thinking when I wear her aptly named Second Skin Bra.

"That bra came together effortlessly," she says. "It has just ten components. No foam, no fussy darts or seams that show under clothes, minimal stitching. The fabric is a microfiber blend of nylon and spandex, knit very tightly to create a smooth, silky touch."

"It's a triumph," I say. "A cup winner, a knockout for the knockers."

"It has been a consistent seller since launch," replies Karunawardhane, who is a 34G. "When I wear it with a button-down shirt, I experience less gaping."

I like bras without foam cups for two reasons: they don't add bulk that makes me feel booby, and they don't suppress my nozzles. My breasts emerged in the 1970s, when silhouettes with twin peaks, like those of Farrah Fawcett, were fashionable. In the 1980s, a period associated with a backlash against feminism, the padded bra came in with a vengeance, creating rounded mountains with no apexes. As a woman in my fifties with a flipped Bert and a wonky Ernie, I am rarely surveyed in a lecherous way. All this to say, the faint outline of my nips through clothes aligns with my feminist politics. I see it as a tiny salute to women's liberation.

o o

"Swimsuits bring out women's greatest insecurities," says Lauren Walker, a swimwear designer at Old Navy. "Because you're outside and you're practically naked." Standing next to the crowd of dress forms clustered near the fit rooms, Walker uses her left arm like a rack, holding a row of paired bathing suits, each style in a medium and an XXL. Too petite for most Old Navy extra-smalls, Walker grew up in Marin County, home to some of the Bay Area's most popular beaches. "Women are so uncomfortable with swimsuits that they don't want to try them on in store," she says. "They feel safer in the comfort of their own home, which is why our swimwear has a greater presence online."

The word "comfortable" gets bandied about by designers so much that its meaning has become a blurry mess for me, so I ask Walker to define comfort.

"Technical comfort is a 'Goldilocks and the Three Bears' situation. It's not too tight, not too loose; it's just right. That's especially important with the first layer. Some high-end brands appeal to women who believe in the saying, 'beauty is pain,' but that's not an Old Navy customer." Walker takes a deep breath. "Emotional comfort is the opposite of 'Oh, I feel uncomfortable in a situation,'" continues Walker. "We also want our customer to feel relaxed and positive."

Speaking of Goldilocks problems, I had a conversation about the discomforts of breast enhancement with a drag queen called Madame Vivien V. Six foot four without heels, Vivien special-ordered "fancy tits" from Switzerland, but they were awkwardly heavy. Then she bought cheaper "foam tits" on Etsy, but they were way too big. After she sliced a few inches off the back of the falsies with a carving knife, she ventured out to the clubs, where people invariably "honked her tits."[13] Various people assigned male at birth (AMAB) have mentioned their difficulty in finding bras due to their height and circumference.[14]

For trans women with belatedly inspired hormonal breasts, the average bra size is likely between a 40A and a 42B.[15]

Old Navy swimwear is generally purchased for vacations and sunbathing. Whatever their bust sizes, customers want the reassurance that their areolae and nipples will not precede them as they emerge from the surf. "Boob popping is not permitted, no ma'am," says Walker. "But my biggest fear is a fabric that is see-through when wet." Old Navy has a plunge-neck one-piece in a shiny, sparkly fabric coming out for summer. "One of the colors is a buff neutral. Let's just say that I've lost some sleep."

Designers usually steer clear of so-called nude and white swimwear to avoid immodest transparency, but also because these colors are owned by intimates. Indeed, color is one way that bikinis have long differentiated themselves from bras and underwear. Beige swimwear upends expectations. A daring choice for Old Navy? I inquire.

"Correct! It's a trend color thanks to SKIMS," explains Walker.

"If a basic bra is beige, what color is a basic swimsuit?" I ask.

Walker pauses and closes her eyes. "My image of a basic swimsuit is a black scoop neck with a supportive tank strap that keeps the girls locked up and in," she says. "That's the foundational suit."

I recognize that iconic black suit, I affirm. It derives from the Victorian bathing costumes that men wore before they won the liberty to wear trunks alone. In those days, women wore dresses with big puffy sleeves, bloomers, and stockings to wade into the water. Their clothes made it impossible to swim. Ironically, the men who swam did breaststroke until the early twentieth century, when they took up front crawl.[16]

One of my heroes is Annette Kellerman, an Australian athlete who beat men in races by swimming a forerunner of the front crawl called the double-armed trudgen, which combined overarm movements with the scissor kicks still used to do the side stroke.[17] Wearing a man's black wool one-piece, she swam the Thames and Seine rivers, set record times, did daring high dives, and popularized "water ballet." (The latter is special to me because I spent much of my childhood on synchronized swimming teams, wearing matching Speedos.)

Kellerman was a household name in the early 1900s. A woman athlete was a novelty rather than a profession, so she made a living as a vaudeville-style entertainer doing "swimming exhibitions." She was also the first actress to perform naked in a Hollywood movie, her nipples peering out from behind curtains of long brown hair. Indeed, her performance in the 1916 movie *A Daughter of the Gods*, which was made by Fox for what was then the biggest budget in film history, led to a ban on nudity in movies the following year.[18] In the 1950s, Kellerman's story was celebrated in a biopic starring Esther Williams. The film's American title was *Million Dollar Mermaid*. A mark of their resistance to hyperbole, the British called it *The One-Piece Bathing Suit*.

Kellerman aligned herself with the suffragists, who were also dress reformers. Obtaining the vote and dress reform were the two high-profile issues of first-wave feminism. As she tells it in *My Story*, Kellerman was arrested on a Boston beach for indecent exposure in 1908 for wearing a man's swimsuit. When she went before the judge, she argued that swimming is an important exercise for human health but the costumes expected of women were like "lead chains," that gave them a better chance of drowning than swimming.[19] Influenced by reports of the importance of exercise on human well-being, the judge concurred with Kellerman, allowing her to wear the suit as long as she concealed her body under a robe until she entered the water.

Aided by the swimmer's publicist, news of her victory spread far and wide, enabling the production of the first modern swimsuit for women, named the Kellerman. Modeled on the men's suit, it was black with a simple scoop neck, but featured an additional short skirt for decorum.

"Our best-selling bathing suit design is a one-piece swim-dress with a modesty panel," announces Walker, interrupting my monologue. "You'll see a revision of the design today during the fitting."

Kellerman has a star on the Hollywood Walk of Fame and made a lasting contribution to women's liberation, I remark. It saddens me that she is all but forgotten.

"Her name may be forgotten, but her impact on product design is not," says Walker. "Her legacy lives on in our swim-dress."

In 1908, a Harvard professor who wrote extensively about physical education declared that Kellerman had the perfect female form. Director of the university's gymnasium, Dudley A. Sargent started measuring women's bodies in 1887, searching for a real woman whose proportions approximated those of the Venus de Milo, an ancient Greek marble sculpture of the goddess of love on display in the Louvre. After measuring thousands of women (in a way oddly similar to the fit model auditions that apparel business insiders call a go-see), Sargent enticed Kellerman into his office for an assessment. He was impressed by her lung capacity, but overwhelmed with joy that her 33–26–38 chest, waist, and hip circumferences were identical to those of the marble Venus. Sargent wrote a paper about Kellerman exploring many more of her body measurements, with the emphatic exception of her champion swimmer's arms, as the Venus de Milo had lost hers many years ago. Such were the preoccupations of male scholars at the turn of the century.

"That is maddening! The audacity to assume he's a judge powerful enough to set the standard," says Walker.

The whole history of bra design is about standardization, I suggest.

"Yes, but there is truly no female ideal at Old Navy. My favorite part of the job is seeing how our suits fit on different bodies. When Amanda, our medium, and Reese, our 2X model, are in the fit room together, I never see one of them as more important or beautiful than the other."

Kellerman used the "Perfect Woman" headline to promote her performances, as can be seen in a poster advertising her New York show, which was directed by William Morris, who founded the talent agency that still bears his name. However, Kellerman was not altogether happy with the objectification this entailed and often joked that she was glad

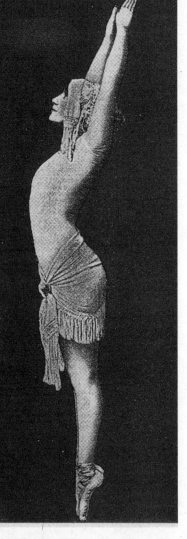

Annette Kellerman, an athlete, dress reform advocate, and innovator in women's swimwear.

"the Lord gave me a homely face . . . and a saving sense of humor."[20] Kellerman often redirected conversations about beauty to health and fitness by publishing books such as *How to Swim* and *Physical Beauty: How to Keep It* (both 1918). Her resolute focus on a strong, active body ran contrary to patriarchal pressures on women's outer appearance.

○ ○

The women's sweater team flow out of the fit room, their arms loaded with stacks of wooly knits. Lauren Walker and I enter to find Amanda Price, the 34C fit model who represents all the "core sizes," and Reese Clayton, a model with a 42D bust who stands in for all the "extended sizes." After the ThirdLove photo shoot, I am struck by how dim and unflattering the lighting is in this fit room. Walker hands Amanda and Reese a pink bikini each and they disappear behind the gray curtain. "Pink is on trend this summer due to the Barbie movie," says the swimwear designer.

Reese appears from behind the curtain in a floral robe wearing socks and flip-flops. Her braids are pulled into a giant side bun and her bright brown eyes are crowned with false lashes and Gucci glasses. A self-declared "jack of all trades," Reese is finishing a degree in social work; she runs a hairstyling business specializing in knotless braids out of her home, and she works Tuesdays and Thursdays as a fit model at Old Navy. The mother of four between the ages of two and eighteen, Reese gave birth naturally twice, then had two caesareans. "I tried to breastfeed all my children," she explained in an earlier interview. "But only the youngest was patient with me. Plus, I got help with his latch because I was in hospital for six days with postpartum preeclampsia."[21]

Working as a fit model has shifted Reese's perception of her body. "I've always been pretty big with heavy boobs," she says, offering as evidence her possession of a credit card from Lane Bryant, a clothing company that celebrates itself as the "pioneers of plus." When Reese first started working for Old Navy, she felt "a little ashamed of the back fat and all the rolls," as she puts it. "But the designers were so sweet. They just wanted to know how they could make their clothes look better on someone like me, so I've become less shy and learned to open up." When a fit model is wearing intimates, swimwear, or sports bras, Old Navy pays $225 an hour. For other clothes, the rate is $150. Reese is thrilled to make more in a day than she would in a week at a regular nine-to-five job. The physical and financial validation of the work has been empowering. "I never thought that somebody would actually care enough to hear my side of this," she explains. "Or that a company would treat me like I mattered. It just blows me away."

Amanda emerges barefoot, wearing the bikini, and takes her position next to Reese. Whatever their size, fit models are under intense pressure to maintain their physical measurements. "A good-paying job comes with requirements that are sometimes stressful," says the curvy Black mom, who jokes that her exercise regime consists of taking the kids to track meets. "We have to stay within our specs. We can't be losing or gaining too much weight." Reese's bosom cascades generously down her front. Maintaining a constant bust is one of the most difficult forms of weight stabilization because breasts are sensitive registers of any surpluses or shortfalls in calories.

For Amanda, maintaining size stability blurs the boundaries between work and play. "If I burn too many calories, I could become a small. If I slack off at the gym and become a large, will I lose my job?" she says. "Sometimes I have to remind myself that I'm bringing more to the table than just my body. I give useful feedback and help the teams understand the on-body reality of their designs."

After announcing the details of these "reference swim samples," Rachel Kraus, the technical-designer-cum-emcee, asks the fit models, "How does the bust feel?"

"Reese's bikini top is looking a little small," announces Walker.

"These girls have not grown!" says Reese with mock indignation.

"The coverage on Amanda is pretty good," says Walker as she carefully straightens the ruffle on the bottom of this feminine design. "Is it holding you well?" she asks Amanda.

"Pretty good," replies the medium fit model. "This style will make a lot of customers happy. It's pretty and really comfortable."

The team returns their gaze to Reese, who sports a poker face. She has an array of tattoos on her shoulders and bosom—butterflies, birds, a rose, and the name Gabrielle in italics.

"What do you think?" says Kraus to her.

"I think my bust is eating this ruffle up," replies Reese with a laugh.

The designers discuss enlarging the ruffle and widening the straps.

"Probably not the suit of choice for women with larger breasts," says Walker with resignation. "Being a swimwear designer, I've had to accept that I cannot please everyone. One design does not fit all."

"Let's move on to the next style," says Kraus.

"Our customers definitely prefer one-pieces," says Walker in an aside to me. "We put a lot of our cross-functional work into perfecting them."

Amanda and Reese emerge in one-piece suits in an orange, brown, and white floral pattern. This "swim dress" was their top seller last summer, so they're carrying it over with a fuller skirt in new colorways and patterns.

"Is this a VIP?" asks one of the merchandisers. A VIP is a "very important print"—one that gets three rounds of strike-offs, or test samples, through which the designer assesses the scale of the pattern and how the fabric absorbs the dye.

"No, we've had dependable color replication with this fabric," replies one of the tech designers.

The swim dresses have a subtle squared neckline with a built-in overskirt attached at the waist, which covers the crotch and upper thigh. To my eye, they have a vintage vibe, which flatters both models' forms.

"I took my seven-year-old to a birthday party at a water park on Saturday," says Reese. "This suit would have been appropriate. I don't want to be all hanging out in front of the kids."

The designers hover and tilt their heads, examining the collarbones, rib cages, and apexes of both women.

"Are we happy with the pads?" asks Kraus, referring to the removable pads, or "cookies," that come with each suit. Positive noises ensue.

"I've been working feverishly on these swim-pad samples," says Walker excitedly. "They're wider with a fresh-shaped projection, made with a new foam quality that doesn't crease or migrate within the cookie mouth." The cookie mouth is the pocket into which the pad is inserted.

These designers go to great lengths to assure their customers of modesty. An adjective with many associations, "modest" means discreet, but it also suggests someone who is humble and self-effacing, which leads me to conclude that some people might interpret a visible apex as self-important or stuck-up. Since I started this research, I see men's nipples through their clothes *all the time,* but no one else, except the occasional gay man, seems to notice them, let alone judge them. I wonder: Could we reframe perceptible feminine nipples so they are not seen as immodest or brazen but as self-assured and self-possessed?

"What's wrong with women's nipples?" I ask the merchant beside me, whom I have not met.

"Nothing," she replies so swiftly that I assume she was expecting the question. "It's just societal norms. We've recently seen a shift, especially in-store—a trend toward lower coverage, lower support items. But the swim dress hit a home run online, especially in the higher sizes."

Walker overhears us talking about nips and chimes in. "Men are jealous that we can nurture life with ours!"

"They are a powerful part of the body," says Reese, while inserting a new cookie into the left side of her suit. "In many African countries, women are free to walk around in their birthday suits. In our country,

men have sexualized that part of our body. They have made it something indecent."

Sexist bias explains the idea that women's breasts are sexual while
men's chests are not, I proclaim. Men's nipples have the same number
of nerve endings as women's nipples. Men's are likely more sensitive
and even more physiologically erogenous than women's because their
nerves are clustered more densely, having not been spread out and
attenuated over a larger bust.

From the perspective of heterosexual women, men's chests are possibly the most sexually alluring part of their bodies. Male strip shows
like Chippendales and Hunk-O-Mania, which cater to the female gaze,
focus on male torsos as much as anything below the waist. Men also
understand the importance of their chests to their attractiveness, or
"pulling power." Studies show that many men have trouble with their
chest self-esteem.[22] By contrast, men with pride in their chests display
photos of themselves topless on dating apps.[23]

The designers inspect Reese's chest now that she has inserted two
firmer foam pads into her swim-dress. Even though the consensus in
the room is that women's nipples are a wholesome part of human life
that needn't be censored, the team has a deep respect for and a commercial remit to please their swim-dress customers, who have no desire
for ostentatious nipples.

o o

As I leave the Gap Inc. building, walking past the large vertical video
screens displaying lifestyle ads for their brands, I have a flash of clarity,
which transforms a mud puddle of research findings into a coherent set
of thoughts. The censorship of women's nipples may be amusing, but it
is not superficial or trivial. It's a deeply ingrained form of suppression
and repression that is integral to male supremacy. For this reason, it's
useful to understand the four ways that feminine nipples are outlawed.

First, nipples are expunged from conversation. The word "apex" is a euphemism derived from a mountain metaphor. While breasts have accumulated hundreds of slang words, nipples have accrued few. Usually, nipples are censored through avoidance or circumlocution. Indecency laws rarely mention them, preferring long-winded workarounds such as "the portion of the breast below the top of the areola."[24] Outside the medical world, uttering the word "nipple" is mildly taboo.[25] I've tested out this hypothesis at parties. When asked, "How was your day?" I reply, "Great. I wrote a few paragraphs about nipples." Most

Representing *Sunshine and Health*, the ACLU argued that American obscenity law discriminated against white breasts.

people ask me to repeat myself, unsure that they've heard me correctly, while the faces of others register shock, followed by amusement.

Second, images of women's nipples are regularly censored from media of all kinds and were effectively illegal in the United States for eighty years between the 1873 Comstock Laws, which suppressed the "Trade in, and Circulation of, Obscene Literature and Articles of Immoral Use" to 1953. During this period, photographs whose content included a woman's nipple could be confiscated by the Postal Service.[26] Despite the federal law, one mass-market magazine was able to publish images of bare-breasted women with impunity. In 1896, *National Geographic* published a photographic portrait of a Zulu groom with his bride, who had strikingly asymmetrical breasts.[27] From then, the respected monthly magazine went on to depict many nipples, all of which belonged to people of color.[28]

The boob color barrier was broken by *Sunshine and Health*, a nudist magazine that showed naked people spending time outside, sunbathing and playing sports, and that often featured a topless woman on its cover. When copies were seized by the post office in 1947, the ACLU took up the case, basically arguing that American obscenity law discriminated against white breasts. In court, the post office retorted that "we are clothed people" and the practices of Indigenous communities were "not the standard by which we should judge these pictures."[29] *Sunshine and Health* eventually won the case on appeal, in June 1953. The verdict was significant because it paved the way for magazines like *Playboy*, whose first issue was published six months later.

While naked female nipples popped into view in the early days of silent cinema, they were swept out of the way in 1934 by the Hays Code, a set of industry guidelines adopted to circumvent government censorship, and didn't officially reappear until the 1960s, when the popularity of risqué European films made clear that the code was out of date. Significantly, the movies needed sexy content to bolster attendance, which was declining due to competition from television. By 1962, TVs

Janet Jackson's nipple show, the most significant video replay in NFL history.

had invaded 90 percent of American households. Tits were officially welcomed into the movies in 1968 when the Motion Picture Association (MPA) established its rating system. To this day, only shirtless men can be seen in a film rated G, for General Audience. A glimmer of breasts still warrants a Parental Guidance (PG) rating, while two excited nipples are PG-13. Any titty action related to sex is R, for Restricted. Breasts alone don't garner the NC-17 rating, which restricts movies to viewers eighteen and older; that honor is reserved for upstanding penises.

The Federal Communications Commission (FCC), which regulates broadcast radio and television, is more likely than the MPA to see women's nipples as indecent, especially if they are met with any public outcry. During the Super Bowl halftime show in 2004, for example, Justin Timberlake pulled off one of the cups of Janet Jackson's bustier, revealing a breast adorned with an unusual piece of body jewelry—a silver star with a hole in the middle for her nipple. Although it was on view for a matter of seconds, "Nipplegate" resulted in the FCC punishing CBS with fines that escalated up to $550,000.[30] By contrast, the courts have decided that cable and streaming channels such as HBO, Showtime, Netflix, Amazon Prime, and Apple TV can ignore the FCC because their viewers intentionally pay for them.

Jackson's "wardrobe malfunction"—or rather, the video clip that led to her nozzle's global fame—convinced three tech bros to leave their jobs at Paypal and set up the video-sharing platform YouTube.[31]

The lawless land of the Internet means that every website and app brand makes its own rules. Porn Hub, XVideo, and other pornography websites are free-the-nipple zones. X, formerly Twitter, long positioned as a proponent of free speech, is replete with nipples, but they come with alerts that say, "Caution: This profile may include potentially sensitive content," and require an extra "yes" click in response to the question, "Do you still want to view it?" Similarly, Reddit allows photos of nipples as long they are tagged #NSFW, which means "Not Safe for Work."

Other major social media have community guidelines that quell the danger of women's "boob hats." A search on the word "nipple" on TikTok yields no results except the explanation: "This phrase may be associated with behavior or content that violates our guidelines." As a result, nipple-related content is always on the move, tricking the algorithms with alterations to search words, such as "n1pple" or "n!pple." Meanwhile, Facebook and Instagram, both owned by Meta, caved in to pressure to allow people to post photos of themselves breastfeeding and in other health-related situations, including breast cancer awareness, mastectomies, and gender affirmation surgeries. In theory, the platforms allow nipples when they are engaged in an act of protest, but in practice, these posts are often taken down. For the most part, nipples need to be pixelated or veiled by virtual pasties. Unfortunately, most algorithms—and presumably the men who write them—have trouble differentiating political activism from sexual availability.[32]

Micol Hebron, an LA-based artist, designed a pasty depicting a male nipple that women can use to cover the apexes of their breasts so that they don't violate Meta's community guidelines. She came up with the idea in 2014 after she and some friends attended an exhibition opening topless. Titled "Thanks for the Mammaries," the art show was raising funds for breast cancer, a disease responsible for the untimely death of Hebron's mother.[33] Images of Hebron were posted on Facebook and Instagram and removed within twenty-four hours. The artist was

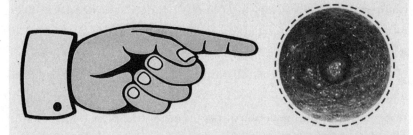

THIS IS A MALE NIPPLE:

If you are going to post pictures of topless women, please use this acceptable male nipple template to cover over the unacceptable female nipples.

(Simply Cut, Resize, and Paste)

THANK YOU FOR HELPING TO MAKE THE WORLD A SAFER PLACE.

Artist Micol Hebron created a protest pasty from a photo of a male nipple.

incensed by the "blatantly sexist double standard" and the platforms' presumption of "a male viewer with cis-hetero sexual desire," as she put it, despite the fact that her followers skewed femme.[34] Hebron posted the absurd male-nipple pasty on Instagram, whereupon it went viral, relayed by the likes of comedian Sarah Silverman, screenwriter Our Lady J, and celebrity blogger Perez Hilton. It circulates to this day.

Breasts are censored from conversations and suppressed in the media, but what about nipples in real life?

It is important to remember that until the 1930s, men all across the United States had to wear tank tops or full one-piece swimsuits to avoid being arrested for indecent exposure. Then men started resisting this regulation of their bodies, possibly inspired by Hollywood transgressions such as the spectacle of Tarzan's hairless nipples in the 1932 film *Tarzan the Ape Man* or, more famously, the tantalizing sight of Clark Gable stripping off his tie, then slowly unbuttoning and discarding his white shirt in 1934's *It Happened One Night*. Indeed, one hot day in 1935, forty-two men were arrested for swimming without torso coverage in Atlantic City and fined $2 each. News of the event led to an epidemic of what was called "bareback bathing."[35] The rebellion continued until a judge in New Jersey, followed by one in New York, lifted the states' respective bans on the public display of male nipples in 1937.[36]

Women took up the same struggle in the 1980s, with campaigns that were variously called "breast freedom" and "free the nipple." As mentioned in chapter 1, Carol Leigh, the prostitute who invented the term "sex work," was involved in the movement, as was a nun you'll meet in chapter 5.[37] These women were reacting to the bizarre inconsistency that women could dance topless to entertain men but were not granted the independence to go top-free on a hot day. (The term "top-free" is preferred by many activists because it avoids the erotic, commercial connotations of "topless.")

The prejudice underlying this discrepancy between lawful and criminal bare breasts is a reminder that "sexual liberation" has been male-defined and is by no means synonymous with women's liberation.[38] Nowadays, most American states allow women the right to protest topless or sunbathe topless—exercising either their freedom of speech or their equal rights—but few women feel comfortable doing so and many are not aware that they have the option.[39]

The final form of nipple censorship is the suppression of the outline of our pointy summits through clothes. Men's nipples poke through their shirts all the time and generally go unnoticed. No one thinks that a man with discernible nipples is inviting sexual attention or being impolite or disrespectful. It may seem trifling, but I am increasingly convinced that hiding this fundamental mammalian marker is integral to women's inequality and disempowerment.

With this in mind, I'm keen to encourage a covert "free the nipple" movement. Sometimes an anecdote says it best. Back in 2016, Serena Williams was playing Wimbledon in a stylish Nike tennis dress. White with a high collar and a racer back, it had a flouncy pleated skirt that swooshed with her movements. She played great tennis in that outfit, winning the quarter-final, which led to her seventh Wimbledon singles title. However, the *Sun* newspaper went with the headline: "Shocked Wimbledon fans slam BBC after it shows Serena Williams' 'distracting' nipples" (see image on page 247). Roger Federer's impertinent apexes were also on display throughout the tournament, but if anyone noticed them, no one mentioned it. When prurient media pretend to be prudish in order to shame individual women, they bring other women into line. Social stigma is powerful and coercive. Resisting it takes strength.

○ ○

"There's a fine line between being a teenage boy and a breast scientist," says Paige Mughannam, a member of the Old Navy "active" team, which oversees sports bras. The technical designer with 38DDDs admits to repeated viewing of full-figured women doing cartwheels in strapless bras on Instagram. She appreciates a brand that promises their customers that they can be upside down at a certain velocity without their breasts falling out of their brassieres.[40] Mughannam has a yellow measuring tape draped around her neck and an elaborate tattoo of golden scissors on her forearm—a mark of pride in her identity as a pattern maker.

"I am not a scientist or a doctor, but I think seriously about their research when I design bras," says her colleague Victoria Quandt, a women's activewear designer. The three of us are standing in the "competitor sample closet" in front of a jumbled rack of twenty sports bras, all turned inside out. A few iconic bras like Nike's Swoosh and Lululemon's Free to Be are evident, but the number of brands I don't recognize is overwhelming. The category has exploded since the first commercial sports bra—the "jock-strap bra," or Jogbra—was launched in 1977. Indeed, the athletic wear business would not be what it is today without Title IX of the Education Amendments of 1972, which prevented all US educational institutions from gender discrimination in their sports programs. As a result, between 1972 and 2012, the number of girls playing high school sports increased by 1,000 percent.[41]

"Breasts don't bounce up and down, but move in a figure-eight pattern like an infinity sign," says Quandt, a medium with a 34D bust. "You could put a woman in a straitjacket and reduce her breast motion to zero, but she wouldn't be able to breathe. Long term, we all aspire to design a bra that she can run a marathon in and sleep in—one bra that does it all." Quandt was a gymnast who took up and taught yoga while working at Macy's, then Athleta. "Short-term, I'm keen to create bras that avoid really big ellipticals and stop your breasts from bottoming out at fast speed, because that's when it hurts." When breasts "bottom out," they whack into the lowest point in their trajectory.

Old Navy's manufacturers test their bras by placing electrical sensors on the apexes of fit models who then walk and run on treadmills. Some companies, such as Nike, also use a "bra bot," a life-sized robot consisting of a torso with substantial fake boobs.[42] The unflagging bra bot gives clean, comparable quantitative results about one bra versus another. But it doesn't deliver insights about real breasts or the human user's experience. Similarly, 3D design systems, such as CLO, are of limited use for bra design because the avatars in their virtual environments have firm hemispherical projections rather than soft, malleable titties.

"Is it true that when a woman runs a marathon, her breasts swing an extra four miles if they're not properly supported?" I ask.[43]

"I haven't heard that . . . but the math adds up," says Quandt, amused.[44] "I'm certain that a well-fitted sports bra improves athletic performance. Discomfort impacts endurance, focus, agility, everything." Quandt feels the thick pad of a navy bra with turquoise trim. "Historically, brands have been concerned with the scale of breast movement—what they call total displacement," she continues. "More recently, they have started to focus on the speed of the movement, meaning that they're okay with a big figure eight if they can slow it down."

It takes me a moment to absorb this information. Annie Sprinkle's *Bosom Ballet* and Dirty Martini's tassel-twirling tits spring to mind. Sports bra makers evidently want their customers' breasts to sway in a graceful waltz rather than bop in a jitterbug or slam in a mosh pit.

The scale of displacement must be a bigger issue for women with bigger boobs. Do Lululemon's bras, which are designed on small-sized fit models, try to control the momentum rather than the magnitude of movement, in other words, titty-time over titty-space?

"We all work with the same manufacturers," says Quandt, resisting my invitation to discuss specific competitors. "They don't come out and say this active brand cares only about speed, but if we study our market research and movement data alongside our competitors' designs, we can figure out who is doing what." During the year ending April 2023, Old Navy was in fifth place in the overall active market behind Nike, Lululemon, Adidas, and Under Armour, which is impressive given that the brand has been associated with weekend barbecues rather than health and fitness. In women's active during the same period, they were in sixth place, knocked down the ranks by their sister Athleta.[45] At the time of writing, Old Navy is the only big-box retailer to have a significant share of the activewear market, including a position in the top ten for sports bras.[46]

"This notion that only skinny women work out is antiquated and just not true," declares Mughannam. "As someone who lives in a plus-sized body myself, these things are important to me. A woman can be fat or super-busty *and also* like to exercise. I appreciate that we are pushing size inclusivity. I feel like we're part of a revolution."

"Fat?" I repeat. "What words do you like best for extended sizes?"

"You would never see a brand announce 'This is our fat lady section,'" replies Mughannam. "But for me personally—curve, plus, extended: it's just verbiage. What is important to me is belonging. If your plus section has a fraction of the product or if the plus version of a bra only comes in black, you're not inclusive. Our Bod Equality initiative means that everything comes in every size and every color. That's why we fit on a medium and a 2X simultaneously."

Quandt's iPhone dings, reminding us that it's time to head to the fit room to see a new sports bra design on Amanda and Reese. As we walk, I marvel at the contrast between the teams' names; the "intimates" designers work on bras and swimwear while the "active" designers make sports bras. If a sports bra is "active," does that mean that an intimate bra is passive? If a sports bra is not an "intimate" or private garment, then could we call it a "public bra"? What do the public-private, active-passive implications of these apparel categories tell us about the culture of breasts?

"It is kind of ridiculous, but somehow not surprising," says Mughannam. "It has to do with sex, how society views female breasts, and how it polices them. A woman in a sports bra at a gym is perfectly acceptable, but God forbid you see her in a lace bra with equal coverage. That is indecent!"

As we enter the area populated by dress forms outside the fit room,

I ask how the designers feel about revealing the outline of their apexes through clothes.

"Personally, I'm free the nipple. But I work in a predominantly female environment. I might feel differently if I worked at a bank or software start-up," replies Quandt as she walks into the fit room.

"I understand that we live in a patriarchal system built without our consent, where only women's nipples are taboo. Even if we don't subscribe to that belief system, we feel it," says Mughannam. "In an ideal world, I'd like to feel sexy and wear whatever I want. But in this reality, I don't want my nipples showing. I'll even insert my own cookie pads into a top to ensure they're hidden because I don't want to be sexualized." Mughannam looks at me glumly. "It's about feeling secure. I feel safe once here, but not on my commute. Men can look at nipples in predatory ways that threaten my sense of personal safety."

o o

"I'll refresh everyone's memory fast so we can get to the fun stuff. This is our new high-support bra with the infinity pad," says Mughannam, nodding at Amanda and Reese, who are standing side by side in black leggings and black sports bra fit samples, both with their arms akimbo so as not to conceal the sides of the bras. While the technical designer rattles off the product number and a long list of features and changes from the last fitting, Quandt shows everyone on the active team the new pad.

"It's a figure eight!" I exclaim, impressed that the way a breast moves has been symbolically integrated into the design. Here's a sports bra that acknowledges the work it's doing.

"How many high-support bras do we have in the assortment at this time?" asks Lisa Sim, the design director of women's activewear. A slim Los Angeleno, Sim worked for five years at elite minimalist brand James Perse, where "we followed the luxury market, designed for ourselves, and never worried about garment cost," she says. Seven years ago, she joined Old Navy, which she sees as the opposite.

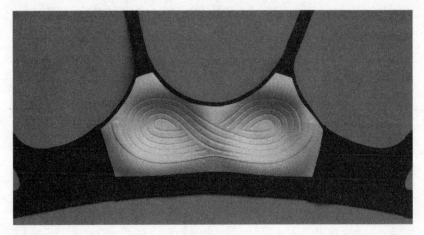

This Old Navy sports bra acknowledges that breasts move in a figure-eight pattern.

"Our compression bra will live. The zip-front will go away," replies Quandt. "By spring 2024, the figure-eight, more of an encapsulation bra, will be the other high-support offering. So, two styles."

The active apparel industry distinguishes between bras that "compress" and those that "encapsulate." Compression bras "smash" the breasts against the chest to minimize movement. They offer security to women who do high-impact exercises like running and jumping. Similar to the binders worn by lesbians and nonbinary and trans folks, they also appeal to people who want to be "one of the guys" at the gym. By contrast, encapsulation bras lift and separate the breasts, creating a more feminine shape and, for some, a sexier feel. As one activewear designer explained, "Personally, I don't love wearing a smasher. I love showing off my figure and I want to feel like a woman even when I am having an intense workout."[47]

As the designers dive into the minutiae of the figure-eight bra, I ask the woman sitting next to me for her job title.

"Director of global merchandising of women's active," says Margaux Foxworth, a fast-talking Stanford alum who has worked for the brand for eight years. "I run the business side of things, about $700 million a year. Sports bras make up about 10 to 15 percent of that. I have to decide how many bras to make, set the sales strategies, manage our AUC [average unit cost], and determine the ticket price for the customer." Foxworth is forever frustrated by the tension between the inordinate human resources soaked up by the complexity of sports bras and the garment's resistance to easy profits. "Sports bras don't drive a ton of margin the way a black legging or a gray sweatshirt does, but bras build credibility in the active space and drive loyalty in general," she says. "If the customer believes that you can make a functional sports bra, then it will help build trust that you have the right materials and technical expertise to create other garments for running, sweating, stretching, and jumping. I have to think about the bigger picture to remind myself and others who analyze the numbers that it would be unwise to exit bras."

Impressed with her openness and articulacy, I ask Foxworth to tell me something about her breasts.

"My boobs are close together," she says, unruffled. "They're not that big—34B½—but they have this beautiful cleavage. Cleavage is in a non-trend cycle, but I still love mine." By "non-trend cycle," she means that high necklines and other cleavage-covering styles are "in" at the moment. She refers to herself as a B½ because she is wearing a bra by ThirdLove, which makes half-sizes.

The design team has finished itemizing the fixes on the 34C. They are now generating a much longer list of changes for the 42D, which has the challenge of supporting a heavier bosom.

Support, I discover, is one of the most subjective of breast sensations. "One woman's medium support is another woman's light support," explains Sim. "People define it for themselves based on their breast size, their fitness activity, and their personal version of modesty." By modesty, the design director is referring to how much breast movement a customer is happy to disclose in public. "Support also has a visual component. Some customers interpret wider shoulder straps or higher necklines as supportive, even if they are not actually lifting the bust in any way."

Support is not just a physical reinforcement; it embodies a load of psychological connotations. A supportive bra can actually offer moral support. In other words, a high-support sports bra can boost, champion, and cheer you on through a marathon, soccer match, or basketball game.

When I discover that the women's active design director has a BA in political science, I launch into a mini-lecture on the relationship between clothes and empowerment. Dress reform was a huge issue for first-wave feminists, not far behind obtaining the vote and accessing higher education, I say. In the United Kingdom and the United States, women protested that the corset didn't just damage their lung capacity and digestion; it was an instrument of oppression that ensured their status as the "weaker sex." Bloomers or knickerbockers (adapted from baggy Turkish trousers that were gathered at the ankle) were popularized in the 1850s by Amelia Bloomer, a women's rights activist and editor of the first newspaper for women, *The Lily*. Enabling greater freedom of movement for activities like cycling and ice skating, bloomers are the most famous form of "rational dress." However, the brassiere was the most successful reform garment, slowly replacing the corset between 1900 and the 1930s, when alphanumeric cup sizes were introduced. I end by asking Sim what she thinks about the politics of bras.

"The changing shape of women's breasts must be political in some way. It has changed so much," replies Sim. "I'm glad that we no longer feel the need to be so padded and lifted and perky."

Men dress for comfort, I remark. They're not wearing stilettos.

"They don't wear push-up bras on their testicles," she says with a laugh.

But what about the politics of sports bras?

"It relates to the accessibility of exercise and wellness, which is a socioeconomic issue," replies Sim. "That is something we try to address. We're keen to help people access fitness."

Patriarchy has not been good for women's health. Bralessness cannot be the only way forward. Part of me would like to imagine the sports bra as a feminist bra.

"Yes, I get that," says Sim. "It's the bra that she's wearing when she burns all her other bras."

5

Holy Mammaries

n the middle of the California redwoods, twenty women who worship nature and ancient goddesses are taking their seats in front of me. It's a Sunday in June, two days before the summer solstice, the longest day of the year. We're all attending a three-day restorative retreat called Fool's Journey, named after the first face card in a tarot deck. As a newcomer to this spiritual subculture, I'm an exemplary fool. Despite this or because of it, I've been asked to give an "offering"—a talk about some of my research on religion and breasts.

"Thank you for coming, everybody," I say as I strip off my T-shirt. In the past, I explain, I would have felt embarrassed giving a top-free talk, even to a group of body-positive women, but recently I sat for a torso portrait. It was a therapeutic experience that makes today's breast-baring oddly effortless.

"A torso portrait?" interrupts a woman with short-cropped silver hair in the front row.

"I'll tell you about it later," I say, raising my silicon orbs with cupped hands. "These boobs are the beginning of my story. Since 1998, American health insurance companies have been required to pay for breast implants after women have had mastectomies for medical reasons. Women have no federal right to breastfeed or to obtain an abortion, but we have the right to fake tits."

A woman with waist-length hair feigns a loud cough, then says, "Misogyny" under her breath, inspiring a round of laughter. She is reclining next to an oval swimming pool, the only semi-luxurious amenity at this nonprofit resort in Lake County, just north of Napa Valley, famous for its wine, and Mendocino, known for its marijuana. The resort has the feel of a summer camp, with rudimentary wood cabins and misshapen mosquito screens.

When my implants first landed, I tell the women, I was struck by the numb inanity of these artificial parts. I realized that my body had lost some sentience. It made me wonder: Why are breasts so often set in opposition to intelligence and seriousness?

After a lot of reading and thinking, I found an answer in an article written thirty years ago by Londa Schiebinger, a historian of science who is now a professor at Stanford. She pieced together evidence that the label "mammal," derived from *mamma*, the Latin word for breast, was not a value-neutral category but a "political act," informed by Christian theology and eighteenth-century ideas that a woman's place was in the home.[1]

Schiebinger did her PhD dissertation on gender and early modern women scientists in the days when it was "professional suicide," as she put it, "to do anything on women because there were no jobs in it." Then, in 1989, she had a child with a fellow historian of science from Harvard. She breastfed her son, who took her surname. By pumping and storing her milk, Schiebinger was able to return to her research shortly after giving birth. While sitting in the New York Public Library consulting one of Comte Buffon's eighteenth-century volumes on natural history, her breasts started leaking. "I took care not to drip on the pages," she explained, "as I was repeatedly confronted with the word 'quadruped.' "[2]

As I recount this, a woman wearing a black T-shirt with a five-pointed star enclosed in a circle—a witchy symbol known as a pentacle—says, "You mean four limbs?"

Many mammals have the remnants of four feet. Humans have arms; bats have wings; dolphins have flippers and bifurcated tails. The ancient Greeks recognized that human beings were animals; Aristotle wrote about quadrupeds around 350 BCE. However, during the Middle Ages, Christian theologians extricated man from nature. As

Schiebinger explains, "Rationality, in their eyes, blessed humans with immortal souls, raising them above brute creation. . . . Holy scripture clearly taught that man was created in God's image."[3]

Mammals actually have many traits in common. We all have fur or hair, so we have been called the hairy ones. We have a constant internal body temperature, a four-chamber heart, a single-bone lower jaw, and three tiny bones connecting the eardrum to the inner ear. We are unique in being born as living creatures rather than eggs. Finally, as infants, we are all sucklers. Intriguingly, only half of all mammals—the females—have mammary glands that regularly produce milk. The male breast tends to be "dry and barren."[4]

Sitting in the library with lactating breasts, Schiebinger wondered who had coined the term "mammal." More importantly, in a world where men are the measure of all things, how exactly did the female mammary gland become the icon of this class of animals?

As I tell this story I pause, suddenly overwhelmed by the sight of many naked breasts. While I have been speaking, roughly half of the women present have stripped off their tops. A few are applying greenish goop to their chests. Oak, the pagan who cofounded Fool's Journey, is entirely naked. She is tall with twinkling blue eyes, long scraggly white hair, and an ample natural bosom. Her robust beauty is reminiscent of the Venus of Willendorf, a Paleolithic stone sculpture.

"Sorry, I just lost my train of thought," I announce, absorbing the diverse shapes and sizes of these spiritual feminists, many of whom have day jobs in caring professions such as therapy, nursing, and teaching.

"Does anyone want a seaweed breast mask?" asks Oak nonchalantly, gesturing toward a big mixing bowl. "It's just a skin mask. You can put it on your face as well." Like many of the pagans assembled here, Oak identifies as a witch. The cofounder of several covens, including Wind Hags with the famed Starhawk, Oak comes from a Wiccan-ish tradition called Reclaiming, which seeks to retrieve the magic of pagan rituals for political purposes.

The Reclaiming movement began in the 1970s to bring together a range of nonsexist sources of spiritual value. They identified with witches as vilified women, then redefined the term to accommodate their identity as counterculture feminists with a penchant for magical thinking. According to Pam Grossman, author of *Waking the Witch*, declaring yourself a witch can be "an act of self-fortification" or a claim to be a "rule breaker, world shaker, no shit-taker."[5]

In embracing nature, Reclaiming witches also welcomed aging and rescued the word "crone," transforming it from an insult designating an ugly old bag to an aspirational label for a wise woman.[6] Although they are sometimes dismissed as romantic white hippies, I respect their enduring concern for the environment and their refusal to glorify youth. In a world where saggy breasts are maligned, here is a community that upholds them as sagacious. Given my interest in reclaiming the feminine top half—wresting breasts away from masculine projection and patriarchal domination—I can learn a lot from mature women who revere the divinity of their own bodies and affirm their physical selves as sources of strength and pleasure.

"Airing your chest feels great," says Marg, an ex-nun with a breast on the right and a mastectomy scar on the left. "The seaweed protects against sunburn."

Schiebinger's story revolves around Carl Linnaeus, a Swedish botanist, zoologist, and physician, I continue. In 1758, Linnaeus published the tenth edition of his *Systema Naturae*, or *Systems of Nature*, which contained two newly invented terms—*Mammalia* and *Homo sapiens*. With intellectual dexterity, his simultaneous coinage effectively linked women to animals and men to a higher intelligence.

"Linnaeus saw nature as divine and science as a spiritual vocation," I say, while applying green gunk to my chest. The eldest son of a Lutheran minister, meant to inherit the parish, he was educated for the priesthood but broke with tradition and became a doctor. He knew the book of Genesis by heart, referred to his study as "the Book of Nature," and gave his scientific lectures in the form of sermons. His students were even called "apostles."[7]

As the father of seven, Linnaeus also campaigned against the "evils" of wet nurses. He imagined that these women guzzled vodka and, as superstition had it, infected babies with their personalities. On his Arctic expeditions, he had admired the Laplanders with whom he spent time—now known as Sámi peoples—particularly their commitment to maternal breastfeeding, which he saw as contributing to their astonishing health and fitness.[8]

Whatever the medical arguments, the moral crusade against wet-nursing arose alongside Europe's democratic movements. The "good mother" of the new democratic nation was expected to retreat into a private sphere where she took care of the children, while enfranchised men of all classes strode out into the public spheres of science, business, and politics.[9] To extend a metaphor, the Enlightenment did not shine brightly on women.

Linnaeus's shrewd nomenclature gave scientific validity to, and effectively revitalized weary belief in, male supremacy. Men were positioned as wise *Homo sapiens*, reflections of divinity, whereas women were associated with mammals, anchored to the earth by their breasts. For this reason, the earliest feminist fights were not for the vote, land ownership, or bodily autonomy, but for permission to attend schools and colleges.[10] Women would be considered inferior animals, incapable of rational thought, for as long as they were barred from learning. Linnaeus actively opposed education for women, including his own daughters, who weren't even allowed to study French, because he wanted them to be "hearty, strong housekeepers, not fashionable dolls."[11]

The term *Mammalia* gained acceptance swiftly in Europe because the term fulfilled a political need, shifting "the laws of nature" away from a world of divine right and holy ordination to one of empirical observation and scientific method. The Germans adopted the category but resisted the Latinate term, choosing the vernacular label *Säugetier*, which translates as "suckling animals"—an apt modification that shifted attention from the female breast to a universal infant instinct.[12]

.."When babies come out, they are not hungry," interjects Bread, a co-leader with Oak of Fool's Journey, who works as a labor and delivery nurse at a top California hospital. "But they have an incredibly strong drive to suckle. With their first breath, they oxygenate their body. A little fish becomes a little mammal. Then they root and show other signs of seeking the breast. In the first hour, they learn how to breathe, suck, and swallow all at the same time."

The drive runs deep, I agree. I once questioned what my history as a bottle-fed baby meant for my relationship to breasts. Today I understand that the relationship goes beyond our own early childhood. It's in our DNA.[13]

"No wonder people have so many feelings, obsessions, and repressions about breasts," declares a pagan sitting in the shade at the back.

Schiebinger's account of Linnaeus reveals how breasts, not vaginas, are the symbolic hub of biological determinism. She pinpoints a key moment when God-given gender roles were converted into natural ones with social destinies. With Linnaeus's reorganization of the animal world, breasts became visual evidence of women's intellectual inferiority and innate subservience.[14]

The story is also a reminder of how religion and science have conspired to privilege male perspectives and justify the subjugation of women. I was brought up by agnostics who revere the empirical world. As an ethnographer, I am expected to be the "village atheist" resisting "the embarrassing possibility of belief."[15] While fundamentalist Jews, Christians, and Muslims have Genesis, social scientists have Charles Darwin, whose theory of evolution and hierarchy of animals is so fundamental to our belief system that we rarely discuss it.[16] In European and American academe, atheist allegiance means that spirituality is dismissed as a private matter, irrational superstition, or "old wives' tales."

"Can we talk about Genesis for a moment?" Oak pipes up, leaning forward. "In the Garden of Eden, a man basically gives birth to a woman via his rib. That is backwards. Then Eve causes problems because she seeks wisdom. What is wrong with that? She eats the apple from the tree of knowledge and learns what? The big insight that she needs to wear a fig leaf?"[17]

Cheers and chuckles reverberate through the group.

"Eve's disobedience," says Marg, the one-breasted ex-nun, "resulted in our fall from Paradise. Catholics see Eve as proof that women and their bodies are conduits of evil that must be controlled, punished, and stigmatized."

"When I was a young dyke in the 1970s," says Nora, a top-free member of the crowd with a tattoo of a great horned owl on her upper arm, "I went to the Michigan Womyn's Music Festival, where we would take off our clothes. The ability to walk through a crowded community at night, completely or partially naked, was utterly transformative. When you remove the men, you expel the fear of harassment, recreating Paradise. It changed my relationship to my body. It gave me another baseline, nourishing a different consciousness. My body understood—viscerally—that the sexist crap we experience under patriarchy was not necessary."

I nod. Others have told me that early women-only events were important to their body positivity. Unfortunately, the Michigan Womyn's Festival excluded trans women and devolved into a platform for bigots, aka "trans-exclusionary radical feminists" (TERFs).

"I am all for gender fluidity," says Oak. "And I understand the importance of safe spaces. I never went to Michigan, but I think back to our solstice rituals at the beach. Men were there, but they knew they were in a feminist setting. Being naked in nature, performing rituals under a full moon or around a fire, is powerful. To be 'sky-clad,' as we say, naked and not sexual with people of different sizes and ages, is beautiful. It's a shame-buster."

Nakedness or naturist nudity, I chime in, retains some innocence. It is not the same as "Live Nude Girls" in makeup and stilettos. What could be more blissful than our birthday suits?[18]

"Birthday suit!" repeats Oak with glee. "One of my spiritual teachers told me that birthdays are the most important pagan holidays because our bodies are divine."[19]

"I used to go to Orr hot springs, a fully nudist hippie paradise back in the day," says Blakey, an English professor and the friend who recommended Fool's Journey as an ethnographic site from which to explore the spirituality of our top halves. "When I'm naked outdoors with others, I know I'm a primate. I don't always remember that I'm a mammal; we are offered a billion ways of forgetting. Seeing ourselves as separate from nature has led to widespread ecocide." Ecocide kills the natural environment in an intentional way, like homicide and suicide.

"Ecocide should be a crime!" exclaims one witch.[20]

"Humans are the apex predator of the globe, but are we really that smart?" asks Blakey. "We are destroying our environment. Animals adapt to their niche, but humans are an invasive species. The fate of invasive species is to destroy habitat. What if our vast intelligence is really the stupidest thing about us?"

Few people acknowledge the superiority of an eagle's eyes, an elephant's memory, a dolphin's relational play, or an ant's ability to cooperate, I say. They see human intelligence as transcendent, disembodied, and somehow independent of the senses. Individually, we may navigate nuance, but as social groups, we still cling to the black-and-white dualisms of mind/body, human/animal, culture/nature, men/women, and brains versus breasts.

A loud cowbell clangs in the distance, signaling time for lunch.

"That was spirit-awakening," says Oak, drawing the session to a close. "In the 1970s, we were all looking at our cooches with speculums, lighting vulva candles, and hanging posters of yoni-flowers by Georgia O'Keeffe. But the breast was not celebrated or even discussed.

Reclaiming our breasts is important work." The group rises and slips back into their T-shirts and blouses. Oak looks around her chair. "I lost my clothes!" she mutters.

While most women head to the dining lodge, a few walk toward their cabins, past the pool dappled with leafy shadows from the trees above. I hear someone say, "Everyone should give their talks topless!"

o o

Marg and I wipe the seaweed mixture off our chests, then jump into the pool. Marg was inspired to be a nun by a priest active in the civil rights movement who taught at her Catholic high school. She joined Sisters of Mercy, a papal order prioritizing spirituality and social justice. After a decade in the convent, Marg left to become a carpenter.

Nuns have a long history of caring for women's bodies as hospital sisters, nurses, and midwives. Back in 2010, Network, the American grassroots organization best known for their activist outreach as Nuns on the Bus, wrote a public letter supporting the Affordable Care Act. Many Mother Superiors, who belonged to the Leadership Conference of Women Religious, signed it. "The bishops condemned the act because it endorsed contraception and abortion," explains Marg. "But the nuns supported it because they felt its attempt to remedy social injustice outweighed the value of strict adherence to Catholic doctrine on sex. The public conflict led to a three-year investigation of the nuns by the Vatican, which ended with the arrival of a new pope."

Pope Francis is an improvement, I say. He invited women to breastfeed in the Sistine Chapel. He doesn't appear to think a woman's breast is, by definition, indecent.

"I grew up in Rochester, New York, the hometown of Susan B. Anthony, where we had a rich community of activists," says Marg. "In the 1980s, a friend of mine was arrested for sunbathing without a top at around the same time they passed a statewide law allowing topless dancing. The juxtaposition drove her crazy, so she recruited all these women to go top-free in the park. One time we went in canoes and pad-dled shirtless on the river where they couldn't arrest us."

I realize Marg's friend must be Ramona Santorelli, the godmother of the movement now called Free the Nipple.[21] Santorelli led the bat-tle and eventually won the right for women to go top-free in New York State, first as a form of protest under the First Amendment and then as an equal right under the Fourteenth Amendment.[22]

"The desire to go top-free is related to a longing for bodily free-dom," says Marg. "Ramona and I had a wonderful adventure, driving from Rochester to San Francisco one summer. We didn't have air con-ditioning, so we were always looking for places to swim. Except in Utah, we swam top-free. It felt great."

I tell Marg that I recently interviewed the first woman to achieve tenure in the Divinity School at Harvard University, Margaret Miles. Miles wrote a great book called *A Complex Delight*, which discusses medi-eval images of the Madonna breastfeeding the baby Jesus as symbols of God's nourishment and love of humanity.[23] While Mary Magdalene is usually presented with two bare breasts, the lactating Madonna, or Madonna del Latte, as the Italians call her, has only one breast bare— sometimes partially obscured by the baby Jesus. She is often so flat on her covered side that she doesn't appear to have a second breast.

"The Virgin's outfits are similar to nuns' habits. They conceal and censor the body," says Marg.

When lecturing about *A Complex Delight*, Miles was sometimes met with protests by Christians who deplored what they called her "breast theology." Miles argued that "the great mystery" of God's devotion to humankind was too complex for one icon. As she told me, "The cruci-fix tells you that God's love for humanity is best exemplified in suffer-ing and sacrifice, in dying for someone else, whereas the nursing breast tells you that God's love for humanity is best exemplified in nursing, nurturing, and the devotion of daily care."[24]

Miles is a specialist on Saint Augustine, the fourth-century theo-

Mary nursing the baby Jesus.

logian. She told me that Augustine contended that human birth is a greater miracle than Christ's resurrection on the grounds that it is much harder to create a new human being than to revive a preexist-ing one.[25]

"Augustine said that?" says Marg. "Wow. That's an amazing acknowl-edgment of the power of women's bodies to generate life."

A few centuries later, Augustine would have been burned at the stake for that heresy. As we climb out of the pool, I catch sight of Marg's asymmetrical chest. I ask whether she misses her lost breast.

"I don't think about it much," replies Marg, toweling herself dry. "I had lobular and ductal, stage one."

In the Middle Ages, they called breast cancer the nun's disease. Nuns didn't die young in childbirth, nor did they benefit from the prophylactics of breastfeeding. Breast cancer scuppered their longevity.

"I have a great recollection of committing a mortal sin in the basement of the convent library," offers Marg as she buttons her shirt. "During my days as a novice, a nun touched my breast, then I touched hers. It was so sweet."

Original sin, venial sins, mortal sins. I'm confused by these echelons of wrongdoing, I admit, as we walk toward lunch.

"Venial sins are minor infractions, like eating meat on Friday," explains Marg. "Mortal sins are serious offenses, everything from kissing and petting to adultery. Original sin derives from Eve. We are all born with original sin because of our fall from Paradise."

Impressed by her lexicon, I ask Marg what the word "holy" means to her.

"Something precious or revered," she replies. "I don't think money is holy, but breasts can be. First, they are close to the heart. Second, they are part of sex. Sex is one of the most sacred things we have. It's a way to connect not just to others, but to ourselves and to the earth. Sex is a portal to the deep mysteries of nature."

o o

"Sarah!" says Oak from across the communal kitchen. "Would you help summon the goddess Artemis to the ritual in the meadow tonight?"

"I'd be delighted," I reply hesitantly. "Anything specific I should do?" As an ethnographer, I respect rites of passage and other rituals as forms of interactive theater that have the power to build community, generate insights, and transform participants in subtle psychological ways.

"Just appeal to her," says Oak. "Explain that we need her help in pursuing justice."

I follow Oak into the dining hall and join a lively table. Those gathered for Fool's Journey see their politics as "intersectional." They are attuned to the advantages of having been born in California with primarily European ancestry and care about the inequities that obstruct universal sisterhood. The busyness of the group allows me to mull over what I've read about Artemis, the goddess of the hunt, animals, and nature.

The people with the oldest known affiliation to Artemis are the Amazons. They were depicted by Homer and other ancient Greeks as savage warrior women who cut off their right breast and lived in women-only tribes. Recent archaeology has discovered the tombs of battle-scarred female skeletons buried with their bows and arrows. Now known as Scythians, these Indigenous nomadic people were likely the first to domesticate horses, which allowed women archers to be as swift and lethal as men when they rode on horseback alongside them. Following existing legends about these "barbarians," Greek writers amplified the disinformation about these fierce women who led relatively egalitarian lives by circulating a bogus etymology for the name Amazon, suggesting that *a-* meant "without" and *mazos* sounded like *mastos*, the Greek word for breast.[26]

Yet Amazon/Scythian women had no need to remove a breast, as archers draw bows against the cheek, some distance from the chest. In the ancient world, mastectomies would have led to certain death. Few things were more terrifying than amputation, so the defamation prevented Amazons from inspiring women to lead more adventurous lives. Moreover, until recent archaeological evidence proved otherwise, the single-breast falsehood fostered the idea that warrior women had never existed, that the Amazons were all myth without any basis in fact.

Echoing the Amazons' lifestyle, one version of the goddess Artemis imagines her as a graceful huntress with a bow and arrow, accompanied by a deer, one of her sacred animals.

The other archetype is a totemic figure adorned with pectoral amu-

Four versions of the pagan power goddess called Artemis by the Greeks and Diana by the Romans.

lets or vessels containing offerings. This version of Artemis was worshipped in Ephesus, a religious center located in present-day Turkey, for roughly ten thousand years and was once housed in a temple so grand that it was deemed one of the Seven Wonders of the World. Ephesus, according to city legends, started out as an Amazonian sanctuary. The Amazons were driven out by the Phrygians who were, in turn, conquered by the Persians, the Greeks, and then the Romans—all of whom claimed Artemis as their own, syncretizing the Ephesian goddess with their own deities. By the Christian era, the votive objects that hung around her chest were interpreted as breasts.[27] Roman copies of the goddess often added nipples to her ambiguous jugs, transforming them into lifelike breasts. The status of nurturer was added to her established identity as an all-powerful political protector. Either way, her mammaries are by no means erotic. Their profusion magnifies her peculiar authority and otherworldliness.

It is worth noting that Saint Paul, the male chauvinist of the Christian apostles, was imprisoned in Ephesus for preaching against Artemis, then known by her Roman name, Diana.[28] While the New Testament implies business motives for Paul's incarceration by pointing to metalsmiths protective of their trade in goddess statuettes, it is also likely that the people of Ephesus were offended by Paul's contempt for the pagan figure on whom they relied for everything from delivering healthy babies to obtaining better credit terms.

In the dining hall at Fool's Journey, the hubbub has died down. Most people at my table have left for a session called "Tarot 101 with Rose." I find myself beside Bread, the labor and delivery nurse, who I learn has been working the night shift for twelve years. She adopted her "magical name" when she was a union representative fighting for "bread and roses." "Witches are fallible like anybody, but we like to think of ourselves as healers, not cursers," Bread explains. "In healing, there is nourishment."

I ask Bread how she interprets the multi-breasted form of Artemis.

"Her body looks like a date palm, a source of sweet sustenance," she says. "She's the deity that assures the community that no one will go hungry."

"Your talk made me think of the creation of the Milky Way," adds Bread. "I love that story. Hera is sleeping. Zeus puts his love child on her breast for feeding. She wakes up, startles, and the milk spurts out with such force that it creates a hundred billion stars. Hera—she was the sister *and* wife of Zeus—put up with a lot of shit." The word "galaxy" comes from *gala*, the Greek word for milk.

o o

After lunch, I head to the art cottage, where Oak is painting eggs using hot beeswax and Ukrainian dyes. It's a restorative activity that encourages conversation. As symbols of birth and rebirth, eggs have been decorated since the Stone Age. Oak has already made good progress painting her egg. It features a naked figure with buoyant breasts, wearing the floppy three-pointed cap of a jester.

Oak makes a living as a therapist who specializes in sexual trauma and body positivity. Her expertise has resulted in exceptional personal poise; she is radiant but serenely grounded. Her engaging presence no doubt contributed to her once being named best psychotherapist in the Bay Area.[29]

"When I was a psychology student in the early 1980s, I worked with a group of incest survivors, trying to heal violence and abuse while also mending myself," says Oak as she peers through her black-rimmed glasses at her egg. "I found the ocean, cycles of the moon, and goddess imagery to be healing. God the Father, not so much."

"Volatile men are an acquired taste," I deadpan as I attempt to make a scallop pattern on my eggshell with a wax pen.

"God is a terrible father," continues Oak, looking up and moving her wild white hair away from her face with the back of her wrist. "He tells Abraham to prove his loyalty by killing his firstborn and then watches

his own kid, Jesus, get crucified. That is crazy-ass behavior. Diagnosti-
cally, all that black-and-white thinking—you're with me, you're against
me, you're ascending to heaven, you're going to hell—suggests he has
borderline personality disorder. He needs a DBT group and a really
good therapist."[30]

"But who would be willing and able to be God's therapist?" I ask.

"Guanyin, the goddess of compassion," says Oak, savoring the
irony. Guanyin is a Buddhist mythical figure, or bodhisattva. She
has reached the state of enlightenment known as nirvana, but delays
leaving the living world in order to help those who are suffering.
"Guanyin is regal and known for her patience. She can sit with suf-

Guanyin, a Buddhist enlightened being known for her compassion.

fering," says Oak, who keeps a statue of the goddess next to the couch in her office.

Guanyin, or Kannon as she is called in Japan, is usually flat-chested. Most Buddhists believe that spiritual enlightenment takes one beyond the specificities of gender. This is why the original Buddha, who lived in the fifth century BCE, and his followers are often depicted as androgynous. More specifically, Guanyin was originally a man, or rather a masculine bodhisattva called Avalokiteśvara, but the pronouns changed to she/her sometime after she migrated from India to China in the first century AD.[31]

"Mary is also fairly flat," says Oak. "I've never seen a voluptuous Mary or a curvy Guanyin."

Oak's therapy clients are often "special victims," as the police say, or survivors of sexual trauma. "Child sexual abuse often involves being felt up by fathers, uncles, and brothers. That is really common," says Oak. "The arrival of breast buds in adolescence is one of the most dangerous times. That's when the shit started for many of the women I've worked with. There are two kinds of girl-child prey. Those of us who were sexually abused pre-breasts and those whose abuse started when they got them."

In West African countries like Cameroon and Guinea-Bissau, the presence of breasts makes women so much more vulnerable to sexual violence that an alarming number of mothers and other female family members subject their pubescent girls to a painful process called breast ironing, whereby their chests are cauterized, pounded, and bound over months to try to delay breast development.[32]

"American girls are getting their breasts earlier," declares Oak. "Of course, some girls rejoice in their arrival, feeling, like, 'Wow, I've got some power.' But others are uncomfortable with the extra attention they receive."[33]

Oak helps her clients accept and sometimes alter their chests. She always starts with an effort at acceptance. "One strategy is to get people to be inside their body. What's actually happening? Where's the energy? Don't worry about being looked at from the outside." Shafts of sunlight stream through the trees into the art cottage. "Another approach is to contemplate memories about body parts. I ask, what's the story so far? When and from whom did you first get this idea that your breasts were unattractive, hazardous, or shameful? Every breast has a story. Let's work on changing the narrative." Although feminists have a reputation for being against plastic surgery, Oak has helped people make the decision to get implants *and* to reduce or remove their breasts. Nevertheless, she hopes for "a culture where you can be gender fluid with breasts or super feminine without them."

Oak tells me that she doesn't do "witch therapy," although she sees it as "pretty much the same magic, setting an intention and working with it." She also thinks that over the years, "therapy has become more witchy, more attuned to the body and the breath."

"As a witch, how do you create magic spells?" I ask as I dunk my eggshell in yellow dye.

"Doreen Valiente defined magic as the art of changing consciousness at will," answers Oak. Active in mid-twentieth-century England, Valiente was a poet and pioneer of the neopagan religion of Wicca. "I see spells as prayers with props. When I teach beginner house magic, we start by sweeping the house with the intention to remove the bad energy."

The transformation of a broom, a tool for domestic chores, into a vehicle for flight is a delicious metaphor for women's liberation, I remark. Some people think that witches are devil worshippers or simply nasty, like the Wicked Witch in *The Wizard of Oz*. They forget about Glinda, the good witch, Mary Poppins, and the old-world "magic" remedies of herbalist apothecaries.

"Everything I make is a spell or an invocation," says Oak, holding up her painted egg to demonstrate. "Spells can involve actions, images, language. Words have power. Your book is a spell."

A magic handkerchief for waving "Goodbye to the Patriarchy."

"I hope so," I say, savoring this surprising thought. "*Tits Up* is about changing consciousness."

"I don't hex," explains Oak. "Magic works best when it's positive. I like to see what I can bring into the world. In my experience, hexing witches don't age well. It's not good for the beauty." Oak dips her waxed egg in a red dye bath, so that the top-free fool on it now has crimson nipples. "Both feminism and witchcraft are about raising consciousness, loving our bodies, and seeing them as holy."

"Are your breasts holy?" I ask.

"I'm sixty-seven and my breasts are as sacred as ever," declares Oak with a laugh. "I don't mind them sagging. In my twenties, I was tits on a stick. It was a relief to age and not get hit on. I truly don't mind that they're falling."

In our culture, saggy is a sin, I point out. Anglo-American culture has intense fear and loathing of aging, especially in women. Apparently, in Mali, "she whose breasts have fallen" is a respectful term for an older woman, not a slur betraying derision or disgust.[34]

For several years, Oak has been working on a series of spells titled "Wave Goodbye to the Patriarchy." Each spell takes the form of an artwork on a found, embroidered handkerchief. "I love how these old hankies hold the emotional energy of women wiping their tears and blowing their noses," explains Oak. Then she prints women-centered images, symbols, and catchphrases on them with multicolored archival ink. Sometimes, Oak strings the hankies together into a prayer flag. Other times, she sends them to people (like feminist Democrats Stacey Abrams and Elizabeth Warren) to put in their handbags, so they're ready to wave away toxic masculinity or male privilege with a flick of the wrist.

Oak made some custom "Wave Goodbye to the Patriarchy" hankies for me on the theme of reclaiming our breasts, which included stamps of a naked witch on a broom, butterflies whose wings flap farewell to male supremacy, a quote from bell hooks declaring "feminism is for everybody," and a trio of multi-breasted Artemis images.

"Artemis delivers strength and protection. She's the original eco-warrior," says Oak. "She has hundreds of breasts and each one can be seen as a different option. She is pro-choice and pro-life."

"Could Artemis be the goddess of the liberated rack?" I ask.

"Maybe," says Oak as she puts her finished egg/spell on the drying rack. "A liberated breast has plenty of choices. Whether to breastfeed or not, you choose. Whether to have plastic surgery, you can go big, small, or flat. Whether to wear a sexy bra, no bra, or no top at all. A liberated rack does what the hell it wants."

o o

As I walk past pines and sequoias toward my cabin, I ponder the polytheism of Oak and other Fool's Journey participants. Their revival of an eclectic, international range of goddesses is an example of the creativity of subcultures. Although women have never ruled the world, we enjoyed greater parity before societies imagined themselves in relation to one male god. As Gerda Lerner explains in her classic tome *The Creation of Patriarchy*, the "symbolic devaluing of women in relation to the divine" coincided with the long process of establishing systemic male dominance and other rigid hierarchical structures.[35]

Prehistory, or the time before written records, was rich in matriarchal power. Almost all of the figures found in Paleolithic excavations are female.[36] Made from stone, clay, bone, or mammoth ivory, these figures resemble the Venus of Willendorf insofar as they are small pocket sculptures with extra-large bosoms—an improbable body type for a nomadic hunter-gatherer on a compulsory Paleo diet. We may never be certain what these sculptures meant to their owners, but they are certainly not maiden goddesses of beauty and love, so it is inaccurate to call them Venuses. The theory I find most compelling for explaining their curious shape is that they are self-portraits made by women looking down at their bodies in an epoch many millennia before the invention of the mirror.[37] From this perspective, giant breasts and fore-

The Venus of Willendorf; made by a pregnant
hunter circa 25,000 BCE?

shortened legs make visual sense. Perhaps Paleolithic women took a break from carving spearheads in early pregnancy to create these amulets to protect themselves from death in childbirth.

Great chasms in time and culture divide these Stone Age little mamas from the hippie feminist revival of goddess worship. By contrast, contemporary Hinduism enjoys a vibrant, continuous goddess tradition. It is also appealingly heterodox insofar as "every Hindu tale has several versions, innumerable interpretations, and no specific place in the canon."[38] While the popularity of Hindu goddesses has not had obvious material benefits for Indian women, it may have fueled the advanced feminist thinking and activism found in Hindu South Asia.[39]

Last month, I had an eye-opening experience in the studio of Chitra Ganesh, an artist whose works are full of figures with astonishing tits. "The divine was inclusive and polymorphous," explained the artist about her Hindu upbringing as I nosed around her workspace, a large

Kali, the Hindu goddess of darkness, destruction, and death,
from Tamil Nadu, eleventh century.

single room overlooking a leafy street near Prospect Park in Brooklyn.
"My family was, like, 'Yes, Jesus. Yes, Krishna. Yes, Durga.'" Immigrants
to New York, Ganesh's parents initially spoke only Tamil to their daughter. They raised her in an environment rich in Hindu mythology out of
"anti-assimilationist" sentiments rather than religious conviction. The
family took long, regular trips to India, where they visited hundreds of
temples—many dedicated to goddesses and occasionally even to their
breasts. According to myth, the bodily remains of Sati, who died by fire
sacrifice, were scattered across the Indian subcontinent. Wherever her
ashes fell, shrines to her body parts were erected. Today, people make

pilgrimage to her relics, including one temple that honors her vagina and five temples devoted to her breasts.[40]

Many of Ganesh's figures have three or even four breasts. "It's a way to think about a nonconforming, disobedient body," explained the artist, whose tiny waist and generous bust are typical of Tamil goddess figures. "I want to complicate this category 'assigned female at birth.' I'd like it to be more capacious." Ganesh went on to tell me that in India, it's not uncommon to see people with six fingers or six toes. "Bodies are less aggressively policed than they are in the West." Indeed, American medicine generally removes the extra nipples and "accessory breast tissue" that usually appear on the "milk line," the axis along which mammals have teats.[41] "Two breasts are appealing and erotic," said Ganesh. "If you add a third one, it is not more exciting. It's weird."

In a piece titled *Black Vitruvian Tiger* depicting a three-breasted character with gold dots for nipples, Ganesh reinterprets Leonardo da Vinci's famous Renaissance drawing of an unclothed European man at the symbolic center of the world. "The ideal universal Western subject is in need of multiple vigorous updates," said Ganesh as I studied the multimedia drawing. Ganesh enjoys using black and brown paper as an inconspicuous skin color and "an antidote to the neutrality of whiteness," as she puts it.

The femme figure's tiger head evokes power figures such as the lion-headed Sekhmet, an Egyptian goddess, and Durga, a major Hindu deity often seen riding a tiger. While traditional depictions of Durga show her holding weapons in her many hands, Ganesh's Vitruvian version is surrounded by rose petals and silk thread, rendering her as the supreme Shakti center of a peaceful new world order. In Hinduism, Shakti is the elemental feminine energy that is the source and sustainer of the universe.

Ganesh often makes paintings with thought and speech bubbles inspired by an Indian comic book series focused on religious legends and historical folklore. In a digital print titled *Charmed Tongue*,

Chitra Ganesh's three-breasted *Black Vitruvian Tiger*, a critique of Leonardo da Vinci's universal man.

the protagonist again has three breasts, but this time each nipple is a brown eye with long lashes on top and red tears on the bottom. Eyes are, as the cliché goes, windows of the soul. Here breasts are an alternate way of sensing, communicating, or even spying. Indeed, Ganesh sees the nipple as a third eye, "a metaphor for extrasensory perception," which "signifies another mode of understanding, such as a somatic knowledge."

Hindu myths, like ancient Greek ones, are often violent. One Tamil epic poem features a breast with the destructive force of a bomb. A woman called Kannagi is heartbroken when she discovers her husband is having an affair with a courtesan. Through a series of mishaps and deceptions, her husband is accused of stealing and

Chitra Ganesh sees nipples as "third eyes."

executed. Kannagi is so angry at the state that she tears off her breast and throws it into the capital, Madurai, where it bursts into flames, burning the city to the ground. Those who survived the fire admired her refusal to be a victim and elevated her into a village goddess, also known as Grama-devis.[42]

When I relayed the story of Kannagi to Ganesh, she smiled with recognition. "My partner and I have been fantasizing about a comic book featuring a menopausal superhero who shoots fire out of her breasts," said Ganesh, who is in her late forties. "Her name would have to be Hot Flash!"

o o

The words "The Divine Rabbi" pop up on my iPhone. A friend and feminist who officiated my wedding, Rabbi Sydney Mintz is returning my call. I've already interviewed her three times, but I am still confused by the convoluted maze of biblical, Talmudic, Midrashic, and Kabbalistic writing that is Judaism. An iconoclastic or aniconic religion, the Jewish tradition offers no visual representations of biblical characters, let alone breasts, so I am missing my favorite repository of cultural connotations. Whatever the case, we can be sure that five thousand years ago, in the Fertile Crescent of the Middle East, people talked about breasts. But in the days before paper, little was written in stone or on sheepskin. Mintz, a reform rabbi at Temple Emanu-El, San Francisco's largest Jewish congregation, has promised to help me understand several instances of what I reckon are sacred breasts.

The most widely known story about breasts derives from the Old Testament and involves my namesake, Sarah, the official matriarch of the Jewish people. I ask Mintz to remind me how Sarah's breast milk was a vehicle for religious conversion.

"Sarah was a hundred years old when she gave birth to Isaac," says Mintz matter-of-factly. "So many doubted that the baby was actually hers. They gossiped that he was a foundling picked up at the market or the son of her handmaiden. Abraham, her husband, decided to hold a great feast to prove otherwise, inviting important locals to bring their infants for her to nurse. But Sarah was like, 'Abraham, what the hell, how can I suckle so many babies at my age?' And Abraham says, 'Honey, don't be so modest. You could feed thousands.' And when the feast happened, her breasts gushed like two fountains, and her milk was so copious that she fed the children of Israel."[43]

Biblical Sarah sounds like the allomothers who donate breast milk to the bank. Their milk flows like springs.[44]

"I often think of Sarah as an early adopter of a milk bank solution," says Mintz. "And what a mitzvah. She wasn't a freak show. She had something to give and was respected for it."

"Sarah had miraculous mammaries!" I declare.

"Literally. Her abundant milk was the miracle that converted skeptics into believers," says Mintz. "Also, in the Talmud, a rabbi says that the Torah is to the human spirit what breast milk is to a hungry infant.[45] And the Torah is *kadosh*, which means sacred or holy."

Mintz did her rabbinical thesis on whores and concubines in the Old Testament.[46] From her, I understand that it features two very different kinds of sex worker: the *zonah* and the *kadeshah*.

"*Zonah* are ordinary prostitutes," says Mintz. "In the Torah, there are many *zonah*. The word appears ninety-three times, probably because Jewish men were forbidden to spill their seed onto the ground. That meant absolutely no masturbating." Mintz goes on to explain that prostitution was both forbidden and condoned. "In Leviticus, it says, don't degrade your daughter by making her a harlot. But in Deuteronomy, the laws about war say that soldiers can take slaves who could become whores. So, disturbingly, the Torah suggests that prostitution is okay for them, but not for us."

"The *kadeshah* were sacred whores," continues Mintz. "*Kadesh* means holy, set apart, consecrated. *Kiddush*, a blessing recited over wine to make Shabbat holy, or *Kaddish*, the mourners' prayer for the dead, or *kiddushin*, the marriage ceremony—all these words come from the same root." We are not certain what acts or rituals the sacred whores performed. "They might have been priestesses performing rites in pagan temples dedicated to fertility or prostitutes who worked nearby," says Mintz.

"Can we assume sacred sex workers had sacred breasts?" I ask.

"I don't see why not," says Mintz.

I was also keen for Mintz's thoughts on one of God's many names in the Hebrew Bible. The third most common, after Yahweh and Elohim, is El Shaddai, which occurs forty-eight times. The term is usually translated as "God Almighty," but *Shaddai* also means mountain and breast. Some scholars translate El Shaddai as "the God with Breasts" and suggest it is consistent with the androgynous, abstract God that appears in parts of the Bible.[47] Others look to the polytheistic roots of monotheism and argue that El Shaddai was more likely two deities—El, a god, and Shaddai, a goddess—who may have been consorts or shared a temple; the blending of their cults led to the compound deity El Shaddai.[48]

"I'm sad that goddess worship was suppressed," says Mintz, "and that the feminine side of divinity is rarely discussed unless you're a Kohenet priestess."[49] The Kohenet Hebrew Priestess Institute is a community that practices "embodied, earth-based feminist Judaism."[50] Mintz likes bringing nature back into Jewish ritual, performing Kiddush Levinah, an outdoor blessing of the new moon, and doing ritual purifications, or *mikveh*, in the ocean.

In *Suckling at My Mother's Breasts: The Image of a Nursing God in Jewish Mysticism*, Ellen Davina Haskell explains that the mystics who wrote the Kabbalah in the thirteenth century conceived the divine as having ten aspects, one of which is feminine and associated with breastfeeding.[51]

"Shekhinah," says Mintz on the other end of the phone, as I catch the smell of roasted carrots in the breeze. "It's like the god—or goddess—that dwells within."

"Yes, shekhinah!" I exclaim. Haskell talks about it as the aspect of God that is willingly in exile among human beings in order to be a conduit between the divine and the natural world. Shekhinah is associated with moonlight, the ebb and flow of the tide, and the Sabbath. Within this, suckling is the primary metaphor for how humans are infused with spirituality. Divinity basically flows through the breast.[52]

o o

Back in the dining hall, I find a seat at the end of a long table near Oak, her Buddhist spouse Max, and my friend Blakey, who is enjoying her fourth annual Fool's Journey long weekend. Blakey has been a generous sounding board for my musings on breasts during many walks on the beach with our sibling mutts. Related through dog ownership, we have a mammalian bond. Blakey is a restrained English professor who was brought up Episcopalian by "Boston Brahmins." When the conversation about *Roe v. Wade* dies down, she turns to me, as if chairing a seminar, and says with genuine curiosity, "During your offering this morning, you mentioned a therapeutic experience that made it easy to give a topless talk. You sat for a painting?"

Last year on Halloween, I went to the Brooklyn studio of an artist called Clarity Haynes. I liked the idea of stripping in pursuit of self-understanding while others dressed up. I pass my phone to Blakey so she can see a photo of Haynes's drawing of my chest.

Over the past twenty years, Haynes has made hundreds of breast portraits. Most artists today work from photographs to the extent that drawing from life is increasingly rare. Life drawing is about an encounter "in real life," where one measure of success is the artist's loyalty to the physicality of her subject.

Haynes discovered the therapeutic potential of breast portraiture

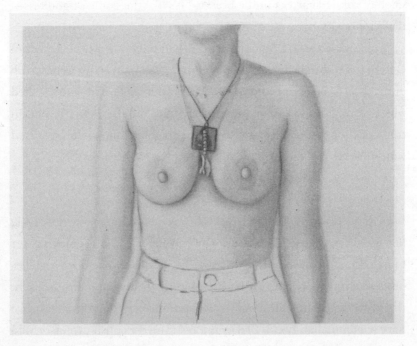

Clarity Haynes's torso portraits are a form of body-image therapy.

by accident. She was working as a stripper a few nights a week so she could spend long days in the studio. She didn't mind the predatory looks cast upon her large breasts if she was being paid for it, but hated being objectified when she was just walking down the street. When she decided to make a breast self-portrait, she didn't know what to expect so was "prepared to see a joke," as she put it. The result was not "a caricature of femininity," but an image that restored her sense of dignity and self-possession.

A few friends asked her to do pastels of their chests, and before long, she was setting up booths and selling in-person breast portraits at women's festivals. She would do three or four portraits a day, while people watched and made encouraging comments. Her sitters often came with significant life experiences etched on their bodies—scars from cancer surgeries or stretch marks from childbirth. Back in her studio, she went on to paint the big, beautiful chests of fat activists and, her favorite subjects, crones. Since her early twenties, she had been fascinated by aging and keen to venerate the wrinkles, creases, and droops that we rarely see in art or media.

Blakey hands my phone to Oak, who peers at my torso portrait through her black-rimmed glasses.

Haynes's studio was an easy place to disrobe, I tell them, because it was full of naked breasts, including some very large-scale paintings of female chests that critics have described as "seated buddhas."[53] After choosing a peachy-pink piece of archival paper, I took my seat next to the window. From about 6 feet away, Haynes squinted at me. She took in my overall shape, then moved to her easel, sketched a few lines in charcoal, and stepped back to stare at my chest with more intense focus. Her gaze felt accurate and authoritative, but nothing like that of a doctor. It was more accepting and appreciative.

"She has a healing gaze," says Oak. "She looks at you as a whole person with a history that is being written and rewritten every day. Everybody talks about the male gaze, but other gazes can have power and influence."

While Haynes was drawing, I vacillated between feelings of inhibi-
tion and exhibitionism before settling into the freedom of being hap-
pily half-naked. After several hours of kind and respectful scrutiny,
my perspective on my top half had shifted. I felt less shame about my
implants and more affection for Bert and Ernie; after all, they're educational puppets with moral and social truths to share. By the time
Haynes finished the work, I felt proud of my breasts and *maybe* even
ready to participate in a top-free public protest.

"Tell us about the necklaces you're wearing," says Oak.

I had curated some amulets: a chain gifted by my sister that says
TITS UP, a newborn hospital bracelet whose beads spell THORNTON,
a heavy gold ring that my wife gave me, a medal for ballroom dancing
that my mother won as a teenager, and a square pendant borrowed from
my friend, writer Terry Castle. I wore them to feel less naked. Indigenous women in hot climates often wear a "social skin" of necklaces,
bracelets, hair ornaments, body paint, etcetera, that communicates
their identity in their culture. By these means, they are not undressed
just because their breasts are bare.[54]

"You have a whole book on your chest," says Oak. "Your shoulders
are not relaxed, which suggests you are doing something brave."

"It's your warrior bosom, your ode to Artemis," declares Blakey,
referring to my protective charms and faint mastectomy scars.

The finished portrait is true to my reconstructed torso, but more
beautiful than my perception of it due to Haynes's thoughtful drafts-
manship. The drawing is prosaic, revealing asymmetrical breasts and
bony middle-aged shoulders, but it also manifests a little poetry, suggesting that I'm a proud proto-crone.

Haynes always hopes that the positive memory of being seen bare-
chested by her will override disagreeable memories related to breasts.
She sees her portraits as a form of "body therapy" for the sitter—a
visual, experiential alternative to talk therapy.

"This drawing is more than a portrait," says Oak, returning my phone. "It was a ritual—a magical act of changing consciousness."

○ ○

Oak and Blakey go back to their cabins to change for the evening's outdoor ritual, leaving Max and me to talk over dessert. Max identifies semi-jokingly as a "cross-dresser" because she wears men's clothes. Raised Jewish, Max officially became a Buddhist almost forty years ago. She doesn't believe in gods or goddesses as much as in the interconnectedness of all living things. She and I share a fascination with the adaptive cunning of raccoons, who disable locks and open doors at speeds that rival primates. Max attends Fool's Journey as Oak's spouse and offers a session on chanting. Between mouthfuls, I ask her if she has any thoughts about the role of breasts in Buddhism.

"I chant every day, twice a day, to become more self-aware, responsible, and happy," says Max slowly, as if she were thinking aloud. "When I chant, I sit up straight and put my hands together in front of my chest. It involves the voice, breathing, and sound vibrations. The universe is vibrating, and when you chant, your body hums with the universe." She pauses and looks at me with a frown. "I'm not sure what exactly that has to do with breasts, but they're there."

I'm intrigued by the centrality of the chest in the cross-legged lotus position and several other body postures through which Buddhists listen to their mind and alter their consciousness. In most representations of the Buddha and his bodhisattvas, the torso is the star. It is more striking and engaging than the face. Often bare and hairless, the Buddha's chest has well-defined nipples and pectorals that are either breast-like or so undeveloped as to be gender-neutral.

"My tradition of Buddhism is not big on anthropomorphic icons," explains Max. Based on the writings of a thirteenth-century Japanese priest, her branch of Buddhism is a lay organization with no paid clergy or hierarchy of authority. "When I chant, I focus on a paper scroll inscribed with calligraphy related to the Lotus Sutra." After the Buddha's death in 486 BCE, there were no portraits of him for 150 years. Just as Jews and Muslims prohibit visual representations of biblical figures like Abraham and Sarah, certain Buddhist traditions are aniconic. Their visual cultures consist of symbols rather than human likenesses.

The thirty-two physical characteristics of a Buddha—sometimes called the Thirty-Two Marks of a Good Man—declare that the Buddha should have a prominent torso, "immense like a lion," and an inconspicuous penis, or more specifically a "well-retracted organ." I understand that an erect penis is a serious obstacle to achieving nirvana, but I'm intrigued that the Buddha is expected to have an outstanding chest. I ask Max if she has any comment.

"No!" she laughs.

Enlightenment is not about accentuating sexual dimorphism. I recently interviewed a Buddhist priest at the Jodo Shinshu Temple in San Francisco's Japantown. She explained that enlightenment is genderless. It is about awakening to a nondual reality where there is no him and her, no me and you, no us and them. She told me a joke: "What's the difference between a Buddhist and a non-Buddhist? The non-Buddhist thinks there is a difference!"[55]

When Alexander the Great invaded northern India in 327 BCE, he brought various genres of ancient Greek art. As a result, many early sculptures of the historical Buddha depict him as a Greek god. For most Buddhist practitioners, however, the historical Buddha is a wise man who became a spiritual leader, not a deity.

The bare torso of the Buddha—like that of Jesus—is a mark of his honesty and openness. Clothes affiliate the wearer with specific social groups and hierarchical ranks. They mask the universal by layering the body with stratification and difference. A naked male chest suggests authenticity, which is a precursor to enlightenment (and resurrection).

"The Buddha's chest is my chest, your chest, everybody's chest. We all have the Buddha nature," says Max patiently, as my dogged queries about specific physicalities go against the grain of her Buddhist love of the immaterial.

From the back of my notebook, I pull out a postcard of Tara, the Buddha-goddess who, for me, epitomizes the beauty of feminine power (see image on page 205). Tara is a Tibetan sister to the Chinese Guanyin and Japanese Kannon, as they all derive from Avalokiteśvara, the original Indian bodhisattva of compassion. However, Guanyin is the listener—her name translates as "the one who perceives the sounds of the world"—while Tara is the watcher. She was born from a tear shed by Avalokiteśvara, the "lord who gazes down at the world," when he was moved by the misery he observed below. Tara is sometimes called the Mother of Liberation because she frees souls from suffering.

White Tara, the specific Tara portrayed in the gilded statue on my postcard, is a conduit not only of compassion but of success in work, healing, and longevity. Made in Kathmandu in the 1400s and now on display in San Francisco's Asian Art Museum, the sculpture is charged with a sublime authority remarkable in a seated figure less than 2 feet high. She peers at me through slitted eyes. A third eye, which affords perception beyond ordinary sight, adorns her forehead, while the eyes on her palms and the soles of her feet evoke her omniscience. A personification of spiritual intelligence, her torso is bare except for a beaded necklace that rides the crest of two pristine hemispheres. Indeed, her breasts are purposely architectural; they are two stupas, dome-shaped shrines that often hold relics such as the remains of Buddhist monks and nuns.

Tibetan Buddhism requires followers to be formally initiated into their esoteric tradition; only then are you permitted to meditate on Tara and visualize her in your mind's eye.[56] In her book on Tara, China Galland, an initiate, recounts her audience with the Dalai Lama, who said to her: "Tara could be taken as a very strong feminist. According to legend, she knew there were hardly any Buddhas who had been enlightened in the form of a woman. So, she determined to retain her female form and to become enlightened only in this female form."[57] An outsider to the practice, I am awed by the way Tara, with her monumental mammaries, embodies such a cerebral practice.[58]

I show the postcard of Tara to Max and ask her opinion.

"I like that it shows a Buddha who is female," she says flatly. "But generally, I feel that statues misrepresent the Buddha nature inherent in all things."

Humbled, I tuck the postcard back into my notebook, keen to protect my secret, inexpert worship. The difference between appreciation and appropriation is a tense topic. When the original culture sees borrowing as a sign of popularity or influence, the debate is easily resolved. However, some cultures perceive the adoption of their heroes as colonial theft, imperial exploitation, or shallow fashion. My admiration for Tara's spiritual physicality may be a means of fortifying my Anglo-American self through Eastern religion.[59] Luckily, my awe will not adversely impact her thousand-year reign.

o o

I'm hit with a blast of outdoor air as I exit the dining hall. Sadly, it's too cold for moon-bathing breasts tonight. I walk past the giant live oak tree, the oval pool, and the arbor toward the small clearing where the rituals take place. A large circle of some thirty canvas chairs awaits the group. On the far, east side of the circle, one of the three men at the retreat, a teacher, sits next to his wife, a photographer. On the near, west side is the eldest participant at Fool's Journey, Betty Jane.

Wearing a red cape with a matching red jester's hat, Betty Jane tells me that she was born in 1927, started menstruating in 1939, and had an abortion in 1947. She breastfed her three children, became a yoga teacher in 1966, divorced in 1974. For the past eighty years, since about the age of fifteen, she has been a member of "the itty bitty titty committee." When she was young, "tits" meant teats and referred specifically to nipples. Betty Jane describes herself as an "equal opportunity spiritual seeker"—a pagan who loves Guanyin and communicates with ancestors through ash altars in the Dagara tradition of western Africa. "What really resonates for me," she adds, "is anything to do with the living spirit of nature."

While I have been absorbed in the arc of Betty Jane's long life, other Fools have gathered. Max, the iconoclastic Buddhist, has taken the seat on my left. Next to her sits my erudite Episcopalian pal Blakey. On the south side of the circle sits Marg, who shared her thoughts about the breasts of Catholic nuns and Mother Mary. No longer bare-breasted, she now wears a parka and a wool beanie. Oak, the therapist whose handkerchiefs "wave goodbye to the patriarchy," stands in the middle of the circle with Bread, who has assisted in the nocturnal births of thousands of babies.

This evening's interactive ceremony starts, like they all do, with a "grounding" visualization that helps bring everyone together. Tonight's ritual is focused on the tarot card Justice, whose attributes are fairness, balance, and the law. A young witch called Sabra casts a circle around the group by drawing a pentacle in the air with a ceremonial knife while facing north, east, south, and then west. Then Sabra moves to the center, looks straight up at the sky, and draws a final pentacle while proclaiming, "The circle is cast and we are between the worlds. The ritual has begun."

Next comes a playful invocation of the elements—earth, wind, fire, and water. One thing that differentiates Fool's Journey from other pagan retreats is the minimal liturgy and extensive use of humor. Oak dislikes any whiff of top-down, dogmatic churchiness or cultish ortho-doxy. Other than sharing a love of Mother Earth and a belief in wom-en's equal rights, the people assembled are welcome to pick and choose their spiritual convictions.

It is time to invoke the deities. Rose, a "Jewitch," summons Hecate, an ancient Greek goddess whom the Romans called Trivia (meaning "three ways").

I've been mulling over how to invite Artemis/Diana. The art historian in me loves reflecting on the power of images, but my atheist upbringing means that I am spiritually limited. When it comes to otherworldliness, I find it hard to believe in much more than the mysteries of DNA. However, I am feeling wishful. I respect the political motives and social good these neo-pagans want to bring into the world. I don't want to fail them.

Luckily, Oak summons Artemis first. She strides around the circle with the full force of her body, arms swinging, her voice rumbling from deep within her chest. "O Artemis, O Diana, mighty goddess of the wild, ruler of both stag and fawn, of all who dwell in your forests, we call and invoke you," she says. "You, the original eco-warrior, join us in our pursuit of Justice. This is a time when we really need you. You remind us that our bodies are holy, our choices are sacred. You, who rule over childbirth and midwifery, defend our power to choose if and when we give birth. Protect our reproductive freedom. Artemis of the many breasts, symbolic tonight of the many choices we make in our short lives, guardian of those choices, join us in our circle as we conjure Justice and choice for all women. We invite and welcome you!"

Oak concludes her invocation, then beckons me with her gaze. I walk a few paces into the center, then my feet seem to sprout roots and I can move no further. With as much conviction as I can muster, I call out hopefully: "Artemis! Can you hear me?" Clouds are rolling by in the twilight. The wind is rustling leaves in the forest's canopy. "You led the Amazons to many victories. We know they were courageous, successful, two-breasted warriors with sharp eyes and great aim. We don't believe the patriarchal poppycock that they cut off one boob." I pause while a few participants cackle. "Artemis, Diana, goddess of many identities, please give us the strength and strategies to go into battle yet again for women's bodily autonomy." I stop, take three steps back, and fall into my chair.

As the theatrical rite continues, I am filled with affection for the people here. They care. They are good souls. I reflect on how academic feminists are often so engulfed in an atheist worldview that they sideline spiritual feminists of all kinds. We could even say they have ignored them as if they were inconvenient boobs. But these witchy women are smart and deep and bring value to the social world, both in their day jobs and in their nightlife. Through being here and researching the place of breasts in spirituality, I have come to understand that there is no necessary opposition between feminism and religion. Women's emancipation is not exclusively secular. In fact, our liberation may be enhanced by flights of fancy and leaps of faith.

While everyone else is focused on the ritual, I notice a deer walking cautiously down a path from the northeast into the meadow. My first thought is: Artemis's sidekick and spirit animal. What a ridiculous coincidence. But then I leap at the opportunity to embrace a delicious sense of the uncanny.

No one appears to have seen her, so I nudge Betty Jane on my right. The ninety-five-year-old eventually spots the creature in the dim light, then beams brightly and says, "That's magic!"

On my left, Blakey and Max have sighted the animal, which now stands motionless, looking at us out of her left eye.

"They are usually so skittish," whispers Blakey. "She understands that we are peaceful humans."

"It's a sign of support from the universe," adds Max.

The deer turns down the path leading toward my cabin, continuing her evening stroll. I am consoled by the enigmatic intelligence of mammals and delighted that eco-feminist yearning has been momentarily rewarded. It's a fitting end to a day dedicated to exploring the diverse universe of holy mammaries.

Toward a
Liberated Rack

I recently asked my niblings, who attend a public high school in an affluent suburb of New York City, what words their friends use for breasts. My nephew, a sixteen-year-old sophomore who socializes with his mates on the soccer team, openly rattled off six terms, starting with "rack" and ending with "tits." My niece, an eighteen-year-old senior, said that the only word the girls in her grade used regularly was "boobs." This disparity in vocabulary is symptomatic of the gender inequalities embodied unconsciously by many Americans. It is also indicative of the larger problem of who defines and controls women's bodies. My hope is that proud "self-labeling with slur terms," as language philosophers call it, can be empowering for girls and women as well as a means of influencing popular culture.[1] Reclaiming slang is one tactic for rescuing a body part from prejudice and unshackling it from shame.

Another strategy central to *Tits Up* is an effort to deepen our understanding of what breasts mean to their owners in different contexts. By these means, I hope to shift the definition of breasts away from the dominant patriarchal version of them as passive erotic playthings. In chapter 1, for example, strippers, burlesque dancers, and full-service sex workers proactively deploy their tits to entertain and make money. In this world, breasts are not sex toys as much as salaried assistants. In chapter 2, the value of mammaries takes a pendulum swing toward the expression of love and commitment. Maternal jugs are about evolutionary function and the intense emotions that have ensured the survival of our species. In chapter 3, form eclipses function as breasts are lifted, augmented, reduced, removed, and reconstructed. They are the flesh that needs to be shaped to conform to the highly social beings that we call our inner selves. In chapter 4, breasts are unruly dissidents that are given neat shapes and physical support by the most technically complex garment made by the apparel industry. For some, nipples are impertinent and in need of the protection of foam cups; for others, they are free-thinking and worthy of the right to roam free. Finally, in chapter 5, breasts are natural mysteries that link us to the sublimity of our mammalian past. They are also protagonists in sacred tales that celebrate their miraculous capacity to save life, create community, and inspire awe.

I hope the complex and contradictory connotations of breasts in *Tits Up* thwart any easy dismissal of them as shallow or superfluous organs. A "rack" is not only a cut of meat close to the ribs and slang for breasts, it is also a framework for hanging clothes and, arguably, cultural baggage. That said, *Tits Up* can be seen as a curated hang of the burdens and benefits of breasts according to expert insiders. Having digested their thoughts, I have a few expectations about the top half of women's liberation.

An emancipated rack has no particular appearance. It may be perky, buxom, or flat; braless or encased in lace; surgically enhanced, a source of nourishment, or a revenue stream. A liberated rack is not dominated by aesthetic criteria. Nor is it subject to the constant pressure of a controlling or objectifying male gaze.

The influence of women's vision is a theme in this book. Strippers actively make eye contact; they look at men in ways that can disrupt and humanize power relations. The ocular exchanges between mother and child, observant doctors and expressive patients, women designers and their fit models, gay photographers and their lingerie muses confound grand theories of the straight male gaze. Indeed, at the end of *Tits Up*, we meet an artist whose therapeutic intent leads to a "healing gaze."

"Is it possible to see *all* breasts as beautiful?" asks Margaret Miles, one of my erudite elder interviewees. "Could we see breasts as reflections of women's experience? Training your eye to see beauty of this kind," she wrote fifteen years ago, would be "a profoundly countercultural act."[2] Indeed, when I hear someone deride their "saggy boobs," I ask them to consider the label "sagacious," a word derived from "sage" that is a synonym for "wise." It amuses me to imagine pendulous breasts as ponderous—weighed down with lived experience. It's a joke, but it's also a plea to reflect on our ageism and to figure out ways to honor the crone.

I look forward to a day when men, women, and people of all genders are broadly aware of the significance of mammaries to human intelligence and sociality. Breasts are not fatuous accessories. They are not dismissible, extraneous add-ons to the neutral, Vitruvian, iconic bodies of men. Without breasts, we could not be human. *Homo sapiens* is distinguished by the superlative communication skills that develop as a result of

Tits up to the late Eve Babitz, seen here with Marcel Duchamp.

the lengthy dependence of human babies on their mother's milk. Infants need to solicit love and, in turn, develop the interactive ability to adore.

In the age of artificial intelligence, when many are scrambling to understand exactly what it means to be human, let us not universalize male experience or sideline the ladies. Indeed, evolutionary evidence indicates that females are the "ancestral sex." As Lucy Cooke writes, "Eve wasn't created out of Adam's rib, it was the other way around. In the beginning there was female and she gave rise to male." The human genome bears witness to this legacy. Women are the default XX and men are XY, wherein the Y is a "runt of a chromosome, stunted and with significantly less genetic material."[3]

Some day, I hope American women will live as freely as men when it comes to the simple things, like a nipple silhouette under a collared shirt. We also deserve to have the joyful sovereignty of a bare-breasted swim on a hot day.

The censorship of female nipples is a self-perpetuating problem. Their sexual charge "owes much of its fascination to full or partial concealment."[4] If our breasts are veiled, it is more difficult for them to shed their status as sex objects. Moreover, when a body part is emblematic of a group of people, its sexiness (or lack thereof) can over-shadow other aspects of our humanity, leading to dehumanization and marginalization.

When I started my research, I did not realize how deeply colonized our breasts are by patriarchy. I didn't think a boob book would take issue with so many laws or that it would lead me into terrain that was historically uncomfortable to mainstream feminism. Sex work, breast-feeding, plastic surgery, fashion, femininity, spirituality, and the pur-suit of beauty are all issues that have been snubbed by the women's movement.

While researching "Hardworking Tits," it became clear that the decriminalization of consenting adult prostitution is a human rights issue of relevance to all women. As I wrote in that chapter, if some women cannot *sell* their bodies without being harassed by the police and organized crime, then none of us actually *own* our bodies. New Zealand was the first country in the world to give women the vote, in 1893, and the first to decriminalize sex work, in 2003. When I spoke with Catherine Healy, who was made a Dame for her leadership in sex-worker rights in New Zealand, she admitted that her home country was still "conflicted." The majority of Kiwis still suffer from "whorepho-bia," but they could not condone the "injustice that the male client was allowed to *pay*, but the sex worker wasn't allowed to *sell*."[5] I hope my readers will consider a woman's right to choose what she does with her own body from this perspective.

Breastfeeding, discussed in "Lifesaving Jugs," is another issue around which the women's movement has not rallied. American femi-nism has foregrounded the right *not* to have children, rather than the rights of women once they've had them. The US government's de facto position on breasts is perverse. First, since 1998, American women have had the right to fake boobs (aka breast reconstructions after mas-tectomies), but we have never been granted the federal right to breast-feed, nor protections that would allow women to feel safe nursing their babies in public.[6] Second, the world's biggest buyer of breast milk substitutes is the US government. It is distributed by the Department of Agriculture through their Women, Children's and Infants offices rather than the Department of Health and Human Services. Is this part of a legacy of treating women as chattel or, for that matter, cattle?

In "Treasured Chests" and "Active Apexes," I investigated two dif-ferent strategies by which women wrestle with the appearance of their top halves: breast surgeries and bra fashions. Feminists have generally condemned women who have cosmetic surgery as dupes of patriarchy, victims of the male gaze, and casualties of beauty norms. Plastic sur-gery can also be seen as a means by which women take ownership of their bodies and attempt to empower themselves in compromised circumstances.[7] Whatever the case, I recommend that we give our sisters a break and let them preside over their own chests.[8]

With a few exceptions, fashion has also been condemned and trivialized.[9] Scouring back issues of *Ms.* magazine for their coverage of breasts (it was mostly about cancer), I came across an article from the mid-1990s that opened with the shocking hook: "I'm a feminist, and I love clothes."[10] For me, style is a creative pleasure. Beauty is an ancient and universal human pursuit. Unlike corsets, a well-designed sports bra can contribute to feminine well-being.

Finally, in "Holy Mammaries," I found myself in a peculiar position—a skeptical agnostic defending spiritualists who believe in magical activism. Their reverence for their own bodies, including their tits, is thought-provoking. In a modern world where breasts are generally considered profane rather than sacred, I was also glad to discover stories about the divinity of breasts in the established faiths of Judaism, Christianity, Hinduism, and Buddhism. Rather than spurning religion for its overarching patriarchal values, I marvel at the power of these specific breast-affirming narratives to unite women, inspire action, and spur change.

So, how can we liberate our top halves? "Most American political movements have over-relied on the legal system," Chase Strangio, a lawyer who works for the ACLU, told me in an interview about chests and breasts. "Our legal system is never going to give us much. It doesn't have robust principles of self-determination, autonomy, or human dignity. All we've got is rights. Rights are created by the state and inherently limited."[11]

In many ways, American women already hold the power to elevate the status of their breasts. What would the world be like if we insisted on owning them and had much greater respect for the choices other women make about their own chests? If the lowly status of dumb boobs is a cornerstone of women's subordination, what if we elevated the gals, not with celebration but with thoughtful appreciation? Would women have a better chance of being seen as whole human beings with intelligence and agency, who merit the bodily autonomy and physical freedoms enjoyed by men? I think so. Our rise depends in part on their higher worth. So, let's stand up, pull our shoulders back, and figure out how to succeed. This is what I hear when a woman hollers, "Tits up!"

ACKNOWLEDGMENTS

It takes a village to write about living cultures. I relish learning through others and rely on their insights. Thank you to the following interviewees, some of whom let me observe them at work and/or endured repeated interrogations in person, on Zoom, over the phone, and in texts and emails: Kelly Adams, Megan Adams, Priscilla Alexander, Kimberly Seals Allers, Maryann Allison, Ghazala Anwar, Marcel Pardo Ariza, Josephine Ashford, Alexander Asseily, Aresha Auzeene, Jill Bakehorn, Joyce Baran, Kat Barlas, Dr. Andrew Barnett, Melissa Barreras, Jonathan Bautista, Robin Wilson Beattie, Robert Behar, Dana Ben-Ari, Kale Bendian, Amy Bessone, Sarah Blaustein, Barbie Bloodgloss, Dr. Kelly Bolden, Amanda Boring, Corinne Botz, Julie Bouchet-Horwitz, Kim Brennecke, Ami Burnham, Heidi Burns, Rose Bush, Tex Buss, Laura Camerlengo, Jeannette Cantone, Sara Carter, Dr. Carolyn Chang, Joey Chang, Abby Chen, Nanci Clarence, Cavan Clark, Julia Clark, Algereese "Reese" Clayton, Mathilde Cohen, Natalie Cohen, Ra'el Cohen, Dr. Tarah Colaizy, Deborah Oak Cooper, Bronwyn Cosgrave, T. Thorn Coyle, Dr. Susan Crowe, Bonnie Cullum, Jill D'Alessandro, Raina Daniels, Dana Donofree, Zackary Drucker, Jeff Durham, Alisha Eastwood, Tana Elise, Sarah Elmer, Brynn Ervin, Teresa Ewins, Charlotte Eyerman, Dominika Fabian, Kristina Fedran, Dr. Julius Few, Kathy Fichtel, Michelle Millar Fisher, Jennifer Dunlop Fletcher, Margaux Foxworth, Dr. Heather Furnas, Jessica Parish Galloway, Chitra Ganesh, Maria Garcia, Brandi Gates-Burgess, Julie Gibson, Helen Ginger (Nguyen Huong), Sonnie Givens, Nash Glynn, Bok Goodall, Laura Gordon, Mr. Gorgeous (Eric Gorsuch), Jenny Gotwals, Ryan Gourley, Helen Gray, Dominique Grisard, Lindsay Groff, Pam Grossman, Anne Grøvslien, Marg Hall, Miki Hamano, Rabbi Jill Hammer, Dian Hanson, Scarlot Harlot (Carol Leigh Szego), Ellen Davina Haskell, Mara Hassan, Kristina Haugland, Clarity Haynes, Dame Catherine Healy, Micol Hebron, Dr. Stephen Henry, Dr. Dawn Hershman, Karen Hodges, Sarah Holme, Kevin Honeycut, Lisa Israel, Isabel Iturrios, Mari-Anna O'Ree Jones, Natalie Kabenjian, Kitty KaPowww, Clare Karunawardhane, Sanjeewa Karunawardhane, Naomi Kelman, Helen Kent-Nicoll, Leticia Kimble, Paul King, Dr. Sangeetha Kolluri, Rachel Kraus, Silpa Kurupati, Ayla Landry, Martha/ Max Lange, Sara Caspi Lee, Vivien Lee, Fabian Licona, Crocodile Lightning (Nat Vikitsreth), Indra Lusero, Emjay Lynn, Dr. Barbara Machado, Lindsey Martin, Miss Dirty Martini (Linda Marraccini), Forrest McGill, Karina Medina, Dr. Zoe Mendelsohn, Dr. Phil Mercado, Shawn Merz, Deena Metzger, Rosemary Meza-DesPlas, Dori Midnight, Midori, Becca Mikesell, Margaret R. Miles, Rabbi Sydney Mintz, Lady Monster, Paige Mughannam, Dr. Rita Mukhtar, Rhonda Mundhenk, Gatita Negra (India Sabater), Daffodil Nicki, Chelsea Nikole, Helen Maria Nugent, Mitsu Okubo, Catherine Opie, Cristina Jade Peña, Gina Peterson, Erin Poh, Jonny Porkpie, Dr. Elisabeth Potter, Jeff Potter, Veronique Powell, Yvonne Simone Powless, Michele Pred, Amanda Price, Victoria Quandt, Carol Queen, Nina Rakhlin, Elysia Joy Ramirez, Omayma Ramzy, Red-Bone (Madeline Latrice Howie), Melanie Reitzel, Jessica Rivers, Jodi Roberts, Angelica Rojas, Ivy Ross, Kate DiMarco Ruck, Alissa Saenz, Pauline Sakamoto, Kempe Scanlan, Londa Schiebinger, Susan Schippmann, Dr. Stephen Seligman, Marie Sena, Reverend Elaine Donlin Sensai, Chen Shen, Lisa Sim, Moscato Sky, Julie Smith, Diane Lynn Spatz, Annie Sprinkle, Dr. Julie Sprunt, Jackie Stacey, Beth Stephens,

Chase Strangio, Susan Stryker, Ellen Susman, Jaqueline Sussman, Dr. Steve Teitelbaum, Heather Thompson, Christy Turlington-Burns, Kim Updegrove, Madame Vivien V (Scott Dennis), Blakey Vermeule, Elliot Vlad, Elle Wagner, Suzy H. Wakefield, Lauren Walker, Gillian Weaver, Jo "Boobs" Weldon, Betty Jane Wilhoit, Leonna Williams, Pepper Williams, Dr. Erin Winston, Whitney Winters, Erin Woods, Leanna Worrell, Susan X. Yee, Heidi Zak, Sabra Zakrzewski, Claire Louise Zimmerman, and a few dozen people who prefer to remain anonymous. A special shout-out to Heidi Hoefinger for guiding me through the complex terrain of sex work and for introducing me to Catherine Healy, Dirty Martini, Jo Weldon, and the late Carol Leigh.

For three years while working on this book, I was a scholar-in-residence at the University of California, Berkeley. I am grateful to my colleagues in the Beatrice Bain Research Group and to Courtney Desiree Morris, Gillian Edgelow, and Stefanie Ebeling for their help in managing twenty-three student apprentices, who contributed valuable research and feedback. Thank you to my apprentices: Sophia Egert-Smith, Shivani Ekkanath, Karah Giesecke, Ai Gu, Eva Hannan, Megha Joshi, Zara Khan, Nathalie Orellana, Jhilmil Pandit, Rebecca Peyriere, Hannah Prior, Roméo Romero, Cate Valinote, Elizabeth Wang, and Raja Yasaswini Sriramoju. Extra thanks to the following students who worked with extra dedication, speed, and efficiency through multiple semesters and holidays: Julian Miguel Bayani, Vestri Lindsey Di Silvestri, Carly Feldman, Keelin Grubb, Eugenia "Snow" Guilfoyle, Ryan Laffin, Char Potes, and Cristina Zito. For further research assistance, thanks also to Laetitia Coustar and Helena Gans.

Thank you to my stellar agents at Wylie: Sarah Chalfant, Rebecca Nagel, Emma Smith, Jessica Bullock, and Sam Sheldon. My deep gratitude to all the smart people at W. W. Norton—particularly my editor Jill Bialosky; her assistant, Drew Elizabeth Weitman; art director Ingsu Liu; project editor Rebecca Munro; and my old pals, Tom Mayer and Elisabeth Kerr.

I am hugely grateful to the friends, family, and colleagues who shared their anecdotes, contacts, multilingualism, and/or intelligent feedback on the proposal or draft chapters, including: Glenn Adamson, Alka Agrawal, Lisa Arellano, Lisa Bloom, Amy Cappellazzo, Terry Castle, Robin Clark, Carol Cohen, David Colt, Natasha Distiller, Bob Fisher, Jon Gans, Dominique Grisard, Madeleine Grynsztejn, Mary Ellen Hannibal, Ellen Haskell, Glen Helfand, Annie Hikido, David Hornik, Kathleen Kelly Janus, Roger Keating, Lou Thornton Keating (my theatrical sister who gave me a necklace that said "Tits Up" way before I chose the title), Kaitlyn Krieger, Jun Li, Anja Manuel, Ederle Man-Son-Hing, Marlo McKenzie, Tina Mendelsohn, Kitty Morgan, Madison Nirenstein, Amber Noland, Daphne Palmer, Jonathan Parker, Stuart Peterson, Hayal Pozanti, Laura Siedel, Jan Silverman, Lesley Silverman, Akio Tagawa, Beverley Talbott, Monte Thornton (my good father), Otto Thornton-Silver (my clever, kind son), Abby Turin, Sarah Wendell, Milly Williamson, and the late Nancy Bechtle. I am indebted to Michael Lewis for sharing his uncanny ability to choose a book topic when he insisted I write about boobs.

Major hugs to the inner circle, who challenged my thinking and gave significant guidance: Marcus Brauchli, Reesa Greenberg, Angela McRobbie, Tabitha Soren, Maja Thomas, and Blakey Vermeule. Finally, the book would not have made it into the world without the trusted trio who read the roughest drafts: my mother, Glenda Thornton, a book lover who wants to see in her mind's eye what she reads; my daughter, Cora Thornton-Silver, a witty wordsmith and practitioner of narrative therapy; and my oldest—but not my eldest—friend, Helge Dascher, a translator with a hearty contempt for slovenly grammar and an annoyingly high bar for jokes.

Tits Up is dedicated to my beloved wife, Jessica, and three magnificent children—Otto, Cora, and Echo.

NOTES

INTRODUCTION: RECLAIMING A PART OF WOMANHOOD

1. See Women's Health and Cancer Rights Act of 1998.
2. Steven Jay Gould, "Male Nipples and Clitoral Ripples," *Columbia: A Journal of Arts and Literature*, no. 20 (Summer 1993): 80–96.
3. Simone de Beauvoir, *The Second Sex*, trans. Constance Borde and Sheila Malovany-Chevallier (New York: Vintage, 2011), 42.
4. William Godwin, *Godwin on Wollstonecraft: Memoirs of the Author of "The Rights of Woman,"* ed. Richard R. Holmes (London: Harper Perennial, 2005), 84.
5. International Society of Aesthetic Plastic Surgery, *ISAPS International Survey on Aesthetic/Cosmetic Procedures Performed in 2020*, 2021.
6. Sarah Blaffer Hrdy, *Mother Nature: Maternal Instincts and How They Shape the Human Species* (New York: Ballantine, 2000), 145.
7. Cat Bohannon, *Eve: How the Female Body Drove 200 Million Years of Human Evolution* (New York: Alfred A. Knopf, 2023), 30–38.
8. Katherine A. Dettwyler, "Beauty and the Breast: The Cultural Context of Breast-feeding in the United States," in *Breastfeeding: Biocultural Perspectives*, edited by Patricia Stuart-Macadam and Katherine A. Dettwyler (New York: Aldine de Gruyter, 1995), 171.
9. Marilyn Yalom, *A History of the Breast* (New York: Ballantine, 1998).
10. George D. Sussman, "Parisian Infants and Norman Wet Nurses in the Early Nineteenth Century: A Statistical Study," *Journal of Interdisciplinary History* 7, no. 4 (1977): 637.
11. Frédéric Courtois et al., "Trends in breastfeeding practices and mothers' experi-

ence in the French NutriNet-Santé cohort," *International Breastfeeding Journal* 16, no. 1 (2021): 1–12.

12. Alfred C. Kinsey, Wardell B. Pomeroy, and Clyde E. Martin, *Sexual Behavior in the Human Male* (Philadelphia: Saunders, 1948), 368.

13. Clellan S. Ford and Frank A. Beach, *Patterns of Sexual Behavior* (Oxford: Harper and Paul B. Hoeber, 1951), 136.

14. Quigley Publishing Company's "Top Ten Money Making Stars Poll" based on a questionnaire sent to movie exhibitors, https://en.wikipedia.org/wiki/Top_Ten_Money_Making_Stars_Poll.

15. Aesthetic Society, *Aesthetic Plastic Surgery National Databank Statistics*, 1997–2022.

16. Fran Mascia-Lees, "Are Women Evolutionary Sex Objects? Why Women Have Breasts," *Anthropology Now* 1, no. 1 (April 2009): 9.

17. Jun Lei, " 'Natural' Curves: Breast-Binding and Changing Aesthetics of the Female Body in China of the Early Twentieth Century," *Modern Chinese Literature and Culture* 27, no. 1 (2015): 163–223.

18. Laura Miller, "Mammary Mania in Japan," *Positions: Asia Critique* 11, no. 2 (Fall 2003): 295.

19. Lauren Walker, interview with the author, March 16, 2023.

20. Viren Swami et al., "The Breast Size Satisfaction Survey: Breast Size Dissatisfaction and Its Antecedents and Outcomes in Women from 40 Nations," *Body Image* 32 (March 1, 2020): 199–217.

21. Diana P. Jones, "Cultural Views of the Female Breast," *Association of Black Nursing Journal* (January/February 2004): 15–21.

22. Esther Newton, *Mother Camp: Female Impersonators in America* (Chicago: University of Chicago Press, 1970).

23. Diane Naugler, "Credentials: Breast Slang and the Discourse of Femininity," *Atlantis* 34, no. 1 (2009): 100.

24. As Lisa Sharik writes, "Women need to reclaim control over their breasts' definitions." Lisa Sharik, "Breasts: From Functional to Sexualized," in *Breasts Across Motherhood*, edited by Patricia Drew and Rosann Edwards (Bradford, Ontario: Demeter Press, 2020), 34.

25. One statistical study found that college students throughout the 1990s associated small breasts with the adjectives "lonely" and "intelligent." Large breasts were associated by both men and women with "sexually active." Stacey Tantleff-Dunn, "Breast and Chest Size: Ideals and Stereotypes Through the 1990s," *Sex Roles* 45, no. 3/4 (August 2001): 239.

26. Annie Sprinkle, interview with the author, January 22, 2022.

27. Fortunately for this effort at reclamation, the soft-porn magazine *Juggs* ceased publication in 2013.

28. International Society of Aesthetic Plastic Surgery. *ISAPS International Survey on Aesthetic/Cosmetic Procedures Performed in 2020*, 2021.

29. See Kirsten Wolf, "The Severed Breast: A Topos in the Legends of Female Virgin Martyr Saints," *Arkiv för nordisk filologi* 112 (1997): 96–112; Bernadette Wegenstein, "Agatha's Breasts on a Plate: 'Ugliness' as Resistance and Queerness," in *On the Politics of Ugliness* (Toronto: Palgrave Macmillan, 2018); Liana De Girolami Cheney, "The Cult of Saint Agatha," *Woman's Art Journal* 17, no. 1 (Spring/Summer 1996): 3–9.

30. As Kathy Davis writes, "Body politics resonate differently in different contexts and what might be considered feminist in one context may be considered ethnocentric or even racist in another." Kathy Davis, "Bared Breasts and Body Politics," *European Journal of Women's Studies* 23, no. 3 (2016): 235.

31. Many important exceptions can be found in my bibliography.

32. Vanessa Olorenshaw, *Liberating Motherhood: Birthing the Purplestockings Movement* (Cork, Ireland: Womancraft Publishing, 2016), 7.

33. Susan Brownmiller, *Femininity* (New York: Simon & Schuster, 1984), 17, 51.

34. Julia Serano, *Whipping Girl: A Transsexual Woman on Sexism and the Scapegoating of Femininity* (Berkeley: Seal Press, 2016), 320.

35. Lucy Cooke, *Bitch: On the Female of the Species* (New York: Basic Books, 2022), 14.

36. Chase Strangio, interview with the author, March 8, 2023.

37. Kate Millett, *Sexual Politics* (Urbana: University of Illinois Press, 1970), 83–84.

CHAPTER 1: HARDWORKING TITS

1. Rachel Shteir, *Striptease: The Untold History of the Girlie Show* (New York: Oxford University Press, 2004), 321.

2. The strip club business is highly fragmented, with no one player generating more than 5% of market revenue. The other large strip club chains are MAL Entertainment, Rick's Cabaret, and Spearmint Rhino. Déjà Vu, which is headquartered in a suburb of Las Vegas, owns strip clubs in six countries (Australia, Canada, France, Mexico, the United Kingdom, and the United States) and the largest strip club in the world, whose website advertises "full-service spa suites." Jeremy Moses, *US Industry Specialized Report: Strip Clubs* (IbisWorld, December 2019), https://dejavutijuana.com/.

3. The industry defines a lap dance as a "strip club service in which a dancer performs one-on-one with a patron, usually for the duration of one song, for a previously set fee." Moses, *Strip Clubs*, 44.

4. See Laura Mulvey, "Visual Pleasure and Narrative Cinema," *Screen* 16, no. 3 (1975).

5. Kimberle Crenshaw, "Demarginalizing the Intersection of Race and Sex: A Black

Feminist Critique of Antidiscrimination Doctrine, Feminist Theory and Antiracist Politics," *University of Chicago Legal Forum* (1989): 139–68.

6. Strip clubs have been popular with ethnographers, who have focused on the balance of power between the dancers and their patrons, discussing it in terms of "mutual exploitation," "resistance," "empowerment," "social control," and "subversion." None of these studies explore breasts in any great depth. See Katherine Frank, "Thinking Critically about Strip Club Research," *Sexualities* 10, no. 4 (2007): 501–17.

7. Sex-worker-rights activists rally on International Whores Day (June 2), International Day to End Violence Against Sex Workers (December 17), and many other occasions. As recently as March 2019, the New York City chapter of the National Organization for Women (NOW–NYC) rallied on the steps of City Hall to demand the continued criminalization of sex work. According to Lorelei Lee, speakers at the event said that sex workers were "ignorant of their own oppression." See Lee, "When she says women, she does not mean me," *We Too: Essays on Sex Work and Survival*, edited by Natalie West with Tina Horn (New York: Feminist Press, 2021), 226–27.

8. This chapter is a composite of many visits to the Condor on my own and with others, including RedBone and Kitty KaPowww.

9. RedBone was crowned in 2019. Due to the Covid-19 pandemic, she reigned for three years.

10. Jenni Nuttall, *Mother Tongue: The Surprising History of Women's Words* (New York: Viking, 2023), 40–41. John Ayto, *The Oxford Dictionary of Modern Slang* (Oxford: Oxford University Press, 2010); "Tit Definition & Meaning," Merriam–Webster; Jonathon Green, "Tits and Ass," *Green's Dictionary of Slang* (Edinburgh: Chambers Harrap, 2011); Sesquiotic (a.k.a. James Harbeck), "Boobs vs. Tits: A First Look," *Strong Language: A Sweary Blog About Swearing*, April 5, 2018, https://stronglang.wordpress.com/2018/04/05/boobs-vs-tits-a-first-look/

11. For example, the "featured categories" on XHamsterLive include the following references to body parts: big tits, small tits, big ass, hairy pussy, and foot fetish. "Big Tits" is cross-referenced with age (Teen 18+, Young 22+, MILF, and Granny) and race (Arab, Asian, Ebony, Indians, Latina, White).

12. Karyn Stapleton, "Gender and Swearing: A Community Practice," *Women and Language* 26, no. 2 (September 22, 2003): 22–34.

13. Yitty is also the name of the shapewear brand cocreated by Lizzo, the musician.

14. Strippers often express frustration with the floor managers who are paid to protect them and enforce the rules, but only do so in exchange for large tips or sexual favors. As Natalie West argues in her book *We Too*, the #MeToo movement needs to embrace sex workers, not ostracize them as "bad girls" who deserve occupational harassment. West and Horn, *We Too*, 10.

15. Norma Jean Almodovar, "Sex Work, Sex Trafficking: Stigma and Solutions," PowerPoint presentation, July 5, 2020, policeprostitutionandpolitics.com.

16. The stylistic differences between stripping and burlesque dancing lie on a continuum. Some strip clubs feature burlesque acts some or all of the time.

17. Dirty's introduction pays tribute to her hero, Jennie Lee, known in the 1940s as Miss 44 and Plenty More. Lee founded the Burlesque Hall of Fame and was an early advocate for the rights of erotic dancers.

18. In *Sex and Social Justice*, Martha Nussbaum outlines "Seven Ways to Treat a Person as a Thing." In her view, "denial of subjectivity" is a key part of the process by which men treat women as objects whose experiences and feelings need not be acknowledged, let alone understood. The other dynamics of objectification are denial of autonomy, inertness, fungibility, instrumentality, violability, and ownership. Martha Nussbaum, *Sex and Social Justice* (Oxford: Oxford University Press, 1999): 218–39.

19. Midori, interview with the author, December 3, 2021.

20. Annie Sprinkle, *Post-Porn Modernist: My 25 Years as a Multimedia Whore* (San Francisco: Cleis Press, 1998).

21. *Bosom Ballet* has been reenacted by other artists. See, for example, Lili Buvat's version on YouTube, https://www.youtube.com/watch?v=ISOeta3Z_Lw.

22. Nurses, teachers, and schoolgirls in uniform are staples of sex-related performance because they erase individual identity, evoke social roles, and suggest power dynamics.

23. The title *Strip Speak* was coined by Sprinkle's collaborator on this work, Willem DeRidder, a Dutch artist who was the European chairman of Fluxus and her boyfriend at the time.

24. As a paid consultant on the HBO series *The Deuce*, Sprinkle shared her thoughts about creativity and sex work with Maggie Gyllenhaal, whose character is a prostitute.

25. Matthew Simmons (Peggy L'Eggs), born 1960, died 2020.

26. Annie Sprinkle, *Post-Modern Pin-Ups Bio Booklet to Accompany the Pleasure Activist Playing Cards* (Richmond, VA: Gates of Heck, 1995), 7–8. In her 2019 book *Pleasure Activism: The Politics of Feeling Good*, adrienne maree brown echoes Sprinkle in defining "pleasure activism" as "the work we do to reclaim our whole, happy, and satisfiable selves from the impacts, delusions, and limitations of oppression and/or supremacy." adrienne maree brown, *Pleasure Activism: The Politics of Feeling Good* (Chico, CA: AK Press, 2019), 13.

27. Dori Midnight is the witch who made the breast elixir. https://dorimidnight.com/apothecary/

28. Carol Leigh, *Unrepentant Whore: Collected Works of Scarlot Harlot* (San Francisco: Last Gasp, 2004).

29. Carol Leigh Szego died November 16, 2022. She gave me permission to use her full name after her death.

30. Rabbi Sydney Mintz, interview with the author, January 12, 2022.

31. For example, Ti-Grace Atkinson argued that "Prostitutes are the only honest women because they charge for their services rather than submitting to a marriage contract, which forces them to work for life without pay." Lacey Fosburgh, "Women's Liberationist Hails the Prostitute," *New York Times*, May 29, 1970, 30.

32. Priscilla Alexander, "Prostitution: A Difficult Issue for Feminists," in *Sex Work: Writings by Women in the Sex Industry*, edited by Priscilla Alexander and Frédérique Delacoste (San Francisco: Cleis Press, 1987/1998), 186.

33. Elizabeth Bernstein, *Temporarily Yours: Intimacy, Authenticity and the Commerce of Sex* (Chicago: University of Chicago Press, 2007), 23.

34. Leigh, *Unrepentant Whore*, 72.

35. Valerie Jenness, "From Sex as Sin to Sex as Work: COYOTE and the Reorganization of Prostitution as a Social Problem," *Social Problems* 37, no. 3 (August 1990): 403–20.

36. Alexander and Delacoste, *Sex Work*.

37. Thomas Meehan, "At Bennington, the Boys are the Co-eds," *New York Times*, December 21, 1969.

38. Priscilla Alexander, interview with the author, January 13, 2022.

39. https://nswp.org/news/sex-workers-belgium-celebrate-historic-vote-decriminalisation-parliament.

40. Topless protest is a semi-regular feature of women's and gay pride marches. It has also been used by FEMEN, a Ukrainian group of anti-Putin activists, and students protesting university fees in Johannesburg, South Africa, among others. See Hlengiwe Ndlovu, "Womxn's Bodies Reclaiming the Picket Line: The 'Nude' Protest during #FeesMustFall," *Agenda* 31, no. 3–4 (October 2, 2017): 68–77.

41. Saundra Weddle, "Mobility and Prostitution in Early Modern Venice," *Early Modern Women: An Interdisciplinary Journal* 14, no. 1 (September 2019): 95–108.

42. Nassim Alisobhani, "Female Toplessness: Gender Equality's Next Frontier," *UC Irvine Law Review* 8, no 2 (2018): 299–330.

43. *Free the Nipple v. City of Fort Collins*, 17–1103 (10th Cir. Colo. 2019).

44. "Heaux" is a faux-French elevation of "ho," African American slang for "whore" popularized in the 1990s, while "THOT" stands for "That Ho/Heaux Over There." thotscholar, aka suprihmbé, aka Femi Babylon, *HeauxThots: On Terminology and Other (Un)Important Things* (Chicago: bbydool press, 2019).

45. As thotscholar writes in *HeauxThots*, "Being able to work inside is a privilege. . . . Prostitution is linked to homelessness, and sex workers who work outdoors generally experience higher levels of criminalization and assault."

46. Leslie Lehr recounts: cheerleader outfits are a key costume in porn; cheerleading

is not considered a sport by Title IX; the January 1980 issue of *Playboy* featured the "NFL's Sexiest Cheerleaders"; the *Playboy* Playmate of 2005 was an Atlanta Falcons cheerleader; diverse NFL teams have been sued by cheerleaders for bullying, body-shaming, and sexual harassment. See Leslie Lehr, *A Boob's Life: How America's Obsession Shaped Me . . . And You.* (New York: Simon & Schuster, 2021).

47. William Safire, "Erotic or Exotic?" *New York Times*, May 21, 2006.

48. Anonymous, interview with the author, December 7, 2021. This interviewee is an example of the adventurous women who choose to sell sex while they travel the world. As Laura María Agustín argues, these women are often erroneously represented as passive victims of trafficking. Laura María Agustín, *Sex Work on the Margins: Migration, Labour Markets and the Rescue Industry* (London: Zed Books, 2007).

49. Resistant to "kink shaming," Dove nevertheless sees it as her professional responsibility to screen out "breeders" with an "impregnation fetish," who want to "ride bareback" or who might engage in "stealthing," because slipping off a condom without a sex worker's consent is a form of rape.

50. See "Operation Do the Math" on Norma Jean Almovodar's policeprostitutionand politics.com website, which shows that the Los Angeles police make more arrests for sex work offenses than for rape.

51. The Prostitute School also gave the attendees tests for HIV and other STDs as well as information about getting onto the federal Women Infants Children (WIC) medical program, if they had kids.

52. Consent is not just about agreeing to have sex, but agreeing on exactly how one has sex. See Janet Hardy and Dossie Easton, *The Ethical Slut* (New York: Ten Speed Press, 1997/2007).

53. Heidi Hoefinger, *Sex, Love and Money in Cambodia: Professional Girlfriends and Transactional Relationships* (New York: Routledge, 2013), 8.

54. Streetwalkers are positioned at the bottom of the "whorearchy." According to Belle Knox, the stratification is arranged according to contact with police as well as intimacy with clients. See also Belle Knox, "Tearing Down the Whorearchy from the Inside," *Jezebel*, July 2, 2014, https://jezebel.com/tearing-down-the-whorearchy -from-the-inside-1596459558; and Mysterious Witt, "What Is the Whorearchy and Why It's Wrong," *An Injustice!*, November 18, 2020, https://aninjusticemag.com/ what-is-the-whorearchy-and-why-its-wrong-1efa654dcb22.

55. Catherine Healy, interview with the author, January 24, 2022.

56. Pole dancing allegedly started in the 1920s, when traveling circuses and fairs featured dancers who used tent poles as props for suggestive movements. In the late 1980s, starting in Canada, many titty bars installed floor-to-ceiling poles when this more acrobatic form of topless theater gained popularity. Beginning in 1991, Déjà Vu clubs held pole dancing competitions every year for a decade.

57. Several academic studies argue that stripping is a creative, expressive outlet that

can heal trauma and even lead to spiritual elation. "Their sensual movements may be a kind of prayer that connects them, even accidentally, to their own perception of the divine." See Bernadette Barton and Constance L. Hardesty, "Spirituality and Stripping: Exotic Dancers Narrate the Body Ekstasis," *Symbolic Interaction* 33, no. 2 (2010): 294.

58. Rita Nakashima Brock and Susan Brooks Thistlethwaite, *Casting Stones: Prostitution and Liberation in Asia and the United States* (Minneapolis: Fortress Press, 1996), 76.

59. David Vine, "Women's Labor, Sex Work and U.S. Military Bases Abroad," *Salon*, October 8, 2017.

60. *Sullivan-Knoff v. City of Chicago*, 16–8297 (7th Cir. IL, 2016). See also Lisa Malmer, "Nude Dancing and the First Amendment," *University of Cincinnati Law Review* 59, no. 4 (1991): 1275–1310; Virginia F. Milstead, "Forbidding Female Toplessness: Why Real Difference Jurisprudence Lacks Support and What Can Be Done about It," *University of Toledo Law Review* 36, no. 2 (Winter 2005): 273–320.

61. See, for example, Department of Justice, U.S. Attorney's Office, Northern District of California, "Gold Club Owner Among Those Indicted for Using Business to Operate Elaborate Money Laundering Scheme," press release, March 19, 2015, https://www.justice.gov/usao-ndca/pr/gold-club-owner-among-those-indicted -using-business-operate-elaborate-money-laundering.

62. Women-run strip clubs are rare to nonexistent. Between 1983 and 2013, San Francisco's Lusty Lady featured live nude dancers in a peep show format. In 1997, the strippers unionized to became the only sex business union in the United States. In 2003, the club was bought by the strippers and began life as a worker cooperative. It closed in 2013. Glen Martin, "S.F. Strip Club Ratifies Union—First in U.S.," *San Francisco Chronicle*, April 11, 1997; Lily Burana, "What It Was Like to Work at the Lusty Lady, a Unionized Strip Club," *Atlantic*, August 21, 2013.

63. In California, Déjà Vu has a reputation for wage theft, charging fees to strippers so they end up paying back their minimum wage and more. See Antonia Crane, "Dispatch from the California Stripper Strike," in West and Horn, *We Too*, 122–23.

CHAPTER 2: LIFESAVING JUGS

1. Diane Lynn Spatz, interview with the author, July 8, 2021, citing Kertin Uvnǎs Moberg and Danielle K. Prime, "Oxytocin effects in mothers and infants during breastfeeding," *Infant* 9, no. 6 (2013).

2. Kate Boyer, "The Emotional Resonances of Breastfeeding in Public: The Role of Strangers in Breastfeeding Practice," *Emotion, Space and Society* 26 (2018).

3. Miriam H. Labbok, "Effects of Breastfeeding on the Mother," *Pediatric Clinics of North America* 48, no. 1 (February 1, 2001); Nancy Mohrbacher and Kathleen Kendall-Tackett, *Breastfeeding Made Simple: Seven Natural Laws for Nursing Mothers*,

2nd ed. (Oakland, CA: New Harbinger, 2010); Colin Binns, MiKyung Lee, and Wah Yun Low, "The Long-Term Public Health Benefits of Breastfeeding," *Asia Pacific Journal of Public Health* 28, no. 1 (2016); Sheeva Rajaei et al., "Breastfeeding Duration and the Risk of Coronary Artery Disease," *Journal of Women's Health* 28, no. 1 (2018).

4. Linda Geddes, "Antibodies in Breast Milk Remain for 10 Months after Covid Infection—Study," *Guardian*, September 27, 2021.

5. One of my favorite ethnographic essays explains how some sensations are beneath consciousness or not experienced as pleasurable until they are labeled and framed as such. Howard S. Becker, "Becoming a Marihuana User," *American Journal of Sociology* 59, no. 3 (November 1953): 235–42.

6. Thank you to Carol Cohen, Mathilde Cohen, Helge Dascher, and Tina Mendelsohn for help with translations.

7. In the Jewish debates of the Talmud, Rabbi Abbahu noted that in humans, the breasts are near the heart, the seat of insight, which nurtures the soul. Rabbis Masna and Yedidyah added that hoofed mammals suckle their young near "the unclean space" of the anus where they can "gaze at the place of nakedness" (the perineum). Interview with Rabbi Sydney Mintz, November 22, 2021.

8. Sarah Blaffer Hrdy, *Mother Nature: Maternal Instincts and How They Shape the Human Species* (New York: Ballantine, 1999), 538.

9. Barry S. Hewlett and Steve Winn reviewed all 258 cultures in Yale University's Human Relations Area Files (eHRAF), a digital database of cultures from around the world, finding that allo-nursing occurred in 97 of the 104 cultures whose records included data about breastfeeding. "Allomaternal Nursing in Humans," *Current Anthropology* 55, no. 2 (2014): 200.

10. Hewlett and Winn, "Allomaternal Nursing in Humans," 206.

11. Hewlett and Winn, "Allomaternal Nursing in Humans," 203.

12. Hrdy is a sociobiologist and lapsed primatologist. She sees nannies, au pairs, and wet nurses as allomothers. As a sociologist interested in capitalism, jobs, and gifts, I do not. For me, the parallels between ancient hunter-gatherers and twentieth-century human allomothers are much stronger when commerce is removed from the equation and some measure of community commitment is present. Hrdy, *Mother Nature*, 109.

13. spermbank.com, accessed September 30, 2021; Hailey Eber, "This L.A. Sperm Bank is More Exclusive Than an Ivy league College," *Los Angeles Magazine*, April 2, 2019.

14. Richard Osbaldiston and Leigh A. Mingle, "Characterization of Human Milk Donors," *Journal of Human Lactation* 23, no. 4 (November 2007).

15. The blood test is paid for by the milk bank. Generally, a mother eligible to donate blood can donate breast milk.

16. Many women swear by the Haakaa hand pump for relieving simple engorgement.

17. For a glimpse into a lactation room, see Corinne May Botz's ten-minute YouTube video "Inside a Lactation Room at the U.S. Capitol."

18. Across the anthropological spectrum, our species has fed its young for anywhere between two and seven years. Katherine A. Dettwyler, "When to Wean: Biological Versus Cultural Perspectives," *Clinical Obstetrics and Gynecology* 47, no. 3 (September 2004).

19. The New York Milk Bank uses volunteers from the Sirens Motorcycle Club, a women's biker organization, to deliver its milk. Its director, Julie Horwitz Bouchet, was inspired by Brazilian postmen who deliver human milk on mopeds. Mathilde Cohen and Hannah Ryan, "From Human Dairies to Milk Riders: A Visual History of Milk Banking in New York City, 1918–2018," *Frontiers: A Journal of Women Studies* 40, no. 3 (2019).

20. In her anthropological account of breast milk sharing in Savannah, GA, Susan Falls found that the typical milk sharer was conservative, Christian, and wary of government and Western medicine. Coming from all over the Democrat-leaning state of California, the donors to the Mothers' Milk Bank are more politically diverse. Although peer-to-peer milk sharers are not the same as milk bank donors, most of the bank donors I interviewed had also shared milk. Susan Falls, *White Gold: Stories of Breast Milk Sharing* (Lincoln: University of Nebraska Press, 2017), xiv.

21. Holder pasteurization method heats the milk to 62.5°C (144°F) for half an hour, then rapidly cools it to 4°C (39°F).

22. According to one report, there was a "lactation bar" in Tokyo that provided breast milk shots to male clientele or a drink directly from the breast of a lactating mother for a higher price. Kazutaka Shimanaka, "Lactating Ladies Nurse Customers at Kabukicho Milk Bar," *Tokyo Reporter*, August 6, 2009.

23. In the United States, women with college degrees have children an average of seven years later than those without higher education, which is why San Francisco has the oldest mothers in America (average age thirty-two). Women in other developed countries, such as Switzerland, Japan, Spain, Italy, and South Korea, become new mothers at age thirty-one on average. Quoctrung Bui and Claire Cain Miller, "The Age That Women Have Babies: How a Gap Divides America," *New York Times*, August 4, 2018.

24. Heartfelt thanks to milk donors Raphaela Lipinsky DeGette and Britt Barrett, our midwife connector, Ami Burnham, and our emergency courier, Blakey Vermeule.

25. Sakamoto helped leading neonatologist and pediatrician Katsumi Mizuno set up the milk bank at the Showa University Koto Toyosu Hospital in Tokyo.

26. Ronald Cohen and Katherine McCallie, "Feeding Premature Infants: Why, When and What to Add to Human Milk," *Journal of Parenteral and Enteral Nutrition* 36, no. 1 (2021): 20s–24s.

27. Mashriq Alganabi et al., "Recent Advances in Understanding Necrotizing Entero-colitis," *F1000Research* 8 (January 25, 2019).

28. Kim Updegrove, interview with the author, April 24, 2021. See A. Lucas et al., "Breast milk and subsequent intelligence quotient in children born preterm," *Lancet*, February 1, 1992; Sean C. L. Deoni et al., "Breastfeeding and Early White Matter Development: A Cross Sectional Study." *NeuroImage*, May 28, 2013.

29. The four multinational companies that enjoy a 90% market share in the United States are Mead Johnson, Abbott, Perrigo, and Nestlé.

30. Molly Fischer, "Biomilq and the New Science of Artificial Breast Milk," *New Yorker*, March 6, 2023.

31. Christina Jewett, "Justice Department Investigating Troubled Infant Formula Plant," *New York Times*, January 21, 2023.

32. *Paris Is Burning*, directed by Jennie Livingston (Off-White Productions, 1990); *Pose* (FX, 2018); RuPaul, "Call Me Mother," track 6 on *American* (RuCo, 2017).

33. People assigned male at birth can establish lactation by taking hormones. How-ever, it is still unclear whether they can produce enough milk to nourish a baby to the age of six months. See Tamar Reisman and Zil Goldstein, "Case Report: Induced Lactation in a Transgender Woman," *Transgender Health* 3, no. 1 (January 1, 2018); Emily Trautner et al., "Knowledge and practice of induction of lactation in trans women among professionals working in trans health," *International Breast-feeding Journal* 15, no. 63 (July 16, 2020); Mathilde Cohen, "The Lactating Man," in *Making Milk: The Past, Present and Future of Our Primary Food*, edited by Mathilde Cohen and Yoriko Otomo (New York: Bloomsbury, 2017).

34. One in four unmarried mothers live below the poverty line in the United States. Black infants are 50% more likely than white infants to be born preterm and 200% more likely to be born very prematurely. The percentage of preterm births in the United States is 12%, the same as Thailand (12%) and marginally less than Myan-mar (12.4%). Robin Bleiweis et al., "The Basic Facts About Women in Poverty," Center for American Progress, August 3, 2020; Krista Sigurdson et al., "Racial/ Ethnic Disparities in Neonatal Intensive Care: A Systematic Review," *Pediatrics* 144, no. 2 (August 2019); "Born Too Soon: The Global Action Report on Preterm Birth," World Health Organization/March of Dimes, 2012.

35. Important exceptions include *Our Bodies, Ourselves* by the Boston Woman's Health Book Collective, first published in 1970 and still in print in an updated edition. In Britain, a burgeoning "maternal feminism" movement puts motherhood as a role, status, and experience at the center of its political mission. See Vanessa Oloren-shaw, *Liberating Motherhood: Birthing the Purplestockings Movement* (Cork, Ireland: Womancraft Publishing, 2016).

36. The Family and Medical Leave Act (FMLA, 1993) applies only to employees at companies with at least fifty people, who have worked for at least a year for a min-

imum of twenty-five hours a week. In other words, 44% of US workers were not eligible for family or medical leave in 2019. Only 20% of those who took leave did so to take care of a new child—birthed, adopted, or fostered. California instituted state-paid family leave in 2002, the first of nine states to do so. The others are Colorado, Connecticut, Massachusetts, New Jersey, New York, Oregon, Rhode Island, and Washington.

37. Ayla Landry, interview with author, April 7, 2021. Mohrbacher and Kendall-Tackett, *Breastfeeding Made Simple*; Nils Bergman, Ginger Carney, and Susan M. Ludington-Hoe, "Kangaroo Care for the Preterm Infant," *Infant, Child, and Adolescent Nutrition* 2, no. 3 (June 2010): 33–39.

38. Helen Gray, interview with the author, July 6, 2021.

39. Germany has recently reintroduced raw milk at some of their banks, but the initiative remains at the experimental stage.

40. With the rare outpatient exception, donor human milk is extended only to infants in hospital, and peer-to-peer milk sharing is relatively rare.

41. Jonathan Y. Bernard, Emmanuel Cohen, and Michael S. Kramer, "Breast Feeding Initiation Rate across Western Countries: Does Religion Matter? An Ecological Study," *BMJ Global Health* 1, no. 4 (November 1, 2016).

42. Here Islam is in agreement with Judaism, as halal food rules echo kosher law (e.g., no pork, no carnivorous animals, regulated slaughtering). The Talmud discusses breastfeeding duration in a number of contexts and in most cases recommends a duration of twenty-four months (*Ketuvot* 60a, b; *Even Haezer* 143:8). Rabbi Sydney Mintz, interview with the author, November 22, 2022.

43. "The Average American Bra Size Is Now a 34 DD," *Racked*, July 22, 2013.

44. Zoe Mendelsohn, interview with the author, August 8, 2021.

45. The European Commission bans the use of corn syrup solids and other forms of sucrose from breast milk substitutes. America, a major corn producer with a powerful agriculture lobby, does not. High-sugar baby food has been linked to the American obesity and diabetes epidemic.

46. Depending on the year and the exact definition of breastfeeding, France's low-ebb breastfeeding rates are rivaled by Ireland and/or Britain.

47. Jean-Jacques Rousseau, philosopher of the French Revolution, put maternal breastfeeding at the center of his vision for a new society. On this topic, however, his influence was short-lived and limited in France to a small circle of the cultural elite. By 1783, "the fashion for maternal nursing among Parisian women had passed." George Sussman, *Selling Mother's Milk: The Wet Nursing Business in France* (Urbana: University of Illinois Press, 1982), 27.

48. Elisabeth Badinter, *The Conflict: How Modern Motherhood Undermines the Status of Women* (New York: Henry Holt, 2010), 1, 68, 85, 77, 94.

49. Mathilde Cohen, "Should Human Milk Be Regulated?," *UC Irvine Law Review* 9

(2019): 557–634. Also, Saad S. Al-Shehri et al., "Breast Milk–Saliva Interactions Boost Innate Immunity by Regulating the Oral Microbiome in Early Infancy," *PLOS One* 10, no. 9, September 1, 2015.

50. Tanya Cassidy and Fiona Dykes with Bernard Mahon, *Banking on Milk: An Ethnography of Donor Human Milk Relations* (New York: Routledge, 2019), 101.

51. Melitta Weiss-Adamson, ed., *Regional Cuisines of Medieval Europe* (London: Routledge, 2002), 58.

52. Sylvie Corbet, "France Legalizes IVF for Lesbians and Single Women," AP News, June 29, 2021.

53. Julie P. Smith, "A commentary on the carbon footprint of milk formula," *International Breastfeeding Journal* 14, no. 1 (December 2019).

54. These are 2019 statistics. While the pandemic helped many women who could work from home to breastfeed for longer, low-income women in manual jobs did not enjoy that privilege. Additionally, WIC offices were mostly closed from March 2020 to October 2021, so their clients were unable to access prenatal breastfeeding classes, free breast pumps, or face-to-face lactation support for eighteen months.

55. Women with lower levels of education are less persuaded by scientific evidence and less able to "negotiate the hypersexualization of the breast." Danielle Groleau, Catherine Sigouin, and Nicole Anne D'souza, "Power to Negotiate Spatial Barriers to Breastfeeding in a Western Context: When Motherhood Meets Poverty," *Health & Place* 24 (November 1, 2013).

56. Alison Stuebe, "How Often Does Breastfeeding Just Not Work?," *Breastfeeding Medicine*, October 15, 2012.

57. Bernice L Hausman, "Women's Liberation and the Rhetoric of 'Choice' in Infant Feeding Debates," *International Breastfeeding Journal* 3, no. 1 (2008).

58. Kimberly Seals Allers, *The Big Letdown: How Medicine, Big Business, and Feminism Undermine Breastfeeding* (New York: St. Martin's Press, 2017), 53, 40.

59. The dairy industry's influence over WIC can also be seen in the diet endorsed by their monthly food package prescriptions, which includes 5 gallons of milk for a pregnant woman (8 gallons if there is another child at home), 2 pounds of cheese, and a quart of yogurt. Brandi Gates-Burgess, interview with the author, October 14, 2021.

60. Kim Updegrove, interview with the author, April 24, 2021.

61. Andrea Freeman, "Unmothering Black Women: Formula Feeding as an Incident of Slavery," *Hastings Law Journal* 69, no. 6 (2017).

62. In Canada, Vancouver's BC Women's Provincial Milk Bank has also been in continuous operation since 1974.

63. Testing pregnant women for HIV is important because early use of antiretroviral treatment can ensure an HIV-free baby. An "undetectable" viral load is when treatment has reduced the virus to such a low level that it cannot be detected by

standard blood tests. People with an undetectable viral load are not cured, but they cannot pass HIV on through sex or pregnancy.

64. Peña even has a Health Savings Account for expenses not covered by insurance, but "reimbursables" are tied to an IRS list, which includes everything from infertility treatment and penile implants to insoles and menstrual pads. It includes breast pumps and milk storage bags, but not donor milk.

65. For example, in 2020, Stanford's Lucile Packard Children's Hospital accepted a donation of $250,000 from Similac.

CHAPTER 3: TREASURED CHESTS

1. Dr. Chang's quotes were culled during multiple surgeries, office visits, and formal sit-down interviews: May 3, 2019; July 29, 2020; May 1, 2022; August 28, 2022; September 1, 2022; October 22 and 27, 2022; November 2, 3, and 4, 2022; December 2, 9, and 29, 2022; and several follow-ups by phone and text in January 2023.

2. The three sources of the statistics in this paragraph are American Society of Plastic Surgeons, *2020 Plastic Surgery Statistics Report*, 2021; International Society of Aesthetic Plastic Surgery, *International Survey on Aesthetic/Cosmetic Procedures performed in 2020*, 2021; and the Aesthetic Society statistical reports published between 1997 and 2022, including their most recent, *Aesthetic Plastic Surgery National Databank: Statistics 2020–2021.*

3. A brochure for Allergan's Natrelle implants warns: "Breast implants are not life-time devices. . . . You will likely need additional surgeries. . . . Many of the changes to your breasts following implantation are irreversible. If you choose to have your implants removed and not replaced, you may experience unacceptable dimpling, puckering, wrinkling, or other cosmetic changes. . . . The health consequences of a ruptured silicone gel-filled breast implant have not been fully established." *Natrelle Silicone-Filled Breast Implants and Natrelle Inspira Breast Implants: Important Factors Breast Augmentation and Reconstruction Patients Should Consider* (Irvine, CA: Allergan, 2017), 4, 5.

4. Julius Few, interviews with the author, March 28 and April 21, 2022.

5. As one of my interviewees put it, "Perfection is not beauty. It is just weird." Alissa Saenz, interview with the author, November 15, 2022.

6. Kathleen M. Higgins, "Beauty and Its Kitsch Competitors," in *Beauty Matters*, edited by Peg Zeglin Brand (Bloomington: Indiana University Press, 2000), 87–111.

7. T. Y. Stevens, "Which Cities Have the Most Plastic Surgeons per Capita?," surgery plasticsurgeon.com, March 7, 2016.

8. The FDA, or Food and Drug Administration, is a federal agency of the US Department of Health and Human Services.

9. Many plastic surgeons will not operate on a patient with a BMI over 30. Dr. Bolden's preferred BMI cutoff is 34.

10. American Academy of Medical Colleges website, "Active Physicians by Sex and Specialty, 2021" and "Active Physicians Who Identified as Black or African-American, 2021." See also Rachael Payne et al., "Women Continue to Be Underrepresented in Plastic Surgery: A Study of AMA and ACGME Data from 2000–2013," *Plastic and Reconstructive Surgery—Global Open* 5, no. 9S (September 2017): 37.

11. According to the Centers for Disease Control and Prevention, approximately 2% of all infants born in the United States every year are conceived using "assisted reproductive technology," a statistic that rises to 2.7% in the state of California. In urban areas, particularly those with affluent older mothers like San Francisco, one in twenty babies are likely IVF or born with the aid of some reproductive technology.

12. Jacqueline Sanchez Taylor, "Fake Breasts and Power: Gender, Class and Cosmetic Surgery," *Women's Studies International Forum* 35, no. 6 (2012): 458–66.

13. Dr. Barbara Machado, interview with the author, April 27, 2021.

14. Rebecca Scofield, " 'Nipped, Tucked, or Sucked': Dolly Parton and the Construction of the Authentic Body," *Journal of Popular Culture* 49, no. 3 (2016): 662, 673.

15. Alexander Edmonds, *Pretty Modern: Beauty, Sex, and Plastic Surgery in Brazil* (Durham, NC: Duke University Press, 2010), 52.

16. V. Shakespeare and K. Postle, "A Qualitative Study of Patients' Views on the Effects of Breast-Reduction Surgery: A 2-Year Follow-up Survey," *British Journal of Plastic Surgery* 52, no. 3 (April 1, 1999): 198–204.

17. Edmonds, *Pretty Modern*, 76.

18. International Association of Aesthetic Plastic Surgery, *ISAPS International Survey 2020*.

19. Viren Swami et al., "The Breast Size Satisfaction Survey (BSSS): Breast Size Dissatisfaction and Its Antecedents and Outcomes in Women from 40 Nations," *Body Image* 32 (March 1, 2020): 199–217.

20. Diana Dull and Candace West, "Accounting for cosmetic surgery: The accomplishment of gender," *Social Problems* 38 (1991): 54–70.

21. Skin necrosis is caused by infection and poor blood flow.

22. American Society of Plastic Surgeons, *2020 Plastic Surgery Statistics Report* (ASPS National Clearinghouse of Plastic Surgery Procedural Statistics 2021), 7, 25.

23. American Association of Plastic Surgeons, *2020 Plastic Surgery Statistics Report.*

24. Naomi Wolf, *The Beauty Myth: How Images of Beauty Are Used Against Women* (New York: Harper Perennial, [1991] 2002), 242. See also Sheila Jeffreys, *Beauty and Misogyny: Harmful Cultural Practices in the West* (New York: Routledge, 2005), 154.

25. "Like dieting and much exercise, surgery can be understood as a self-punishment

necessary to bring her body into line." Iris Marion Young, *On Female Body Experience: Throwing Like a Girl and Other Essays* (New York: Oxford University Press, 2005), 93, 94.

26. Melissa Febos, "The Feminist Case for Breast Reduction," *New York Times*, May 10, 2022.

27. Trinne Annfelt, "More Gender Equality—Bigger Breasts? Battles over Gender and the Body," *Nora: Nordic Journal of Women's Studies* 10, no. 3 (November 2010): 135.

28. Rita Felski, " 'Because It Is Beautiful': New Feminist Perspectives on Beauty," *Feminist Theory* 7, no. 2 (August 2006): 281.

29. Eleanor Heartney, foreword to *Beauty Matters*, edited by Peg Zeglin Brand (Bloomington: Indiana University Press, 2000), xv.

30. Roni Y. Kraut et al., "The Impact of Breast Reduction Surgery on Breastfeeding: Systematic Review of Observational Studies," *PLOS One* 12, no. 10 (2017): e0186591.

31. Dr. Stephen Henry, interview with the author, November 19, 2022.

32. Dr. Elisabeth Potter, interviews with the author, January 14 and 25, 2021, and November 5, 2022. Participant observation in Austin, TX, November 14 and 15, 2022.

33. "Flap" is a medical term for a living block of tissue transferred with a nourishing blood supply. DIEP refers to the deep inferior epigastric perforator, the blood vessels that serve subcutaneous abdominal fat.

34. We were at St. David's Medical Center in Austin, TX, one of 175 hospitals owned by Hospitals Corporation of America. It sees a large portion of the breast cancer surgeries in central Texas. Of the twenty-five operating rooms, seven were occupied by ten different breast oncology and reconstructive plastic surgeries. Dr. Potter was participating in three of those surgeries: two double DIEP flap reconstructions (i.e., four breasts) and one insertion of expanders after mastectomy.

35. Doctors no longer say that breast cancer is "in remission" but that there is "no evidence of disease." Many breast cancer survivors have blood draws every three months to confirm as much.

36. Hina Panchal and Evan Matros, "Current Trends in Post-Mastectomy Breast Reconstruction," *Plastic Reconstructive Surgery* 140, no. 5 (November 2017): 7S–13S. See also Ian J. Saldanha et al., "Implant-Based Breast Reconstruction after Mastectomy for Breast Cancer: A Systematic Review and Meta-Analysis," *Plastic and Reconstructive Surgery—Global Open* 10, no. 3 (March 2022): e4179.

37. Saldanha, "Implant-Based Breast Reconstruction," e4179.

38. Some insurance companies resist paying for a flat closure, saying it is part of the mastectomy. However, a glance at before-and-after photos makes clear the difference between a standard mastectomy scar and an aesthetic flat closure.

39. Triple negative means the patient's cancer cells do not have estrogen or progesterone receptors (ER or PR) and do not make a protein called HER2.

NOTES TO PAGES 139-146

40. Prepectoral breast reconstruction is gaining in popularity due to "decreased post-operative pain, shortened length of hospital stay, quicker return to activities, elimination of animation deformity, decreased operative time, and decreased capsular contracture rates." Adam M. Goodreau et al., "Revising Prepectoral Breast Reconstruction," *Plastic and Reconstructive Surgery* (March 2022): 579–84.

41. The FDA's "Breast Implant Labeling Guidance," September 29, 2020, declares that patients with a history of radiation therapy (or planned radiation following breast implant placement) are at a higher risk for poor surgical outcomes.

42. A flap "fails" when the transferred tissue dies. With only three failed flaps in the past five years, Potter and Henry's failure rate is a mere 0.3%. With regard to post-op complications, in the past three years, only seven patients have needed remedial surgery, resulting in a takeback rate of just 2%. The most common reason for takeback was bleeding in the breast pocket (hematoma) in circumstances where the reconstruction was taking place immediately after the mastectomy, a surgery with a high risk of bleeding in itself. Data supplied by Dr. Steven Henry, January 16, 2023.

43. *Diagnostic and Statistical Manual of Mental Disorders, Fifth Edition, Text Revision (DSM-5-TR)* (American Psychiatric Association, March 18, 2022), 271–72.

44. *DSM-5-TR*, 512.

45. The diagnoses of "homosexuality," "transsexualism," and "gender identity disorder" relate to the first, third, and fourth editions of the *Diagnostic and Statistical Manual of Mental Disorder*, respectively published in 1952, 1980, and 1994. For the record, the second edition of the *DSM* was published in 1968.

46. Cora Thornton-Silver, in conversation with the author, February 27, 2023.

47. Cyrus Grace Dunham, "A Year Without a Name," *New Yorker*, August 19, 2019.

48. The American Society of Plastic Surgeons reported 8,548 masculinizing chest surgeries, but only 4,035 trans feminine augmentations in 2020. *2020 Plastic Surgery Statistics Report*, 26.

49. Access to gender-affirming healthcare is a key determinant in wellness. Transgender people have high rates of substance abuse, depression, suicidal ideation, suicide attempts, and death by suicide. Ledibabari M. Naage et al., "Health Insurance Coverage of Gender-Affirming Top Surgery in the United States," *Plastic and Reconstructive Surgery* 144, no. 4 (2019): 824, 832.

50. Jack Halberstam, *Trans: A Quick and Quirky Account of Gender Variability* (Berkeley: University of California Press, 2017), 23.

51. Thank you to Char Potes for this perspective.

52. A diagnosis of gender dysphoria is required by all insurers. 96% of insurers provided coverage for trans masculine mastectomies, while only 68% underwrote trans feminine augmentations on the grounds that they were "not medically necessary." Ngaage, "Health Insurance Coverage," 826–27.

53. I accompanied Drucker as a friend rather than a formal ethnographer. The doctor was unaware that I was researching a book.

54. Susan Stryker, "My Words to Victor Frankenstein above the Village of Chamounix: Performing Transgender Rage," *Journal of Lesbian and Gay Studies* 1, no. 3 (June 1, 1994): 245.

55. Anonymous, interview with the author, August 16, 2022.

56. Daniel C. Richardson et al., "Small Penises and Fast Cars: Evidence for a Psychological Link," manuscript, University College London, 2023.

CHAPTER 4: ACTIVE APEXES

1. In America, 30% of clothing store customers shop at Old Navy. Alexander Kunst, "Old Navy brand profile in the United States 2022," *Statistica*, May 25, 2023.

2. Karen Korellis Reuther, "Shrink It and Pink It: Gender Bias in Product Design," *Harvard Advanced Leadership Initiative: Social Impact Review*, October 25, 2022.

3. Jonny Porkpie, interview with the author, December 18, 2021.

4. According to Alvanon, the average American woman was a size 18 in 2022, up from a size 14 in 2017. The mean weight for women twenty years old and over was 171 pounds in 2016. Suzanne Kapner, "Old Navy Made Clothing Sizes for Everyone. It Backfired," *Wall Street Journal*, May 20, 2022.

5. Roxane Gay, "Fifty Years Ago, Protesters Took on the Miss America Pageant and Electrified the Feminist Movement," *Smithsonian Magazine*, January 2018.

6. Beth Kreydatus, "Confronting the Bra Burners: Teaching Radical Feminism with a Case Study," *History Teacher* 41, no. 4 (August 2008): 490–91.

7. Hilary Hinds and Jackie Stacey, "Imaging Feminism, Imaging Femininity: The Bra-Burner, Diana, and the Woman Who Kills," *Feminist Media Studies* 1, no. 2 (2001): 153–77.

8. Most women fasten their bra in the front and turn it around on their body. Nearly everyone in the bra business used to do it that way before they worked on intimates, according to Laura Gordon.

9. Steven Jay Gould, "Male Nipples and Clitoral Ripples," *Columbia: A Journal of Arts and Literature*, no. 20 (Summer 1993): 80–96.

10. The models' day rates include permission to use the resulting photographs for a year.

11. Claire Zimmerman (wardrobe stylist).

12. Heidi Zak, "An Open Letter to Victoria's Secret," *New York Times*, November 18, 2018.

13. Madame Vivien V, interview with the author, January 17, 2022.

14. Bok Goodall, interview with the author, November 17, 2021.

15. Brands like TomboyX make a huge range of breast coverings for lesbians, trans

men, and nonbinary people, whereas companies that specialize in "expressing the
woman within" like En Femme promote prosthetic "silicone breast forms" more
heavily than brassieres, probably because trans women's breasts do not need the
same degree of physical support.

16. Charles Sprawson, *Haunts of the Black Masseur: The Swimmer as Hero* (New York:
Pantheon, 1992).

17. The Australians adopted the swimming styles of Indigenous peoples and became
the fastest swimmers in the world by doing front crawl, now called freestyle. See
Sprawson, *Haunts of the Black Masseur.*

18. Peter Catapano, "The Perfect Woman: Annette Kellerman and the Spectacle of
the Female Form," *Proteus: A Journal of Ideas* 25, no. 2 (Fall 2008).

19. Annette Kellerman, *My Story*, quoted in Emily Gibson with Barbara Firth, *The
Original Million-Dollar Mermaid: The Annette Kellerman Story* (Crows Nest, Australia:
Allen & Unwin, 2005).

20. Gibson with Firth, *The Original Million-Dollar Mermaid*, 61.

21. Preeclampsia is a high blood pressure disorder related to abnormalities in the
placenta.

22. Stacey Tantleff-Dunn, "Breast and Chest Size: Ideals and Stereotypes through the
1990s," *Sex Roles* 45, no. 3/4 (August 2001): 231–42.

23. Cora Thornton-Silver, "Top 10 Male Dating App Photo Cliches," *La Tonique*, September 15, 2021.

24. In the case of *People v. Santorelli*, New York Penal Law section 245.01 defined indecent exposure with these anatomical coordinates.

25. Kate Burridge, "Taboo, Euphemism, and Political Correctness," *Encyclopedia of
Languages and Linguistics*, 2nd ed. (Amsterdam: Elsevier, 2006), 455.

26. As is typical of American law, nipples are not mentioned explicitly, but swept up
into regulation of human nudity that is assumed to be indecent, obscene, lewd,
and/or immoral. Comstock Laws (Act for the Suppression of Trade in, and Circulation of, Obscene Literature and Articles of Immoral Use), 1873.

27. Mark Collins Jenkins, *National Geographic: 125 Years* (Washington, DC: National
Geographic Society, 2013), 33.

28. So-called "ethnographic nudity" was allowed by the Hays Code, which created
standards for Hollywood movies in 1934.

29. Brian Hoffman, "A Certain Amount of Prudishness: Nudist Magazines and the
Liberalization of American Obscenity Law, 1947–1958," *Gender and History* 22, no.
3 (November 2010): 722–23; see also Brian Hoffman, *Naked: A Cultural History of
American Nudism* (New York: New York University Press, 2015).

30. CBS contested the fine and, eight years after the event, won its battle with the FCC.

31. According to Jawed Karim. See Jim Hopkins, "Surprise! There's a third YouTube
co-founder," *USA Today*, October 11, 2006.

32. As one law professor writes, feminist activists "unleash their breasts rather than unveil them . . . they convey not submission, passive sexual availability, or obsessive concern for the viewer, but victory, protest and aggression." Libby S. Adler, "A Short Essay on the Baring of Breasts," *Harvard Women's Legal Journal* 23 (2000): 224–25.

33. The exhibition was curated by Bettina Hubby at a space called For Your Art run by Bettina Korek.

34. Micol Hebron, interview with the author, January 21, 2021.

35. Petula Dvorak, "Men were once arrested for baring their chests on the beach," *Washington Post,* January 5, 2019.

36. The liberation of the naked male chest runs contra to the history of formal European fashion where men, before the twentieth century, exposed the skin of only their face and hands. Women, by contrast, revealed their bare arms, then shoulders and upper bust with low-cut necklines. As John Harvey writes, "Power . . . wears more clothes than service." John Harvey, "Showing and Hiding: Equivocation in the Relations of Body and Dress," *Fashion Theory* 11, no. 1 (April 2015): 71, 82.

37. Brenna Helppie-Schmieder, "The Constitution and Societal Norms: A Modern Case for Female Breast Equality," *DePaul Journal of Women, Gender and the Law* 5, no. 1 (2015): [iii]–47.

38. Ariel Levy, *Female Chauvinist Pigs: Women and the Rise of Raunch Culture* (London: Simon & Schuster, 2005).

39. The exposure of feminine nipples or breasts below the top of the areola is banned outright in Utah, Indiana, and Tennessee.

40. See UK brand Curvy Kate, which specializes in bras with cups sized from D to K.

41. Amy L. Ladd, "The Sports Bra, the ACL, and Title IX—The Game in Play," *Clinical Orthopedics and Related Research* 472, no. 6 (April 11, 2014).

42. Meredith Clark, "Nike invents 'boob robot' to innovate sports bra technology," *Independent,* May 27, 2022.

43. "Support for all: why we re-engineered our entire sports bra portfolio," news.adidas.com, February 9, 2022.

44. Joanna Wakefield-Scurr, a professor of Biomechanics and Breast Health at Portsmouth University, is the authority on breast movement and the likely source of this figure. She consults for Old Navy and, according to Quandt, just about everyone in the sports bra space.

45. These data are from NPD, a firm that offers market research and industry expertise, provided to me by Gap Inc.

46. The ranking of women's active/sports bras (May 2022 through April 2023) was Nike 8.2%, Lululemon 5.5%, Victoria's Secret 3.3%, Adidas 2.8%, Calvin Klein 2.8%, Under Armour 2.7%, Aerie 2.7%, Hanes 2.1%, Athleta 1.6%, and Old Navy 1.4%. NPD 2023.

47. Susan X. Yee, interview with the author, April 3, 2023.

CHAPTER 5: HOLY MAMMARIES

1. Londa Schiebinger, "Why Mammals Are Called Mammals: Gender Politics in Eighteenth-Century Natural History," *American Historical Review* 98, no. 2 (April 1993): 382.

2. Londa Schiebinger, interview with the author, March 1, 2021.

3. Schiebinger, "Why Mammals Are Called Mammals," 385, 386.

4. Schiebinger, "Why Mammals Are Called Mammals," 389.

5. For an overview of witches in popular culture as well as a compelling analysis of the way men accuse feminists of "witch hunts," see Pam Grossman, *Waking the Witch: Reflections of Women, Magic and Power* (New York: Gallery Books, 2019).

6. Ninety-five-year-old Betty Jane, the oldest participant at Fool's Journey, who obtained a degree in German in the 1940s, told me that "crone" happens to be the German word for "crown."

7. Lisbet Koerner, *Linnaeus: Nature and Nation* (Cambridge, MA: Harvard University Press, 1999), 22–24.

8. Koerner, *Linnaeus*, 70.

9. Jean-Jacques Rousseau revered Linnaeus and advocated maternal nursing not for health reasons but so that women would fulfill their moral destiny under the laws of nature, bringing up citizens of the nation-state. Famed for his hypocrisy, the philosopher of the French Revolution abandoned at least five of his offspring to the foundling hospital, where they would meet certain death without the benefit of a wet nurse.

10. In the late seventeenth century, Mary Astell argued that the causes of women's deficiencies, including the perception that they were less intelligent than men, arose from poor education. She called for individual self-improvement and all-female educational establishments. Mary Astell, *A Serious Proposal to the Ladies*, ed. Sharon L. Janson (Steilacoom, WA: Saltar's Point Press, 2014).

11. Wilfred Blunt, *Linnaeus: The Compleat Naturalist* (Princeton: Princeton University Press, 2001), 177.

12. Theo Gill, "The Story of the Word—Mammal," *Popular Science Monthly*, no. 61 (November 1901–April 1902): 436.

13. Nancy Mohrbacher and Kathleeen Kendall-Tackett, *Breastfeeding Made Simple: Seven Natural Laws for Nursing Mothers*, 2nd ed. (Oakland, CA: New Harbinger, 2010).

14. Both breasts and black skin have been positioned in inverse relationship to intelligence. In her influential essay "No Humans Involved," Sylvia Wynter argues that jobless Black males have been deemed "I.Q. lacking" and "the least equal" of humans in an American capitalist culture where economics is the "master discipline in the place of theology." Sylvia Wynter, "No Humans Involved: An Open Letter to My Colleagues," *Forum N.H.I.: Knowledge for the 21st Century* 1, no. 1 (Fall 1994): 56, 42, 48.

15. Katherine P. Ewing, "Dreams from a Saint: Anthropological Atheism and the Temptation to Believe," *American Anthropologist* 96, no. 3 (September 1994): 573, 571.

16. Charles Darwin, *On the Origin of Species*, 1859.

17. For feminist critiques of Genesis, see Ilana Pardes, "Creation According to Eve," *Countertradition in the Bible: A Feminist Approach* (Cambridge, MA: Harvard University Press, 1992), 13–37.

18. Following Kenneth Clark, art historians have long waxed lyrical about the differences between the nude and the naked. Most of it assumes that a white male art connoisseur can differentiate between the elevated, ideal "nude" and the salacious "naked." For me, the debate is unhelpful due to its sexism, elitism, and ethnocentrism. Kenneth Clark, *The Nude: A Study in Ideal Form* (New York: Pantheon, 1956).

19. In her book on the Reclaiming community, Jone Salomonsen describes the group's nudity or naturalism as a "ritualized symbol" of "trust and love" that is "associated with pride, vulnerability, sensuality, honesty, and equality." Jone Salomonsen, *Enchanted Feminism: Ritual, Gender and Divinity among the Reclaiming Witches of San Francisco* (New York: Routledge, 2002), 225.

20. Ten countries, including Vietnam, Ecuador, Ukraine, and France, have criminalized ecocide, the intentional causing of long-term severe damage to the natural environment.

21. In 2014, *Free the Nipple*, directed by and starring Lina Esco, was released. I assume the fiction film was inspired by the activism of Ramona Santorelli and other earlier feminists.

22. *The People v. Ramona Santorelli and Mary Lou Schloss*, 80 N.Y.2d 875, 600 N.E.2d 232, 587 N.Y.S.2d 601 (New York Appeals, July 7, 1992).

23. Margaret R. Miles, *A Complex Delight: The Secularization of the Breast, 1350–1750* (Berkeley: University of California Press, 2008).

24. Margaret Miles, interviews with the author, January 8, 2021 and May 26, 2022. Miles was born in 1937, taught at Harvard from 1978 to 1996, then was dean of the Graduate Theological Union in Berkeley, CA, until she retired.

25. Margaret R. Miles, *Augustine on Beautiful Bodies* (Eugene, OR: Cascade Books, 2024).

26. "Amazon" may derive from the ancient Iranian word for warriors, *ha-mazon*. See Adrienne Mayor, *The Amazons: Lives and Legends of Warrior Women Across the Ancient World* (Princeton: Princeton University Press, 2014).

27. Lynn R. LiDonnici, "The Images of Artemis Ephesia and Greco-Roman Worship: A Reconsideration," *Harvard Theological Review* 85, no. 4 (October 1992): 389–415.

28. *Who Wrote the Old Testament*, directed by Caryl Ebenezer (MagellanTV, 2002).

29. "The 39th edition of Best of the Bay," *Bay Guardian* 48, no. 3 (October 16–22, 2013).

30. DBT stands for dialectical behavioral therapy, which is often prescribed for peo-

ple with borderline personality disorder, bipolar disorder, and other psychiatric conditions.

31. Thank you to Ai Gu for her research in Chinese and English. See Huang Lele, "The Ambiguity of the Gender of Avalokiteśvara," *Asia Social Issues* 1, no. 2 (2022); Robert Wilf, "The Transition of Guanyin: Reinterpreting Queerness and Buddha Nature in Medieval East Asia," Religious Studies Honors Papers, Ursinus College, 2020; Ying Huang, "Songzi Guanyin and Koyasu Kannon: Revisiting the Feminization of Avalokiteśvara in China and Japan," Master of Arts thesis, University of Alberta, 2019; Krista K. Rodin, "Empress Influence on the Establishment and Rise in Popularity of the Virgin Mary and Kuan Yin," *Journal of Literature and Art Studies* 6, no. 11 (November 2016): 1396–1406.

32. In Cameroon, up to a quarter of women between ten and eighty-two years of age were found to have undergone breast ironing. See Alessandra Glover Williams and Fiona Finlay, "Breast ironing: An under-recognised form of gender-based violence," *Archives of Diseases in Childhood*, no. 105 (2020): 90–91. See also African Health Organization, "Breast Ironing Fact Sheet," https://aho.org/fact-sheets/breast-ironing-fact-sheet/.

33. Thelarche, the medical term for when breast buds develop, usually precedes menarche, or the first period, by two to three years. The causes of early breast development, an international phenomenon, may include stress and related higher cortisol levels, exposure to endocrine-disrupting chemicals, obesity and higher body mass indexes, and the melatonin-disrupting effects of blue light. See Jessica Winter, "Why more and more girls are hitting puberty early," *New Yorker*, October 27, 2022.

34. Katherine A Dettwyler, "Beauty and the Breast: The Cultural Context of Breastfeeding in the United States," in *Breastfeeding: Biocultural Perspectives*, edited by Patricia Stuart-Macadam and Katherine A. Dettwyler (New York: Aldine de Gruyter, 1995), 168–217.

35. Gerda Lerner, *The Creation of Patriarchy* (New York: Oxford University Press, 1986), 10, 201.

36. Kamala Ganesh, "Mother Who Is Not a Mother: In Search of the Great Indian Goddess," *Economic and Political Weekly*, October 20–27, 1990.

37. LeRoy McDermott, "Self-Representation in Upper Paleolithic Female Figurines," *Current Anthropology* 37, no. 2 (April 1996): 227–75.

38. Devdutt Pattanaik, *The Man Who Was a Woman and Other Queer Tales from Indian Lore* (New York: Routledge, 2002), 4.

39. Alf Heitebeitel and Kathleen M. Erndl, eds., *Is the Goddess a Feminist: The Politics of South Asian Goddesses* (New York: New York University Press, 2000).

40. Shrines to Sati's breasts are found at the following Indian temples: Mangla Gauri in Bihar (both breasts); Devi Talab Mandir in Jalhandar (right breast); Shakti Tri-

purmalini in the Punjab (left breast); Tara Tarini Temple in Odisha (left breast); Bajreshwari Temple in Kangra, Himachal Pradesh (left breast). Sunita Pant Bansal, *Hindu Pilgrimage: A Journey through the Holy Places of Hindus All Over India* (New Delhi: V & S Publishers, 2012). See tourist and government websites for further details.

41. Melanie Reitzel, interview with the author, January 25, 2021.

42. Anannya Bohidar, "Worshipping Breasts in the Maternal Landscape of India South," *Asian Studies* 31, no. 2 (2015): 247–53; Pattanaik, *The Man Who Was a Woman*, 102. Potent breasts are central to the plots of several Tamil myths. See Maheshvari Naidu, "Inscribing the Female Body: Fuzzy Gender and Goddess in a South Indian Saiva Marriage Myth," *Journal for the Study of Religion* 21, no. 1 (2008): 19–35; Maheshvari Naidu, "Marriage as Reaffirming Sacred Space," *Nidan: International Journal for Indian Studies* 11 (December 1999): 52–76.

43. As Ellen Davina Haskell explains, full accounts of the miraculous nursing occur in rabbinical texts that date from the fifth through the seventh century CE. All versions reflect on the phrase in Genesis, "Sarah would suckle children." The plural "children" is the trigger for the rabbinical embellishments. Ellen Davina Haskell in correspondence with the author, July 13, 2022. For further detail, see Jordan Rosenblum, " 'Blessings of the Breasts': Breastfeeding in Rabbinic Literature," *Hebrew Union College Annual* 87 (2016): 145.

44. See chapter 2, "Lifesaving Jugs."

45. The passage reads: "That the Torah bestows grace upon those who study it. 'Let her breasts satisfy you at all times'; why were matters of Torah compared to a breast? Just as with a breast, whenever a baby searches it for milk to suckle, he finds milk in it, so too, with matters of Torah. Whenever a person meditates upon them, he finds new meaning in them" (Eruvin 54b: 3).

46. Sydney Mintz, "Co-Wives, Sisters and Concubines in the Genesis Narrative," rabbinical thesis, Hebrew Union College–Jewish Institute of Religion, New York, 1997.

47. David Biale, "The God with Breasts: El Shaddai in the Bible," *History of Religions* 21, no. 3 (February 1982): 240–56.

48. Harriet Lutzky, "Shadday as a Goddess Epithet," *Vetus Testamentum* 48, fasc. 1 (January 1998): 15–36.

49. The Kohenet Hebrew Priestess Institute "reclaims and innovates embodied, earth-based feminist Judaism." See: kohenet.org.

50. https://kohenet.org.

51. Ellen Davina Haskell, *Suckling at My Mother's Breasts: The Image of a Nursing God in Jewish Mysticism* (Albany: State University of New York Press, 2012). Thank you to Jill Hammer, the cofounder of the Kohenet Hebrew Priestess Institute, for recommending this book.

52. Ellen Davina Haskell, interview with the author, June 30, 2022.

53. Beth Gersh-Nesic, "Radical Acceptance," *Clarity Haynes: Radical Acceptance* (Brooklyn: Tabla Rasa Gallery, 2011).

54. Misty L. Bastian, "The Naked and the Nude: Historically Multiple Meanings of *Oto* (Undress) in Southeastern Nigeria," in *Dirt, Undress, and Difference: Critical Perspectives on the Body's Surface*, edited by Adeline Masquelier (Bloomington: Indiana University Press, 2005), 41.

55. Reverend Elaine Donlin Sensai, interviews with the author, August 31 and September 14, 2022.

56. Jeff Durham, associate curator of Himalayan art at the Asian Art Museum of San Francisco, explains that Tibetan meditation is a visualization process. Put simply, for example, the Buddhist practitioner looks at the sculpture of White Tara for so long that they can replicate her image in complete three-dimensional detail in their mind's eye. The visualization is the worship, the offering, and the philosophical practice. Interview with the author, February 26, 2021.

57. China Galland, *Longing for Darkness: Tara and the Black Madonna* (New York: Penguin, 1990), 95.

58. In the Tibetan tradition, Tara has risen to the status of a fully qualified Buddha, above a bodhisattva, which syncretizes her early position as a devi or Hindu goddess. For a theological argument about the validity of claiming Tara as a feminist icon, see Raymond Lam, "Legitimizing Legitimization: Tara's Assimilation of Masculine Qualities in Indo-Tibetan Buddhism and the Feminist 'Reclaiming' of Theological Discourse," *Feminist Theology* 22, no. 2 (2014): 157–72.

59. See Shefali Chandra, "India Will Change You Forever: Hinduism, Islam, and Whiteness in the American Empire," *Signs* 40, no. 2 (Winter 2015): 488.

CONCLUSION: TOWARD A LIBERATED RACK

1. Mihaela Popa-Wyatt, "Reclamation: Taking Back Control of Words," Special Issue on Non-Derogatory Uses of Slurs, edited by Bianca Cepollaro and Dan Zeman. *Grazer Philosophische Studien* 97 (March 2020).

2. Margaret Miles, *A Complex Delight: The Secularization of the Breast, 1350–1750* (Berkeley: University of California Press, 2008), 140.

3. Lucy Cooke, *Bitch: On the Female of the Species* (New York: Basic Books, 2022), 13, 26, 27.

4. Brenna Helppie-Schmieder, "The Constitution and Societal Norms: A Modern Case for Female Breast Equality," *DePaul Journal of Women, Gender and the Law* 5, no. 1 (2015): 26.

5. Catherine Healy, interview with the author, January 24, 2022.

6. See New York State Breastfeeding Mother's Bill of Rights, https://www.health.ny.gov/publications/2028.pdf.

7. Kathy Davis, "Remaking the She-Devil: A Critical Look at Feminist Approaches to Beauty," *Hypatia* 6, no. 2 (Summer 1991): 22.

8. As the distinguished Black social theorist bell hooks once wrote, "We can be sisters . . . united in our appreciation for diversity, united in our struggle to end sexist oppression. See bell hooks, "Sisterhood: Political Solidarity between Women," *Feminist Review*, no. 23 (1986): 138.

9. See, for example, Angela McRobbie, "Bridging the Gap: Feminism, Fashion and Consumption," *Feminist Review* 55, no. 1 (March 1997).

10. Angela Bonavoglia, "What's *Ms.* doing at the fall fashion shows?" *Ms.* 6, no. 2 (September/October 1995).

11. Chase Strangio, interview with the author, March 8, 2023.

BIBLIOGRAPHY

Adler, Libby S. "A Short Essay on the Baring of Breasts." *Harvard Women's Legal Journal* 23 (2000).

Agustín, Laura María. *Sex Work on the Margins: Migration, Labour Markets and the Rescue Industry*. London: Zed, 2007.

Al-Shehri, Saad S., et al. "Breast Milk-Saliva Interactions Boost Innate Immunity by Regulating the Oral Microbiome in Early Infancy." *PLOS One* 10, no. 9 (September 1, 2015).

Alexander, Priscilla, and Frédérique Delacoste, eds. *Sex Work: Writings by Women in the Sex Industry*. San Francisco: Cleis, 1998.

Alganabi, Mashriq, et al. "Recent Advances in Understanding Necrotizing Enterocolitis." *F1000 Research* 8 (January 25, 2019).

Alisobhani, Nassim. "Female Toplessness: Gender Equality's Next Frontier." *UC Irvine Law Review* 8, no. 2 (2018).

Allergan. *Natrelle Silicone-Filled Breast Implants and Natrelle Inspira Breast Implants: Important Factors Breast Augmentation and Reconstruction Patients Should Consider*. Irvine, CA: Allergan, 2017.

Allers, Kimberly Seals. *The Big Letdown: How Medicine, Big Business, and Feminism Undermine Breastfeeding*. New York: St. Martin's, 2017.

Almodovar, Norma Jean. "Operation Do the Math." policeprostitutionandpolitics.com.

———. "Sex Work, Sex Trafficking: Stigma and Solutions." PowerPoint presentation, July 5, 2020. policeprostitutionandpolitics.com.

American Academy of Medical Colleges (AAMC) website. "Active Physicians by Sex and Specialty, 2021."

———. "Active Physicians Who Identified as Black or African-American, 2021."

American Psychiatric Association. *Diagnostic and Statistical Manual of Mental Disorders, Fifth Edition, Text Revision DSM-5-TR, March 18, 2022.*

American Society for Aesthetic Plastic Surgery. Statistical reports, 1997 through 2022.

———. Aesthetic Plastic Surgery National Databank: Statistics 2020–2021.

American Society of Plastic Surgeons. *2020 Plastic Surgery Statistics Report.* Arlington Heights, IL: ASPS National Clearinghouse of Plastic Surgery Procedural Statistics, 2021.

Annfelt, Trinne. "More Gender Equality—Bigger Breasts? Battles over Gender and the Body." *Nora: Nordic Journal of Women's Studies* 10, no. 3 (November 2010).

Astell, Mary. *A Serious Proposal to the Ladies,* ed. Sharon L. Janson. Steilacoom, WA: Saltar's Point, 2014.

"The Average American Bra Size Is Now a 34 DD." *Racked,* July 22, 2013.

Ayto, John. *The Oxford Dictionary of Modern Slang.* Oxford: Oxford University Press, 2010.

Babitz, Eve. "Eve Babitz on the Time She Played Chess Nude with Marcel Duchamp: Looking Back at the Allure of the 1960s LA Art Scene," *Literary Hub via New York Review of Books,* October 9, 2019.

Badinter, Elisabeth. *The Conflict: How Modern Motherhood Undermines the Status of Women.* New York: Henry Holt, 2010.

Bakehorn, Jill. "Making Politics Explicit: Depicting Authenticity in Women-Made Pornography." In *Introducing the New Sexuality Studies,* 3rd ed., edited by Nancy Fischer et al. New York: Routledge, 2016.

Bansal, Sunita Pant. *Hindu Pilgrimage: A Journey through the Holy Places of Hindus All Over India.* New Delhi: V & S, 2012.

Baraldi, Girardi, et al. "Intimate Partner Violence and the Practice of Breastfeeding." *Journal of Nursing UFPE / Revista de Enfermagem UFPE* 13 (July 2019).

Barton, Bernadette, and Constance L. Hardesty. "Spirituality and Stripping: Exotic Dancers Narrate the Body Ekstasis." *Symbolic Interaction* 33, no. 2 (2010).

Bastian, Misty L. "The Naked and the Nude: Historically Multiple Meanings of *Oto* (Undress) in Southeastern Nigeria." In *Dirt, Undress, and Difference: Critical Perspectives on the Body's Surface,* edited by Adeline Masquelier. Bloomington: Indiana University Press, 2005.

Beauvoir, Simone de. *The Second Sex.* Translated by Constance Borde and Sheila Malovany-Chevallier. New York: Vintage, 2011.

Becker, Howard. "Becoming a Marihuana User." *American Journal of Sociology* 59, no. 3 (November 1953).

Bergman, Nils, Ginger Carney, and Susan M. Ludington-Hoe. "Kangaroo Care for the Preterm Infant." *ICAN: Infant, Child, & Adolescent Nutrition* 2, no. 3 (June 2010).

Bernard, Jonathan Y., Emmanuel Cohen, and Michael S. Kramer. "Breast Feeding Initiation Rate across Western Countries: Does Religion Matter? An Ecological Study." *BMJ Global Health* 1, no. 4 (November 1, 2016).

Berney, Adrienne. "Streamlining Breasts: The Exaltation of Form and Disguise of Function in 1930s' Ideals." *Journal of Design History* 14, no. 4 (January 1, 2001).

Bernstein, Elizabeth. *Temporarily Yours: Intimacy, Authenticity and the Commerce of Sex.* Chicago: University of Chicago, 2007.

Biale, David. "The God with Breasts: El Shaddai in the Bible." *History of Religions* 21, no. 3 (February 1982).

Binns, Colin, MiKyung Lee, and Wah Yun Low. "The Long-Term Public Health Benefits of Breastfeeding." *Asia Pacific Journal of Public Health* 28, no. 1 (2016).

Bleiweis, Robin, et al. "The Basic Facts About Women in Poverty." Center for American Progress, August 3, 2020.

Blum, Virginia L. *Flesh Wounds: The Culture of Cosmetic Surgery.* Berkeley: University of California Press, 2003.

Blunt, Wilfred. *Linnaeus: The Compleat Naturalist.* Princeton: Princeton University Press, 2001.

Bogaert, Anthony F., Deborah A. Turkovich, and Carolyn L. Hafer. "A Content Analysis of *Playboy* Centrefolds from 1953 through 1990: Changes in Explicitness, Objectification, and Model's Age." *Journal of Sex Research* 30, no. 2 (1993).

Bohannon, Cat. *Eve: How the Female Body Drove 200 Million Years of Human Evolution.* New York: Alfred A. Knopf, 2023.

Bohidar, Anannya. "Worshipping Breasts in the Maternal Landscape of India South." *Asian Studies* 31, no. 2 (2015).

Boone, Meghan. "Lactation Law." *California Law Review* 106, no. 6 (2018).

Boston Woman's Health Book Collective. *Our Bodies, Ourselves.* New York: Simon & Schuster, 2011.

Botz, Corinne May. "Inside a Lactation Room at the U.S. Capitol." *YouTube*, posted May 19, 2021.

Boyer, Kate. "The Emotional Resonances of Breastfeeding in Public: The Role of Strangers in Breastfeeding Practice." *Emotion, Space and Society* 26 (2018).

Brock, Rita Nakashima, and Susan Brooks Thistlethwaite. *Casting Stones: Prostitution and Liberation in Asia and the United States.* Minneapolis: Fortress, 1996.

Brown, Adrienne Maree. "The Pleasure Dome: Nipples Are Magic." *Bitch Media*, July 26, 2017.

———. *Pleasure Activism: The Politics of Feeling Good.* Chico, CA: AK, 2019.

Brownmiller, Susan. *Against Our Will: Men, Women, and Rape.* New York: Fawcett Columbine, 1993.

———. *Femininity.* New York: Simon & Schuster, 1984.

Bui, Quoctrung, and Claire Cain Miller. "The Age That Women Have Babies: How a Gap Divides America." *New York Times*, August 4, 2018.

Burana, Lily. "What It Was Like to Work at the Lusty Lady, a Unionized Strip Club." *Atlantic*, August 21, 2013.

Burke, Jill. "Sex and Spirituality in 1500s Rome: Sebastiano Del Piombo's 'Martyrdom of Saint Agatha'." *Art Bulletin* 88, no. 3 (September 2006).

Burridge, Kate. "Taboo, Euphemism, and Political Correctness." *Encyclopedia of Languages and Linguistics,* 2nd ed. Amsterdam: Elsevier, 2006.

Buvat, Lili. "Recherche Solo: Inspired by Annie Sprinkle's Bosom Ballet." *YouTube.* No date.

Cassidy, Tanya, and Fiona Dykes, with Bernard Mahon. *Banking on Milk: An Ethnography of Donor Human Milk Relations.* New York: Routledge, 2019.

Catapano, Peter. "The Perfect Woman: Annette Kellerman and the Spectacle of the Female Form." *Proteus: A Journal of Ideas* 25, no. 2 (Fall 2008).

Chandra, Shefali. "India Will Change You Forever: Hinduism, Islam, and Whiteness in the American Empire." *Signs* 40, no. 2 (Winter 2015).

Chao, Y. Antonia. "Drink, Stories, Penis, and Breasts: Lesbian Tomboys in Taiwan from the 1960s to the 1990s." *Journal of Homosexuality* 40, no. 3–4 (May 21, 2001).

Cheney, Liana De Girolami. "The Cult of Saint Agatha." *Woman's Art Journal* 17, no. 1 (Spring–Summer 1996).

Clark, Kenneth. *The Nude: A Study in Ideal Form.* New York: Pantheon, 1956.

Clark, Meredith. "Nike Invents 'Boob Robot' to Innovate Sports Bra Technology." *Independent,* May 27, 2022.

Coffey, Julia, and Jessica Ringrose. "Boobs and Barbie: Feminist Posthuman Perspectives on Gender, Bodies, and Practice." In *Practice Theory and Education: Diffractive Readings in Professional Practice,* edited by Julianne Lynch. New York: Routledge, 2017.

Cohen, Mathilde. "The Lactating Man." In *Making Milk: The Past, Present and Future of Our Primary Food,* edited by Mathilde Cohen and Yoriko Otomo. New York: Bloomsbury, 2017.

———. "Regulating Milk: Women and Cows in France and the United States." *American Journal of Comparative Law* 65, no. 3 (November 13, 2017).

———. "Should Human Milk Be Regulated?" *UC Irvine Law Review* 9, no. 3 (March 2019).

———. "Toward an InterSpecies Right to Breastfeed." *Animal Law* 26 (2020).

———, and Hannah Ryan. "From Human Dairies to Milk Riders: A Visual History of Milk Banking in New York City, 1918–2018." *Frontiers: A Journal of Women Studies* 40, no. 3 (2019).

———, and Yoriko Otomo, eds. *Making Milk: The Past, Present and Future of Our Primary Food.* London and New York: Bloomsbury, 2017.

Cohen, Ronald, and Katherine McCallie. "Feeding Premature Infants: Why, When and What to Add to Human Milk." *Journal of Parenteral and Enteral Nutrition,* 36, no. 1 (January 2012).

Coleman, Barbara J. "Maidenform(ed): Images of American Women in the 1950s." *Gender Journal*, no. 21 (June 1995).

Coleman-Bell, Ramona. " 'Droppin' It like It's Hot': The Sporting Body of Serena Williams." In *Framing Celebrity: New Directions in Celebrity Culture*, edited by Su Holmes and Sean Redmond. London: Routledge, 2006.

Cooke, Lucy. *Bitch: On the Female of the Species*. New York: Basic Books, 2022.

Corbet, Sylvie. "France Legalizes IVF for Lesbians and Single Women." AP News, June 29, 2021.

Courtois, Frédéric, et al. "Trends in Breastfeeding Practices and Mothers' Experience in the French NutriNet-Santé Cohort." *International Breastfeeding Journal* 16, no. 1 (2021).

Craig, R. D., and P. A. Sykes. "Nipple Sensitivity Following Reduction Mammaplasty." *British Journal of Plastic Surgery* 23, no. 2 (April 1970).

Crais, Clifton, and Pamela Scully. *Sara Baartman and the Hottentot Venus: A Ghost Story and a Biography*. Princeton: Princeton University Press, 2010.

Crane, Antonia. "Dispatch from the California Stripper Strike." In *We Too: Essays on Sex Work and Survival*, edited by Natalie West with Tina Horn. New York: Feminist, 2021.

Craw, Victoria. " 'Breasts Meant She's OK to Rape.' " *Morning Bulletin*, October 12, 2017.

Crenshaw, Kimberle. "Demarginalizing the Intersection of Race and Sex: A Black Feminist Critique of Antidiscrimination Doctrine, Feminist Theory and Antiracist Politics." *University of Chicago Legal Forum* 1989, article 8.

Cunningham, Patricia A. *Reforming Women's Fashion, 1850–1920: Politics, Health, and Art*. Kent, OH: Kent State University, 2003.

Cunnington, C. Willett, and Phillis Emily Cunnington. *The History of Underclothes*. New York: Dover, 1992.

Cusack, Carmen M. "Boob Laws: An Analysis of Social Deviance within Gender, Families, or the Home (Etudes 2)." *Women's Rights Law Reporter* 33, no. 2/3 (2011).

Dadhich, J. P., Julie P. Smith, Alessandro Iellamo, and Adlina Suleiman. "Climate Change and Infant Nutrition: Estimates of Greenhouse Gas Emissions from Milk Formula Sold in Selected Asia Pacific Countries." *Journal of Human Lactation* 37, no. 2 (May 2021).

Darwin, Charles. *On the Origin of Species*. 1859.

Davis, Angela. *Women, Race and Class*. New York: Vintage, 1983.

Davis, Kathy. "Bared Breasts and Body Politics." *European Journal of Women's Studies* 23, no. 3 (July 2016).

———. *Reshaping the Female Body: The Dilemma of Cosmetic Surgery*. New York: Routledge, 1995.

Deoni, Sean, et al. "Breastfeeding and Early White Matter Development: A Cross Sectional Study." *NeuroImage* 82 (November 2013).

Deshotels, Tina, and Craig J. Forsyth. "Strategic Flirting and the Emotional Tab of Exotic Dancing." *Deviant Behavior* 27, no. 2 (March 1, 2006).

———, Mollie Tinney, and Craig J. Forsyth. "McSexy: Exotic Dancing and Institutional Power." *Deviant Behavior* 33, no. 2 (February 1, 2012).

Dettwyler, Katherine A. "Beauty and the Breast: The Cultural Context of Breastfeeding in the United States." In *Breastfeeding: Biocultural Perspectives*, edited by Patricia Stuart-Macadam and Katherine A. Dettwyler. New York: Aldine De Gruyter, 1995.

———. "Can Paleopathology Provide Evidence for 'Compassion'?" *American Journal of Physical Anthropology* 84, no. 4 (1991).

———. "Styles of Infant Feeding: Parental/Caretaker Control of Food Consumption in Young Children." *American Anthropologist* 91, no. 3 (1989).

———. "When to Wean: Biological Versus Cultural Perspectives." *Clinical Obstetrics and Gynecology* 47, no. 3 (September 2004).

Dodsworth, Laura. *Bare Reality: 100 Women, Their Breasts, Their Stories.* London: Pinter & Martin, 2019.

Dull, Diana, and Candace West. "Accounting for Cosmetic Surgery: The Accomplishment of Gender." *Social Problems* 38 (1991).

Dunham, Cyrus Grace. "A Year Without a Name." *New Yorker*, August 19, 2019.

Dvorak, Petula. "Men Were Once Arrested for Baring Their Chests on the Beach." *Washington Post*, January 5, 2019.

Eber, Hailey. "This L.A. Sperm Bank Is More Exclusive Than an Ivy league College." *Los Angeles Magazine*, April 2, 2019.

Edmonds, Alexander. " 'The Poor Have the Right to Be Beautiful': Cosmetic Surgery in Neoliberal Brazil." *Journal of the Royal Anthropological Institute* 13, no. 2 (June 1, 2007).

———. *Pretty Modern: Beauty, Sex, and Plastic Surgery in Brazil.* Durham, NC: Duke University Press, 2010.

Eileraas, Karina. "Sex(t)Ing Revolution, Femen-Izing the Public Square: Aliaa Magda Elmahdy, Nude Protest, and Transnational Feminist Body Politics." *Signs: Journal of Women in Culture and Society* 40, no. 1 (September 2014).

Eller, Cynthia. "Divine Objectification: The Representation of Goddesses and Women in Feminist Spirituality." *Journal of Feminist Studies in Religion* 16, no. 1 (2000).

Ellis-Petersen, Hannah. "How Formula Milk Firms Target Mothers Who Can Least Afford It." *Guardian*, February 26, 2018.

Ephron, Nora. "A Few Words About Breasts." *Esquire*, May 1972.

Ewing, Katherine P. "Dreams from a Saint: Anthropological Atheism and the Temptation to Believe." *American Anthropologist* 96, no. 3 (September 1994).

Falls, Susan. *White Gold: Stories of Breast Milk Sharing.* Lincoln: University of Nebraska Press, 2017.

Febos, Melissa. "The Feminist Case for Breast Reduction." *New York Times*, May 10, 2022.

Fefferman, Marie, et al. "Rates of Bilateral Mastectomy in Patients with Early-Stage Breast Cancer." *Journal of the American Medical Association* 6, no. 1 (January 18, 2023).

Felski, Rita. " 'Because It Is Beautiful': New Feminist Perspectives on Beauty." *Feminist Theory* 7, no. 2 (August 2006).

Finnbogadóttir, Hafrún, and Li Thies-Lagergren. "Breastfeeding in the Context of Domestic Violence: A Cross-Sectional Study." *Journal of Advanced Nursing* 73, no. 12 (December 2017).

Firestone, Shulamith. *The Dialectic of Sex*. New York: Bantam, 1970.

Fischer, Kirsten. "The Imperial Gaze: Native American, African American, and Colonial Women in European Eyes." In *A Companion to American Women's History*, edited by Nancy A. Hewitt. London: John Wiley & Sons, 2008.

Fischer, Molly. "Biomilq and the New Science of Artificial Breast Milk." *New Yorker*, March 6, 2023.

Flynn, Meagan. "A Transgender Woman Is Challenging Chicago's Definition of the Female Breast." *Washington Post*, November 29, 2018.

Fooladi, Marjaneh M. "A Comparison of Perspectives on Breastfeeding Between Two Generations of Black American Women." *Journal of the American Academy of Nurse Practitioners* 13, no. 1 (January 1, 2001).

Forbes, Gordon B., and David A. Frederick. "The UCLA Body Project II: Breast and Body Dissatisfaction among African, Asian, European, and Hispanic American College Women." *Sex Roles* 58, no. 7–8 (April 2008).

Ford, Clellan S., and Frank A. Beach. *Patterns of Sexual Behavior*. Oxford: Harper and Paul B. Hoeber, 1951.

Fosburgh, Lacey. "Women's Liberationist Hails the Prostitute." *New York Times*, May 29, 1970.

Foss, Katherine A., and Ken Blake. " 'It's Natural and Healthy, but I Don't Want to See It': Using Entertainment-Education to Improve Attitudes Toward Breastfeeding in Public." *Health Communication* 34, no. 9 (July 29, 2019).

Frank, Katherine. "Thinking Critically about Strip Club Research." *Sexualities* 10, no. 4 (2007).

Freadman, Anne. "Breasts Are Back! Colette's Critique of Flapper Fashion." *French Studies* 60, no. 3 (July 1, 2006).

Freeman, Adam J., David R. Senn, and Douglas M. Arendt. "Seven Hundred Seventy-Eight Bite Marks: Analysis by Anatomic Location, Victim and Biter Demographics, Type of Crime, and Legal Disposition." *Journal of Forensic Sciences* 50, no. 6 (November 2005).

Freeman, Andrea. "Unmothering Black Women: Formula Feeding as an Incident of Slavery." *Hastings Law Journal* 69, no. 6 (2017).

Friedan, Betty. *The Feminine Mystique*. New York: Dell, 1979.

Galland, China. *Longing for Darkness: Tara and the Black Madonna.* New York: Penguin, 1990.

Ganesh, Kamala. "Mother Who Is Not a Mother: In Search of the Great Indian Goddess." *Economic and Political Weekly,* October 20–27, 1990.

Gay, Roxane. "Fifty Years Ago, Protesters Took on the Miss America Pageant and Electrified the Feminist Movement." *Smithsonian Magazine,* January 2018.

Geddes, Linda. "Antibodies in Breast Milk Remain for 10 Months after Covid Infection—Study." *Guardian,* September 27, 2021.

Geggel, Laura. "Why Do Men Have Nipples?" *LiveScience,* June 17, 2017.

Gerber, Douglas E. "The Female Breast in Greek Erotic Literature." *Arethusa* 11, no. 1/2 (1978).

Gersh-Nesic, Beth. "Radical Acceptance." In *Clarity Haynes: Radical Acceptance.* Brooklyn: Tabla Rasa Gallery, 2011.

Gibson, Emily, with Barbara Firth. *The Original Million-Dollar Mermaid: The Annette Kellerman Story.* Crows Nest, Australia: Allen & Unwin, 2005.

Giffney, Noreen. *The Culture–Breast in Psychoanalysis.* New York: Routledge, 2021.

Giles, Fiona. "Making Breastfeeding Social: The Role of Brelfies in Breastfeeding's Burgeoning Publics." In *Social Experiences of Breastfeeding: Building Bridges between Research, Policy and Practice,* edited by Sally Dowling et al. Bristol, UK: Policy, 2018.

Gill, Theo. "The Story of the Word—Mammal." *Popular Science Monthly,* no. 61 (November 1901–April 1902).

Gilman, Sander L. *Making the Body Beautiful: A Cultural History of Aesthetic Surgery.* Princeton: Princeton University Press, 1999.

Godwin, William. *Godwin on Wollstonecraft: Memoirs of the Author of "The Rights of Woman,"* ed. Richard R. Holmes. London: Harper Perennial, 2005.

"'Gold Club' Owner among Those Indicted for Using Business to Operate Elaborate Money Laundering Scheme." United States Attorney's Office: Northern District of California, March 19, 2015.

Golden, Janet Lynne. *A Social History of Wet Nursing in America: From Breast to Bottle.* New York: Cambridge University Press, 1996.

Goodreau, Adam M., et al. "Revising Prepectoral Breast Reconstruction." *Plastic and Reconstructive Surgery,* March 2022.

Gott, Suzanne. "Golden Emblems of Maternal Benevolence." *African Arts* 36, no. 1 (2003).

Gould, Steven Jay. "Male Nipples and Clitoral Ripples." *Columbia: A Journal of Arts and Literature,* no. 20 (Summer 1993).

Green, Jonathon. *Green's Dictionary of Slang.* Edinburgh: Chambers Harrap, 2011.

Groleau, Danielle, Catherine Sigouin, and Nicole Anne D'souza. "Power to Negotiate Spatial Barriers to Breastfeeding in a Western Context: When Motherhood Meets Poverty." *Health & Place* 24 (November 1, 2013).

Grossman, Pam. *Waking the Witch: Reflections of Women, Magic and Power.* New York: Gallery, 2019.

Guthrie, Elspeth, Eileen Bradbury, Peter Davenport, and Frederick Souza Faria. "Psychosocial Status of Women Requesting Breast Reduction Surgery as Compared with a Control Group of Large-Breasted Women." *Journal of Psychosomatic Research* 45, no. 4 (October 1998).

Haiken, Elizabeth. *Venus Envy: A History of Cosmetic Surgery.* Baltimore: Johns Hopkins University Press, 1997.

Halberstam, Jack. *Trans: A Quick and Quirky Account of Gender Variability.* Berkeley: University of California Press, 2017.

Hanna, Judith. " 'Toxic Strip Clubs': The Intersection of Religion, Law and Fantasy." *Theology and Sexuality* 16, no. 1 (April 2, 2010).

Hanson, Dian. *The Little Big Book of Breasts: The Compact Age of Natural Curves.* Cologne: Taschen, 2021.

Harari, Yuval Noah. *Sapiens: A Brief History of Humankind.* New York: Harper Perennial, 2015.

Hardy, Janet, and Dossie Easton. *The Ethical Slut.* New York: Ten Speed, 2017.

Harvey, John. "Showing and Hiding: Equivocation in the Relations of Body and Dress." *Fashion Theory* 11, no. 1 (April 2015).

Haskell, Ellen Davina. *Suckling at My Mother's Breasts: The Image of a Nursing God in Jewish Mysticism.* Albany: State University of New York Press, 2012.

Hausman, Bernice L. "Women's Liberation and the Rhetoric of 'Choice' in Infant Feeding Debates." *International Breastfeeding Journal* 3, no. 1 (2008).

Heartney, Eleanor. Foreword to *Beauty Matters*, edited by Peg Zeglin Brand. Bloomington: Indiana University Press, 2000.

Heitebeitel, Alf, and Kathleen M. Erndl, eds. *Is the Goddess a Feminist: The Politics of South Asian Goddesses.* New York: New York University Press, 2000.

Helppie-Schmieder, Brenna. "The Constitution and Societal Norms: A Modern Case for Female Breast Equality." *DePaul Journal of Women, Gender and the Law* 5, no. 1 (2015).

Hewlett, Barry S., and Steve Winn. "Allomaternal Nursing in Humans." *Current Anthropology* 55, no. 2 (April 2014).

Higgins, Kathleen M. "Beauty and its Kitsch Competitors." In *Beauty Matters*, edited by Peg Zeglin Brand. Bloomington: Indiana University Press, 2000.

Hinds, Hilary, and Jackie Stacey. "Imaging Feminism, Imaging Femininity: The Bra-Burner, Diana, and the Woman Who Kills." *Feminist Media Studies* 1, no. 2 (January 2001).

Hinson, Tyonne D., et al. "Factors That Influence Breastfeeding Initiation Among African American Women." *Journal of Obstetric, Gynecologic and Neonatal Nursing* 47, no. 3 (May 2018).

Hite, Shere. *The Hite Report*. New York: Dell, 1987.

Hoefinger, Heidi. *Sex, Love and Money in Cambodia: Professional Girlfriends and Transactional Relationships*. New York: Routledge, 2013.

Hoffman, Brian. "A Certain Amount of Prudishness: Nudist Magazines and the Liberalization of American Obscenity Law, 1947–1958." *Gender and History* 22, no. 3 (November 2010).

———. *Naked: A Cultural History of American Nudism*. New York: New York University Press, 2015.

Holla-Bhar, Radha, et al. "Investing in Breastfeeding—the World Breastfeeding Costing Initiative." *International Breastfeeding Journal* 10, no. 1 (February 23, 2015).

Hollander, Anne. *Seeing Through Clothes*. Berkeley: University of California Press, 1993.

Holliday, Ruth, and Jacqueline S. Taylor. "Aesthetic Surgery as False Beauty." *Feminist Theory* 7, no. 2 (2006).

Hooks, Bell. "Sisterhood: Political Solidarity Between Women." *Feminist Review*, no. 23 (1986).

Horta, Bernardo L., Fernando P. Hartwig, and Cesar G. Victora. "Breastfeeding and Intelligence in Adulthood: Due to Genetic Confounding?" *Lancet Global Health* 6, no. 12 (December 1, 2018).

———, et al. "Long-Term Consequences of Breastfeeding on Cholesterol, Obesity, Systolic Blood Pressure and Type 2 Diabetes: A Systematic Review and Meta-Analysis." *Acta Paediatrica* 104, no. S467 (2015).

Hrdy, Sarah Blaffer. *Mother Nature: Maternal Instincts and How They Shape the Human Species*. New York: Ballantine, 1999.

Huang, Ying. "Songzi Guanyin and Koyasu Kannon: Revisiting the Feminization of Avalokiteśvara in China and Japan." Master of Arts thesis, University of Alberta, 2019.

International Society of Aesthetic Plastic Surgery. *ISAPS International Survey on Aesthetic/Cosmetic Procedures Performed in 2020* (2021).

Ionescu, Carla. "Feeding the World: Reconsidering the Multibreasted Body of Artemis Ephesia." In *Bearing the Weight of the World*, edited by Alys Einion and Jen Renaldi. Coe Hill, ON: Demeter, 2018.

Jain, Lochlann. "Cancer Butch." *Malignant: How Cancer Becomes Us*. Berkeley: University of California Press, 2013.

Jeffreys, Sheila. *Beauty and Misogyny: Harmful Cultural Practices in the West*. New York: Routledge, 2005.

Jenkins, Mark Collins. *National Geographic: 125 Years*. Washington, DC: National Geographic Society, 2013.

Jenness, Valerie. "From Sex as Sin to Sex as Work: COYOTE and the Reorganization of Prostitution as a Social Problem." *Social Problems* 37, no. 3 (August 1990).

Jewett, Christina. "Justice Department Investigating Troubled Infant Formula Plant." *New York Times*, January 21, 2023.

Jones, Diana P. "Cultural Views of the Female Breast." *Association of Black Nursing Journal* 15, no. 1 (January/February 2004).

Jordan, Jessica Hope. *The Sex Goddess in American Film, 1930–1965.* Amherst, NY: Cambria, 2009.

Kapner, Suzanne. "Old Navy Made Clothing Sizes for Everyone. It Backfired." *Wall Street Journal*, May 20, 2022.

Katan, Tania. *My One-Night Stand with Cancer.* Los Angeles: Alyson, 2005.

Kellerman, Annette. *Physical Beauty: How to Keep It.* New York: George H. Doran Company, 1918.

Kennard, Jerry. "Why Do Men Have Nipples?" *Verywell Health*, October 21, 2022.

Kinsey, Alfred C., Wardell B. Pomeroy, and Clyde E. Martin. *Sexual Behavior in the Human Male.* Philadelphia: Saunders, 1948.

———, et al. *Sexual Behavior in the Human Female.* Philadelphia: Saunders, 1953.

Knox, Belle. "Tearing Down the Whorearchy from the Inside." *Jezebel*, July 2, 2014.

Koerner, Lisbet. *Linnaeus: Nature and Nation.* Boston: Harvard University Press, 1999.

Kraut, Roni Y., et al. "The Impact of Breast Reduction Surgery on Breastfeeding: Systematic Review of Observational Studies." *PLOS One* 12, no. 10 (2017).

Kreydatus, Beth. "Confronting the Bra Burners: Teaching Radical Feminism with a Case Study." *History Teacher* 41 (August 4, 2008).

Kunst, Alexander. "Old Navy Brand Profile in the United States 2022." *Statistica*, May 25, 2023.

Labbok, Miriam H. "Effects of Breastfeeding on the Mother." *Pediatric Clinics of North America*, 48, no. 1 (February 1, 2001).

Ladd, Amy L. "The Sports Bra, the ACL, and Title IX—The Game in Play." *Clinical Orthopedics and Related Research* 472, no. 6 (April 11, 2014).

Lam, Raymond. "Legitimizing Legitimization: Tara's Assimilation of Masculine Qualities in Indo-Tibetan Buddhism and the Feminist 'Reclaiming' of Theological Discourse." *Feminist Theology* 22, no. 2 (2014).

Latteier, Carolyn. *Breasts: The Women's Perspective on an American Obsession.* New York: Haworth, 1998.

Lee, Lorelei. "When She Says Women, She Does Not Mean Me." In *We Too: Essays on Sex Work and Survival*, edited by Natalie West with Tina Horn. New York: Feminist, 2021.

Lehr, Leslie. *A Boob's Life: How America's Obsession Shaped Me . . . And You.* New York: Simon & Schuster, 2021.

Lei, Jun. " 'Natural' Curves: Breast-Binding and Changing Aesthetics of the Female Body in China of the Early Twentieth Century." *Modern Chinese Literature and Culture* 27, no. 1 (2015).

Leigh, Carol. *Unrepentant Whore: Collected Works of Scarlot Harlot.* San Francisco: Last Gasp, 2004.

Lele, Huang. "The Ambiguity of the Gender of Avalokiteśvara." *Asia Social Issues* 1, no. 2 (March/April 2022).

Lenning, Alkeline van, and Ine Vanwesenbeeck. "The Ever-Changing Female Body: Historical and Cultural Differences in Playmates' Body Sizes." *Feminism & Psychology* 10, no. 4 (November 2000).

Lerner, Gerda. *The Creation of Patriarchy*. New York: Oxford University Press, 1986.

Levin, Roy J. "The Breast/Nipple/Areola Complex and Human Sexuality." *Sexual and Relationship Therapy* 21, no. 2 (May 2006).

———, and Cindy Meston. "Nipple/Breast Stimulation and Sexual Arousal in Young Men and Women." *Journal of Sexual Medicine* 3, no. 3 (2006).

Levy, Ariel. *Female Chauvinist Pigs: Women and the Rise of Raunch Culture*. London: Simon & Schuster, 2005.

LiDonnici, Lynn R. "The Images of Artemis Ephesia and Greco-Roman Worship: A Reconsideration." *Harvard Theological Review* 85, no. 4 (October 1992).

Lintott, Sheila. "Feminist Aesthetics and the Neglect of Natural Beauty." *Environmental Values* 19, no. 3 (August 1, 2010).

Lorde, Audre, and Sonia Sanchez. *A Burst of Light and Other Essays*. Mineola, NY: Ixia, 2017.

Lucas, A., et al. "Breast Milk and Subsequent Intelligence Quotient in Children Born Preterm." *Lancet* 339, no. 8788 (February 1, 1992).

Lutz, Catherine A., and Jane L. Collins. *Reading National Geographic*. Chicago: University of Chicago Press, 1993.

Lutzky, Harriet. "Shadday as a Goddess Epithet." *Vetus Testamentum* 48, fasc. 1 (January 1998).

Malmer, Lisa. "Nude Dancing and the First Amendment." *University of Cincinnati Law Review* 59, no. 4 (1991).

Mascia-Lees, Fran. "Are Women Evolutionary Sex Objects? Why Women Have Breasts." *Anthropology Now* 1, no. 1 (2009).

Masquelier, Adeline, ed. *Dirt, Undress, and Difference: Critical Perspectives on the Body's Surface*. Bloomington: Indiana University Press, 2005.

Matelski, Elizabeth M. *Reducing Bodies: Mass Culture and the Female Figure in Postwar America*. New York: Taylor & Francis, 2017.

Mayor, Adrienne. *The Amazons: Lives and Legends of Warrior Women Across the Ancient World*. Princeton: Princeton University Press, 2014.

McDermott, LeRoy. "Self-Representation in Upper Paleolithic Female Figurines." *Current Anthropology* 37, no. 2 (April 1996).

McKay, James, and Helen Johnson. "Pornographic Eroticism and Sexual Grotesquerie in Representations of African American Sportswomen." *Social Identities* 14, no. 4 (July 1, 2008).Insert new entry:

McRobbie, Angela. "Bridging the Gap: Feminism, Fashion, and Consumption." *Feminist Review* 55, no 1 (March 1997).

Meehan, Thomas. "At Bennington, the Boys are the Co-eds." *New York Times*, December 21, 1969.

Megarry, Jessica. "Under the Watchful Eyes of Men: Theorising the Implications of Male Surveillance Practices for Feminist Activism on Social Media." *Feminist Media Studies* 18, no. 6 (2018).

Midori. *The Seductive Art of Japanese Bondage*. Emeryville, CA: Greenery, 2001.

———. *Wild Side Sex: The Book of Kink: Educational, Sensual, and Entertaining Essays*. Los Angeles: Daedalus, 2005.

Miles, Margaret R. *Carnal Knowing: Female Nakedness and Religious Meaning in the Christian West*. Boston: Beacon, 1989.

———. *A Complex Delight: The Secularization of the Breast, 1350–1750*. Berkeley: University of California Press, 2008.

———. *Augustine on Beautiful Bodies*. Eugene, OR: Cascade Books, 2024.

Miller, Laura. "Mammary Mania in Japan." *Positions: Asia Critique* 11, no. 2 (May 1, 2003).

Millett, Kate. *Sexual Politics*. Urbana: University of Illinois Press, 1970.

Milstead, Virginia F. "Forbidding Female Toplessness: Why Real Difference Jurisprudence Lacks Support and What Can Be Done about It." *University of Toledo Law Review* 36, no. 2 (Winter 2005).

Mintz, Sydney. "Co-Wives, Sisters and Concubines in the Genesis Narrative." Rabbinical thesis, Hebrew Union College–Jewish Institute of Religion, New York, 1997.

Moberg, Kertin Uvnäs, and Danielle K. Prime. "Oxytocin Effects in Mothers and Infants during Breastfeeding." *Infant* 9, no. 6 (2013).

Mohrbacher, Nancy, and Kathleen Kendall-Tackett. *Breastfeeding Made Simple: Seven Natural Laws for Nursing Mothers*. 2nd ed. Oakland, CA: New Harbinger, 2010.

Moses, Jeremy. *US Industry Specialized Report: Strip Clubs*. IbisWorld, December 2019.

Mulvey, Laura. "Visual Pleasure and Narrative Cinema." *Screen* 16, no. 3 (1975).

Naage, Ledibabari M., et al. "Health Insurance Coverage of Gender-Affirming Top Surgery in the United States." *Plastic and Reconstructive Surgery* 144, no. 4 (2019).

Nagle, Jill, ed. *Whores and Other Feminists*. New York: Routledge, 1997.

Naidu, Maheshvari. "Inscribing the Female Body: Fuzzy Gender and Goddess in a South Indian Saiva Marriage Myth." *Journal for the Study of Religion* 21, no. 1 (2008).

———. "Marriage as Reaffirming Sacred Space." *Nidan: International Journal for Indian Studies* 11 (December 1999).

Naugler, Diane. "Credentials: Breast Slang and the Discourse of Femininity." *Atlantis* 34, no. 1 (2009).

Ndlovu, Hlengiwe. "Womxn's Bodies Reclaiming the Picket Line: The 'Nude' Protest during #FeesMustFall." *Agenda* 31, no. 3–4 (October 2, 2017).

Newton, Esther. *Mother Camp: Female Impersonators in America*. Chicago: University of Chicago Press, 1970.

Nussbaum, Martha. *Sex and Social Justice*. Oxford: Oxford University Press, 1999.

Nuttall, Jenni. *Mother Tongue: The Surprising History of Women's Words.* New York: Viking, 2023.

Olorenshaw, Vanessa. *Liberating Motherhood: Birthing the Purplestockings Movement.* Cork, Ireland: Womancraft, 2016.

Osbaldiston, Richard, and Leigh A. Mingle. "Characterization of Human Milk Donors." *Journal of Human Lactation* 23, no. 4 (November 2007).

Panchal, Hina, and Evan Matros. "Current Trends in Post-Mastectomy Breast Reconstruction." *Plastic Reconstructive Surgery* 140, no. 5 (November 2017).

Pardes, Ilana. *Countertradition in the Bible: A Feminist Approach.* Cambridge, MA: Harvard University Press, 1992.

Paris Is Burning. Documentary film directed by Jennie Livingston. Off-White Productions, 1990.

Pattanaik, Devdutt. *The Man Who Was a Woman and Other Queer Tales from Indian Lore.* New York: Routledge, 2002.

Payne, Rachael, et al. "Women Continue to Be Underrepresented in Plastic Surgery: A Study of AMA and ACGME Data from 2000–2013." *Plastic and Reconstructive Surgery—Global Open* 5, no. 9S (September 2017).

Popa-Wyatt, Mihaela. "Reclamation: Taking Back Control of Words," Special Issue on Non-Derogatory Uses of Slurs, edited by Bianca Cepollaro and Dan Zeman. *Grazer Philosophische Studien* 97 (March 2020).

Rajaei, Sheeva, et al. "Breastfeeding Duration and the Risk of Coronary Artery Disease." *Journal of Women's Health* 28, no. 1 (2018).

Ratajkowski, Emily. *My Body.* New York: Henry Holt, 2021.

Reisman, Tamar, and Zil Goldstein. "Case Report: Induced Lactation in a Transgender Woman." *Transgender Health* 3, no. 1 (January 1, 2018).

Reuther, Karen Korellis. "Shrink It and Pink It: Gender Bias in Product Design." *Harvard Advanced Leadership Initiative: Social Impact Review*, October 25, 2022.

Rich, Adrienne C. *Of Woman Born.* New York: W. W. Norton, 1995.

Richardson, Daniel C., et al. "Small Penises and Fast Cars: Evidence for a Psychological Link." Manuscript, University College, London, 2023.

Rodin, Krista K. "Empress Influence on the Establishment and Rise in Popularity of the Virgin Mary and Kuan Yin." *Journal of Literature and Art Studies* 6, no. 11 (November 2016).

Rosenblum, Jordan. "Blessings of the Breasts: Breastfeeding in Rabbinic Literature." *Hebrew Union College Annual* 87 (2016).

Runnebaum, Achim. "Tokyo Serves Up Lactation Bars." *Japan Daily* (blog), February 25, 2016.

Safire, William. "Erotic or Exotic?" *New York Times*, May 21, 2006.

Saldanha, Ian J., et al. "Implant-Based Breast Reconstruction after Mastectomy for

Breast Cancer: A Systematic Review and Meta-Analysis." *Plastic and Reconstructive Surgery—Global Open* 10, no. 3 (March 2022).

Salomonsen, Jone. *Enchanted Feminism: Ritual, Gender and Divinity among the Reclaiming Witches of San Francisco.* New York: Routledge, 2002.

Sanchez Taylor, Jacqueline. "Fake Breasts and Power: Gender, Class and Cosmetic Surgery." *Women's Studies International Forum* 35, no. 6 (2012).

Sanders, Teela, and Kate Hardy. "Devalued, Deskilled and Diversified: Explaining the Proliferation of the Strip Industry in the UK." *British Journal of Sociology* 63, no. 3 (2012).

Schiebinger, Londa. "Why Mammals Are Called Mammals: Gender Politics in Eighteenth-Century Natural History." *American Historical Review* 98, no. 2 (April 1993).

———. *Nature's Body: Gender in the Making of Modern Science.* Boston: Beacon, 1993.

———. *Has Feminism Changed Science?* Cambridge, MA: Harvard University Press, 1999.

Scofield, Rebecca. " 'Nipped, Tucked, or Sucked': Dolly Parton and the Construction of the Authentic Body." *Journal of Popular Culture* 49, no. 3 (2016).

Serano, Julia. *Whipping Girl: A Transsexual Woman on Sexism and the Scapegoating of Femininity.* Berkeley: Seal, 2016.

Sesquiotic. "Boobs vs. Tits: A First Look." *Strong Language: A Sweary Blog About Swearing,* April 6, 2018.

"Sex Workers in Belgium Celebrate Historic Vote for Decriminalisation in Parliament." Global Network of Sex Work Projects, nswp.org, March 25, 2022.

Shakespeare, V., and K. Postle. "A Qualitative Study of Patients' Views on the Effects of Breast-Reduction Surgery: A 2-Year Follow-up Survey." *British Journal of Plastic Surgery* 52, no. 3 (April 1, 1999).

Sharik, Lisa. "Breasts: From Functional to Sexualized." In *Breasts Across Motherhood,* edited by Patricia Drew and Rosann Edwards. Bradford, ON: Demeter, 2020.

Sherfey, M. J. "Some Biology of Sexuality." *Journal of Sexual and Marital Therapy* 1, no. 2 (Winter 1974).

Shimanaka, Kazutaka. "Lactating Ladies Nurse Customers at Kabukicho Milk Bar." *Tokyo Reporter,* August 6, 2009.

Shteir, Rachel. *Striptease: The Untold History of the Girlie Show,* New York: Oxford University Press, 2004.

Sigurdson, Krista, et al. "Racial/Ethnic Disparities in Neonatal Intensive Care: A Systematic Review." *Pediatrics* 144, no. 2 (August 2019).

Smith, Julie P. "A Commentary on the Carbon Footprint of Milk Formula." *International Breastfeeding Journal* 14, no.1 (December 2019).

———. " 'Lost Milk?' Counting the Economic Value of Breast Milk in Gross Domestic Product." *Journal of Human Lactation,* July 12, 2013.

———, and Alessandro Iellamo. "Wet Nursing and Donor Human Milk Sharing in Emergencies and Disasters: A Review." *Breastfeeding Review* 28, no. 3 (November 2020).

Smith, Merril D. *Cultural Encyclopedia of the Breast.* Lanham, MD: Rowman & Littlefield, 2014.

Smith, Molly, and Juno Mac. *Revolting Prostitutes: The Fight for Sex Workers Rights.* Brooklyn: Verso, 2018.

Spiegel, Maura, and Lithe Sebesta. *Breast Book: Attitude, Perception, Envy and Etiquette.* New York: Workman, 2002.

Sprawson, Charles. *Haunts of the Black Masseur: The Swimmer as Hero.* New York: Pantheon, 1992.

Sprinkle, Annie. *Post-Modern Pin-Ups Bio Booklet to Accompany the Pleasure Activist Playing Cards.* Richmond, VA: Gates of Heck, 1995.

———. *Post-Porn Modernist: My 25 Years as a Multimedia Whore.* San Francisco: Cleis Press, 1998.

———, and Elizabeth Stephens with Jennie Klein. *Assuming the Ecosexual Position: The Earth as Lover.* Minneapolis: University of Minnesota Press, 2021.

"Sri Lanka Ranks First in the World for Breastfeeding." *Nation,* April 28, 2002.

Stapleton, Karyn. "Gender and Swearing: A Community Practice." *Women and Language* 26, no. 2 (September 22, 2003).

Steinem, Gloria. "A Bunny's Tale." *Show,* May 1963.

———. "A Bunny's Tale, Part II." *Show,* June 1963.

Steiner, Claudia A., et al. "Trends in Bilateral and Unilateral Mastectomies in Hospital Inpatient and Ambulatory Settings, 2005–2013." *Healthcare Cost and Utilization Project,* March 2016.

Stevens, T. Y. "Which Cities Have the Most Plastic Surgeons Per Capita?" surgery-plasticsurgeon.com, March 7, 2016.

Steyn, Mark. "The Maestro of Jiggle TV: Aaron Spelling (1923–2006)." *Atlantic,* September 1, 2006.

Stjernfelt, Frederik, and Anne Mette Lauritzen. *Your Post Has Been Removed: Tech Giants and Freedom of Speech.* Copenhagen: Springer, 2020.

Strangio, Chase. "Can Reproductive Trans Bodies Exist?" *CUNY Law Review* 19, no. 2 (2015).

Stryker, Susan. "My Words to Victor Frankenstein above the Village of Chamounix: Performing Transgender Rage." *Journal of Lesbian and Gay Studies* 1, no. 3 (June 1, 1994).

———. *Transgender History.* Berkeley: Seal, 2008.

Stuebe, Alison. "How Often Does Breastfeeding Just Not Work?" *Breastfeeding Medicine,* October 15, 2012.

"Support for All: Why We Re-Engineered Our Entire Sports Bra Portfolio." news.adidas.com, February 9, 2022.

Sussman, George D. "Parisian Infants and Norman Wet Nurses in the Early Nineteenth Century: A Statistical Study." *Journal of Interdisciplinary History* 7, no. 4 (1977).

———. *Selling Mother's Milk: The Wet Nursing Business in France*. Chicago: University of Illinois Press, 1982.

Swami, Viren, et al. "The Breast Size Satisfaction Survey (BSSS): Breast Size Dissatisfaction and Its Antecedents and Outcomes in Women from 40 Nations." *Body Image* 32 (March 1, 2020).

Taussig, Michael. *Beauty and the Beast*. Chicago: University of Chicago Press, 2012.

"The 39th Edition of Best of the Bay." *Bay Guardian* 48, no. 3 (October 16–22, 2013).

Thornton-Silver, Cora. "Top 10 Male Dating App Photo Cliches." *La Tonique*, September 15, 2021.

thotscholar. *HeauxThots: On Terminology and Other UnImportant Things*. Chicago: bbydool, 2019.

Trautner, Emily, et al. "Knowledge and Practice of Induction of Lactation in Trans Women among Professionals Working in Trans Health." *International Breastfeeding Journal* 15, no. 63 (July 16, 2020).

Vine, David. "Women's Labor, Sex Work and U.S. Military Bases Abroad." *Salon*, October 8, 2017.

Warner, Marina. *Monuments and Maidens: The Allegory of the Female Form*. New York: Atheneum, 1985.

———. *Alone of All Her Sex: The Myth and the Cult of the Virgin Mary*. New York: Vintage, 1983.

Weddle, Saundra. "Mobility and Prostitution in Early Modern Venice." *Early Modern Women: An Interdisciplinary Journal* 14, no. 1 (September 2019).

Wegenstein, Bernadette. "Agatha's Breasts on a Plate: 'Ugliness' as Resistance and Queerness." In *On the Politics of Ugliness*, edited by Sara Rodrigues and Ela Przybylo. Toronto: Palgrave Macmillan, 2018.

Weiss-Adamson, Melitta, ed. *Regional Cuisines of Medieval Europe*. London: Routledge, 2002.

Weldon, Jo. *Burlesque Handbook*. New York: Dey Street, 2010.

West, Natalie, with Tina Horn. *We Too: Essays on Sex Work and Survival*. New York: Feminist, 2021.

Who Wrote the Old Testament. Documentary film, directed by Caryl Ebenezer. MagellanTV, 2002.

Wiener, Margaret. "Breasts, (Un)Dress, and Modernist Desires in the Balinese–Tourist Encounter." In *Dirt, Undress, and Difference: Critical Perspectives on the Body's Surface*, edited by Adeline Marie Masquelier. Bloomington: Indiana University Press, 2005.

Wilf, Robert. "The Transition of Guanyin: Reinterpreting Queerness and Buddha Nature in Medieval East Asia." Religious Studies Honors Papers, Ursinus College, Collegeville, PA, 2020.

Williams, Alessandra Glover, and Fiona Finlay. "Breast Ironing: An Under-Recognised Form of Gender-Based Violence." *Archives of Diseases in Childhood*, no. 105 (2020).

Williams, Florence. *Breasts: A Natural and Unnatural History.* New York: W. W. Norton, 2012.

Wilson, George Thomas. "The Elusive White Breast on the Pages of National Geographic." National Geographic: Collector's Corner, May 27, 2017. http://ngscollectors.ning.com/.

Winter, Jessica. "Why More and More Girls are Hitting Puberty Early." *New Yorker,* October 27, 2022.

Witt, Mysterious. "What Is the Whorearchy and Why It's Wrong." *An Injustice!* November 18, 2020.

Wolf, Kirsten. "The Severed Breast: A Topos in the Legends of Female Virgin Martyr Saints." *Arkiv för nordisk filologi* 112 (1997).

Wolf, Naomi. *The Beauty Myth: How Images of Beauty Are Used Against Women.* 1991. New York: Harper Perennial, 2002.

Wollstonecraft, Mary. *A Vindication of the Rights of Woman.* Mineola, NY: Dover, 1996.

Wynter, Sylvia. "No Humans Involved: An Open Letter to My Colleagues." *Forum N.H.I.: Knowledge for the 21st Century* 1, no. 1 (Fall 1994).

Yalom, Marilyn. *A History of the Breast.* New York: Ballantine, 1998.

Young, Iris Marion. *On Female Body Experience: Throwing Like a Girl and Other Essays.* New York: Oxford University Press, 2005.

Yueh, Janet H., et al. "Nipple-Sparing Mastectomy: Evaluation of Patient Satisfaction, Aesthetic Results, and Sensation." *Annals of Plastic Surgery* 62, no. 5 (May 2009).

Zak, Heidi. "An Open Letter to Victoria's Secret." *New York Times,* November 18, 2018.

Zhou, Yufan. "From Victoria's Secret to ThirdLove: Changes in Bra from the Perspective of Feminism." *Advances in Social Science, Education and Humanities Research 631,* January 17, 2022.

ILLUSTRATION CREDITS

1   Farrah Fawcett. Photo by Bruce McBroom. Courtesy of the Farrah Fawcett Foundation.

3   Eugene Delacroix, *Liberty Leading the People*, 1831 (detail). Louvre Museum, Paris.

5   J. Howard Miller. *Rosie the Riveter: We Can Do It!* 1942. Smithsonian, Washington, DC.

14   Betty Grable, 1943. Photo by Frank Powolny. Twentieth Century Fox.

15   Marilyn Monroe with Tony Curtis and Jack Lemmon in publicity still for *Some Like It Hot*, Los Angeles, 1959. Michael Ochs Archives / Getty Images.

17   Left: Dogon wood sculpture from Mali, encapsulated in resin by artist Matthew Angelo Harrison, *Forward Majesty*, 2021. Courtesy of the artist and Jessica Silverman. Right: Japanese geishas, 1924. CPA Media Pte Ltd / Alamy Stock Photo.

24   Votes for Women, 1908, Museum of London.

26   Laverne Cox and honoree Chase Strangio attend Hammer Museum's Eighteenth Annual Gala in the Garden on October 8, 2022, in Los Angeles, CA. Photo by Emma McIntyre / Getty Images for Hammer Museum.

29   Vixen Photography, *Portrait of Redbone*.

32   Barbie Bloodgloss. Photo by Jane Blade / Queer Occult.

37   David Lawrence Byrd, *Portrait of Jo Weldon*, 2020.

46   Annie Sprinkle, *Bosom Ballet*, 1990–91. Documentation by Leslie Barany. Courtesy of Annie Sprinkle.

61   Marco Andrea Felix, *Portrait of Crocodile Lightning*, 2020.

65   Carey Fruth, *Portrait of Kitty KaPo*www.

73   Tabitha Soren, *Tabitha and Walker*, 2023. ©Tabitha Soren.

79   Pygmies breastfeeding babies in the forest, Republic of Congo. Photo by André Quillien / Alamy Stock Photo.

85   Loie Hollowell, *Milk Fountain*, 2020–21. © Loie Hollowell. Courtesy of Pace Gallery and Jessica Silverman.

96   Jayne Mansfield, *The Girl Can't Help It*, 1956. Twentieth Century Fox / Courtesy of the Everett Collection.

105 ElectraGraphics

111 ElectraGraphics

114 ElectraGraphics

127 Top: Dolly Parton, Lily Tomlin, and Jane Fonda at the premiere of *Nine to Five*. Photo by Betty Galella. Ron Galella Collection / Getty Images. Bottom: Cardi B. wins best hip-hop video at the MTV Video Music Awards 2019, held at the Prudential Center in Newark, NJ. Doug Peters / EMPICS / Alamy stock photo.

129 ElectraGraphics

137 *Deena Metzger as the Warrior*. Photo by Hella Hammid, 1977. Courtesy of Deena Metzger and estate of Hella Hammid.

146 ElectraGraphics

147 Zackary Drucker, in collaboration with A. L. Steiner, *Before/After*, 2009 (detail). Courtesy of Zackary Drucker, A.L. Steiner, and Luis de Jesus.

153 Old Navy BOD EQUALITY billboard campaign in New York. Photo by Dia Dipasupil / Getty Images.

159 Old Navy prototype of smoothing, full-coverage, wireless bra. Photo by Phillip Maisel.

162 "Freedom Trash Can" at protest of Miss America pageant, Atlantic City, 1968. Alix Kates Shulman Papers, David M. Rubenstein Rare Book & Manuscript Library, Duke University. © Alix Kates Shulman.

168 Sonnie Givens in 24/7® Classic Uplift Plunge Bra, daydream. Photo by Shawn Merz. Courtesy of ThirdLove.

170 Yvonne Simone Powless in 24/7® Classic T-Shirt Bra, mocha. Photo by Shawn Merz. Courtesy of ThirdLove.

174 Catherine Opie, *Self-Portrait Nursing*, 2004. © Catherine Opie. Courtesy of Regen Projects and Lehmann Maupin.

176 Leonna Williams in 24/7® Second Skin Unlined Bra, taupe. Photo by Shawn Merz. Courtesy of ThirdLove.

183 Annette Kellerman in "The Perfect Woman" William Morris advertisement, 1908.

189 *Sunshine and Health: Official Journal of the American Sunbathing Association* 21, no. 7, July 1952.

191 Janet Jackson performs during the halftime show at Super Bowl XXXVIII on February 1, 2004, in Houston, TX. Photo by Donald Miralle / Getty Images.

193 Male Nipple Pasty meme, 2015. Remastered by Micol Hebron, 2021.

200 Old Navy prototype of high-support sports bra with figure-eight pad. Photo by Phillip Maisel.

205 *The Buddhist Deity White Tara*, 1400–1500, Nepal. The Avery Brundage Collection, Asian Art Museum, San Francisco.

216 Ambrogio Lorenzetti, *Madonna del Latte*, ca. 1325–ca. 1348, Oratory of San Bernardino and Diocesan Sacred Art Museum, Siena, Italy.

219 Top left: *Diana of Versailles*, 125–150 CE, Louvre Museum, Paris. Top right: Artemis of Ephesus, Turkey. Bottom left: Artemis of Ephesus in alabaster and bronze, second century AD. Naples National Archeological Museum / Farnese Collection. Photo by Marie-Lan Nguyen. Bottom right: Diana of Ephesus at Villa d'Este, 1568, in Tivoli, Italy.

222 *Bodhisattva Guanyin*, late fourteenth to fifteenth century (Ming). Collection of the Walters Art Museum, Baltimore, MD.

225 Deborah Oak Cooper, *Waving Goodbye to the Patriarchy*, 2022. One in an unlimited series of handkerchiefs, found and stamped with colored ink. Courtesy of the artist.

228 *Venus of Willendorf*, 25,000 BCE, Natural History Museum, Vienna, Austria.

229 The Hindu goddess Kali, eleventh-century copper alloy sculpture, Tamil Nadu. Collection of the Los Angeles County Museum of Art.

231 Left: Chitra Ganesh, *Black Vitruvian Tiger*. Courtesy of the artist and Wendi Norris Gallery, San Francisco. Right: Leonardo da Vinci, *Vitruvian Man*, ca. 1490. Galleria dell'Accademia, Venice.

232 Chitra Ganesh, *Charmed Tongue*, 2006 (detail). Courtesy of the artist and Wendi Norris Gallery.

236 Clarity Haynes, *The Participant Observer*, 2021. Courtesy of the artist.

247 Serena Williams, Wimbledon, July 1, 2016. Photo by Paul Childs / Reuters.

250 Eve Babitz plays chess with Marcel Duchamp at the Pasadena Art Museum, 1963. © Estate of Julian Wasser. Courtesy of Craig Krull Gallery.

INDEX

Page numbers in *italic* refer to illustrations. Page numbers after 258 refer to notes.

20th Century Fox, 16
50 Cent, 33

Abbott Nutrition, 90
Abercrombie and Fitch, 163
abortion, 27, 91, 104, 206
Abraham (biblical figure), 233
Abrams, Stacey, 226
ACLU, *See* American Civil Liberties Union
Adams, Kelly, 77–78, 80
Adidas, 197
Aesthetic Society, The, *114*, 260, 272
Affordable Care Act, 82, 214
Agatha, Saint, 22
age, 54, 164, 262
ageism, 250
agency, of sex workers, 36, 49
aging, 66, 99, 121, 209, 226, 232, 233, 237, 242, 250, 268, 279
Agustín, Laura María, 265
AIDS pandemic, 106–9
Aka people, 79
Alexander, Priscilla, 50

Alexander the Great, 240
Allergan, 8, 116, 117, 272
Allers, Kimberly Seals, 104
Alloderm, 123
allomothering, 78–80, *79*, 94–95, 109, 267
Alvanon, 161, 276
Amazon Prime, 192
Amazons, in mythology, 218, 244
American Academy of Pediatrics, 108
American Civil Liberties Union (ACLU), 25, 190, 253
American Society of Plastic Surgeons, 272, 275
America's Next Top Model: The College Edition (television program), 169
Amnesty International, 50
amputations, mastectomies as, 11
Anderson, Pamela, 16, 35
androgynous, genderful vs., 64
Angels and Demons (docuseries), 176–77

Anthony, Susan B., 214
Anthropometries (Klein), 47
Antin, Eleanor, 45
apex, 21, 160, 187, 188–89
Apple, 74, 175
apples, as symbols and metaphors, 4, 154, 212
Apple TV, 192
Artemis (goddess), 217–21, *219*, 227, 244–45; *See also* Diana (goddess)
Astell, Mary, 279
Athena (bra), 135
Athleta, 161, 169, 196, 198
Atkinson, Ti-Grace, 264
Augustine, Saint, 215–16
Avalokiteśvara, 223, 241
Avedon, Richard, 173

Babitz, Eve, *250*
Badinter, Elisabeth, 98
ballet, 58
Banana Republic, 161
Bangkok, Thailand, 60
Banking on Milk, 99
Barbie (doll), 32
Barbie (stripper), 30–34, *32*, 59, 68–69
"bareback bathing," 194
Baywatch, 16, 35
BC Women's Provincial Milk Bank, 271
beauty
    and breastfeeding, 76, 84, 98, 259
    definitions of, 40, 41, 58, 118–19, 130, 134, 179, 184, 252, 253, 272
    divergent ideals of, 4, 16–18, 121, 125, 130, 137
    and feminism, 133–34, 251, 273, 274, 284
    and hexing, 226
    and physical changes, 165, 208, 250
    and power, 133–34, 241

Beauty Matters (Heartney), 134
Beauty Myth, The (Wolf), 133
Beauvoir, Simone de, 5
Bechet, Sidney, 62
bereaved donors, 74
Bex (drag king), 64, 66, 67
Big Letdown, The (Allers), 104
Birkenstock, 172
birth justice, 91
Black babies in neonatal intensive care units (NICUs), 119
Black Lives Matter, 119
Black plastic surgeons, 119
Black Vitruvian Tiger (Ganesh), 230, *231*
Black women
    and breast cancer, 138
    and breastfeeding, 91, 101–6, 185, 271
    and sex work, 36, 41, 54
    and words for breast, 19
Blakey (Vermeule), 213, 235–39, 243
Bloomer, Amelia, 202
Bod Equality Initiative (Old Navy), 155, 198
bodily autonomy; *See also* choice, freedom of; freedom
    and formula feeding, 104
    and "free the nipple," 215
    and sex work, 36, 48, 68
    and women's rights, 27, 210, 245, 253–54, 263
body dysmorphia, 143–44
body image, 175–76
Body Imprint (Mendieta), 47
body prints, 47
"body shot" waitresses, 42, 43
Bohannon, Cat, 12
Bolden, Kelly, 120–25, 148
boobs, as term, 19
Bosom Ballet (Sprinkle), 45, *46*, 197, 263
Boston Women's Health Book Collective, 269

bra bots, 196–97
bra-burning, 25, 161–62, *162*
bra design, 21, 153–203, 253
brain development, 89
bralessness, 164
bra math, 158–59
Brazil, 128–30
Bread (witch and labor and delivery nurse), 211, 220–21, 243
breast cancer
  author's experiences with, 2–3, 6–7
  and Black women, 138
  nuns with, 217
  reconstruction surgery following mastectomies, 135–36
  tests for survivors, 274
breastfeeding, 12, 73–109, 252
  and beauty, 76, 84, 98, 259
  benefits to infants, 75, 102
  benefits to mothers, 75, 102
  and Black women, 91, 101–6, 185, 271
  challenges of, 4–6, 87, 93, 97–98, 103–6
  and chest-feeding, 90–91
  downsides of, 77–78
  in France, 96–100
  and HIV, 106–8
  lack of milk supply, 103
  lactation, *See* lactation
  by the Madonna, *73*, 215, *216*
  medical doctors lacking expertise in, 108–9
  in Norway, 92–96
  by people assigned male at birth, 269
  in protestant vs. catholic countries, 94
"breast freedom," 51–52; *See also* "free the nipple"
breast implants, 36–38, 138, 140–41, 272
breast ironing, 223, 281

breast pumps, 82–84, 92, 102, 268
breast reconstruction, 3, 7–10, 134–43, 275
breasts
  appreciation of own, 18
  changes in, over time, 226
  commercialization of, 19, 50, 71, 80, 104, 109, 163, 167, 188, 194, 196, 267
  cultural ideals of, 4
  different contexts for, 248–49
  erotic attraction to, 12–15
  freedom of, 48, 51–52, 164, 194, 215
  liberation of, 9, 68, 76, 136–37, 163, 178, 227, 247, 249–51, 253, 283
  movement of, 196–203
  personality traits associated with large and small ones, 260
  reclamation of, 19–22, 51, 65, 136, 214, 226, 248, 260, 263
  sexualization of, 13, 15–16
  size of, 4
  terms for, 19–21, 34–35, 51, 66, 95–96, 248
Bride of Chucky, 31
brown, adrienne maree, 263
Buddha, 239, 240
Buddhism, 239–42, 283
Buffon, Comte, 207
burlesque, 38, 62–63, 263
Burlesque Hall of Fame, 34
Burlesque Handbook, The (Weldon), 36
buttocks, 41

California Cyrobank, 80
Calvin Klein, 158, 172–73
Cameroon, 281
cam modeling business, 56–57
Canada, 271
"Candy Shop" (50 Cent), 33
Cardi B, 58–59, 126, *127*

Castle, Terry, 238
Catholicism, 94, 212, 214–17
CBS, 192, 277
Centers for Disease Control and
    Prevention (CDC), 108, 273
Chakachas, the, 34
Chang, Carolyn, 10–11, 112–19,
    125–28, 130–34, 142–44, 147,
    149–51
Charmed Tongue (Ganesh), 230–31
Chaturbate, 56
cheerleading, 264–65
Cheetah, the (strip club), 37
chest-feeding, 90–91; *See also*
    breastfeeding
Chicago, IL, 63
choice, freedom of, 104, 107, 136,
    139, 145, 227, 244, 271
Claremont Hotel (Oakland), 7
Clark, Kenneth, 280
Clayton, Reese, 154, 182, 184–88,
    198, 199
cleavage, 124–25, 147–48, 171, 201
Clover Industries, 177–78
Cohen, Mathilde, 96–100
Cohen, Ra'el, 167, 177
Columbia University, 145
comfort, 52, 78, 156–58, 165, 168,
    179, 195, 202, 223
commercialization, *See* breasts, com-
    mercialization of
Complex Delight, A (Miles), 215
Comstock Laws, 190
Condor Club, 30–39, 41–43, 57–60,
    63–64, 67–71, 151
*Conflict, The: How Modern Motherhood
    Undermines the Status of Women*
    (Badinter), 98
consent, 265
Cooke, Lucy, 251
Cordelia, Bea, 63
"corporeal communication"
    (Cohen), 98–99

cow's milk, 86, 89, 92, 99, 100, 108
Cox, Laverne, *216*
COYOTE (Call Off Your Old Tired
    Ethics), 50
Creation of Patriarchy, The (Lerner),
    227
Crocodile Lightning, 60–63, *61*
crone, 209, 238, 250, 279
cross-dressing, 51, 164, 239; *See also*
    drag kings; drag queens
Cross Your Heart bra (Playtex), 161
Curtis, Tony, *15*, 16

dairy industry, 271
Dalai Lama, 241–42
Damiano, Gerard, 44
Darwin, Charles, 211
Darwin, Erasmus, 166
Daughter of the Gods, A (film), 181
Davis, Kathy, 261
DCIS (ductal carcinoma in situ), 2–3
decriminalization, of sex work,
    48–52, 68, 251–52
Deep Throat (film), 44
Déjà Vu (Services, Inc.), 30, 261,
    265, 266
Delacroix, Eugène, 3–4
Delhi, India, 94
DeRidder, Willem, 263
Dettwyler, Katherine, 13, 268, 281
Deuce, The (television program), 263
*Diagnostic and Statistical Manual of
    Mental Disorders* (DSM–V–TR),
    143–44
Diana (goddess), *219*, 220, 244–45;
    See also Artemis (goddess)
Dici bra (WonderBra), 163
DIEP flap surgery, 135, 139–43, 274
Dirty Martini, 39–40
Dirty Martini (dancer), 197
Dita Von Teese Burlesque Gala, 39
DJ Bling, 30, 58, 67
Doda, Carol, 30, 36, 44–45

Dogon peoples, 16, *17*
"domme" (dominatrix), 32, 69
double-armed trudgen, 180
Dove, Nova, 52–57, 265
drag kings, 64, 66
drag queens, 19, 40, 90, 179
DREAM (Driving Racial Equity in
    Aesthetic Medicine) initiative,
    121
dress reform, 21, 181, *183*, 202
Drucker, Zackary, 146–48, *147*, 276
DSM–V–TR (*Diagnostic and Statisti-
    cal Manual of Mental Disorders*),
    143–44
Duchamp, Marcel, *250*
ductal carcinoma in situ (DCIS), 2–3
Dunham, Cyrus Grace, 145
Durga (goddess), 230
Durham, Jeff, 283

eating disorders, 58
ecocide, 213
Edmonds, Alexander, 129
education, 210, 279
Educational Amendments of 1972,
    196
eHARF (Human Relations Area
    Files), 267
El Shaddai, 234–35
"End Demand" model, 50
En Femme, 277
environmental impact, of formula
    production, 100
Ephesus, 220
Epstein, Jeffrey, 177
equality, 23, 27, 50, 155, 161, 164,
    173, 195, 198, 264, 274, 278,
    280, 283
equal rights, 133, 195, 215, 243
erotic attraction, to breasts, 12–15
escort business, 53–55
ethnicity, 23, 54, 79, 121, 155, 169,
    269

ethnography, 23, 262
European Commission, 270
European Milk Bank Association, 92
Eve (biblical figure), 212
*Eve: How the Female Body Drove 200
    Million Years of Human Evolution*
    (Bohannon), 12
exotic dancing, 54
exoticism, 54
eye contact, 31, 249

Facebook, 192
Falls, Susan, 268
Family and Medical Leave Act
    (FMLA), 92, 269–70
family leave, 91–92
fashion, 16, 113, 170–71, 253
Fawcett, Farrah, *1*, 8, 178
Febos, Melissa, 133
Federal Communications Commis-
    sion (FCC), 191, 192, 277
Federer, Roger, 195
Felski, Rita, 133–34
female gazes, 22, 188, 237
femininity, 24–25, 60, 62, 117, 147,
    161, 163, 186, 200, 224, 230,
    235, 275
feminism
    and beauty, 133–34, 251, 273, 274,
        284
    and bras, 161–63
    and breasts, 23–27
    discrimination against trans
        women, 32, 212
    and education, 210, 279
    in France, 98
    intersectional, 32
    and motherhood, 91
    and plastic surgery, 9, 133
    second-wave, 51
    and sex work, 32, 52
Fichtel, Kathy, 163
First 5 LA, 109

fit models, 154–61

flat closures (after mastectomies), 136–37, 274

Fleetwood Mac, 113

flesh, as term, 122

FMLA (Family and Medical Leave Act), 92, 269–70

Fool's Journey retreat, 206–45

Ford, Christine Blasey, 9

formula (breast milk substitutes), 13–14, 89–90, 92–93, 97, 100, 104

Fox (Film Corp), 181

Foxconn, 74

Foxworth, Margaux, 200–201

France, 13, 96–100, 106

Francis, Pope, 214

Frankenstein (Shelley), 6

freedom
  of being naked/top-free, 212, 215, 237–38
  breast pump enabled, 82
  of breasts, 48, 51–52, 164, 194, 215
  of choice (reproductive), 104, 244
  of expression/speech, 52, 63, 195, 266
  from femininity, 24–25, 161
  of physical movement, 164, 202, 254
  sexual, 35

"free the nipple," 51–52, 194, 215

Free to Be bra (Lululemon), 135, 196

FUPA (fatty upper pubic area), 124

Gable, Clark, 194

Galland, China, 241–42

Ganesh, Chitra, 228–32

Gap Inc., 161, 188

Garden of Eden (strip club), 42

Gates-Burgess, Brandi, 91, 100–106

gay male gaze, 173

gender
  ambiguity/neutrality, 145, 223, 239, 281, 282
  binary, 63
  and bralessness, 164
  breasts/chests as defining, 2, 7, 9, 25, 51, 114, 135, 145
  cis-, 26, 144–45, 148, 194
  discrimination, 52, 196, 264, 278, 283
  dysphoria, 91, 143–44, 275
  fluidity/variability, 63, 145, 212, 224, 275
  identity, 60, 64–66, 98, 135, 177
  identity disorder, 144, 275
  as a journey, 66
  nonbinary, 60–62, 64, 66, 145, 200, 277
  polarization, 4
  presentation, 25, 64
  reappraisals of, 25–26
  roles, 177, 211
  war, 33

gender-affirming healthcare, 7, 61–62, 143–49, 192, 275

genderful, 64, 145

Genesis (biblical book), 211, 212, 282

Gentlemen Prefer Blondes (film), 16

Germany, 270

"Girls, Girls, Girls" (Mötley Crüe), 38

Givens, Sonnie, *168*, 168–69, 171, 173–75

glamour, 119

God, 221–22, 234–35

"Goodbye Yellow Brick Road" (Elton John), 149

Gordon, Laura, 156, 158–66, 276

Gourley, Ryan, 113, 115, 116, 118, 126, 130, 132, 142, 149–51

"Go Your Own Way" (Fleetwood Mac), 113

Grable, Betty, *14*, 15

grandmothers
  allo-nursing by, 78–79
  influence of, 94
Grossman, Pam, 209
Grøvslien, Anne, 92–96
Guanyin (bodhisattva/deity), *222*,
  222–23, 241
Gyllenhaal, Maggie, 263
gynecomastia, 114; *See also* "moobs"
  (man boobs)
Gypsy Rose Lee, 40

Haakaa hand pump, 268
Halberstam, Jack, 145
Handmaid's Tale, The (television pro-
  gram), 8
Harvard University, 22, 48, 182, 207,
  215
Harvey, John, 278
Haskell, Ellen Davina, 235, 282
Haynes, Clarity, 236–38
Hays Code, 190–91, 277
HBO, 192
Health Savings Accounts, 272
Healy, Catherine, 58, 252
Heartney, Eleanor, 134
Hebron, Micol, 193–94
Hecate (goddess), 243–44
Henry, Steven, 141
Hera (goddess), 221
heroes, 80
Hewlett, Barry S., 267
hexing, 226
Higgins, Kathleen, 119
high-capacity breast milk donors,
  77, 82
Hilton, Perez, 194
Hinduism, 228–32
HIV
  and breastfeeding, 106–8
  and pregnancy, 271–72
HMBANA (Human Milk Banking
  Association of North America), 88

Hoefinger, Heidi, 56
Holder pasteurization, 268
Holme, Sarah, 156
holy, as term, 217
housewives, as sex workers, 55–56
Howard University Hospital, 120
How to Swim (Kellerman), 184
Hrdy, Sara Blaffer, 12, 78, 79, 267
Human Milk Banking Association
  of North America (HMBANA),
  88
human milk banks, 20–21, 73–109,
  252
Human Relations Area Files
  (eHRAF), 267
human rights, 6, 20, 23, 36, 48-50,
  52, 102, 133, 195, 202, 214, 243,
  251-253, 259, 262, 263, 283
Human Rights Watch, 50
humans
  as animals, 207–8
  and our place in nature, 213
  what makes us human, 12, 250–
  51, 253

IFIF (Iron-Fortified Infant Formula)
  program, 105
Instagram, 192, 194
insufficient glandular tissue (IGT),
  102–3
intelligence, 12, 89, 117, 177, 207,
  209, 213, 241, 245, 250–51, 254,
  260, 269, 279
Interfilière (lingerie convention), 166
"International Klein Blue," 47
Internet, 20, 192
intersectional feminism, 32
intimates, as term, 165–66
Iron-Fortified Infant Formula (IFIF)
  program, 105
Islam, 94–95, 270
Issey Miyake, 172
It Happened One Night (film), 194

Jackson, Janet, *191*, 191–92
Jacquemus, 172
Jaipur, India, 94
James Perse, 199
Jane, Betty (Wilhoit), 242–45, 279
Japan, 16, *17*, 54
Jax, 177
Jodo Shinshu Temple, 240
Jogbra, 196
John, Elton, 149
Johnson and Johnson, 117
Jones, Rashida, 160
Judaism, 232–35, 270
Juggs magazine, 260
jugs, as term, 21, 95–96
"Jungle Fever" (the Chakachas), 34
Juvéderm, 116

Kadeshah, 234
KakaoTalk, 53
Kali (goddess), *229*
Kannagi (legendary Tamil woman), 231–32
Kannon, 223, 241; *See also* Guanyin (bodhisattva/deity)
KaPowww, Kitty, 64–67, *65*, 145
Kardashian, Kim, 41, 169
Karunawardhane, Clare, 177–78
kathoey, 60–63
Kavanaugh, Brett, 9
Kellerman, Annette, 180–84, *183*
Kellogg Foundation, 102
kink-shaming, 265
Kinsey report, 14
Kissush Levinah, 235
kitsch, 119
Klein, Yves, 47
Knox, Belle, 265
Kohenet Hebrew Priestess Institute, 235
Kohenet priestesses, 235
Kolkata, India, 94
Kraus, Rachel, 155, 158–60, 185–87

lactation; *See also* breastfeeding
and evolution, 12
as fetish, 56, 268
and premature babies, 88–89
"ladyboys," 60–63
Lakoff, Robin, 49
Lane Bryant, 184
Lang, Fritz, 149
language
in plastic surgery, 122
related to sex workers, 264
terms for breasts, 19–21, 34–35, 51, 66, 95–96, 248
trans terminology, 144–45
Language and Woman's Place (Lakoff), 49
lap dances, 33, 38–39, 261
Laplanders, 210
Larry Flynt's Hustler Club, 42
laws, about exposing breasts, 52, 63
Leadership Conference of Women Religious, 214
Lee, Jennie, 263
Lee, Lorelei, 262
Lee, Vivien, 74–77, 84
legalization, of sex work, 50
Lehr, Leslie, 264–65
Leigh, Carol (Scarlot Harlot), 48–52, 194
Lemmon, Jack, *15*, 16
Leonardo da Vinci, 230
Lepore, Amanda, 40
Lerner, Gerda, 227
letdown, 76–77
Levi Strauss (apparel), 157, 175
liberated woman, 45, 62, 82
Liberating Motherhood (Olorenshaw), 23–24
liberation; *See also* freedom
of breasts, 9, 68, 76, 136–37, 163, 178, 227, 247, 249–51, 253, 283
mother of, 241
sexual, 194

of women, 23–27, 161, 163, 178, 182, 195, 224, 245

Liberty Leading the People (Delacroix), *3*, 3–4

Lily, The, 202

Linnaeus, Carl, 209–11

love, 12, 22, 43, 48, 55–56, 60, 74, 75, 78, 84, 98, 109, 119, 182, 215, 241, 243, 248, 251, 265, 280

love of one's own breasts, 7, 22, 36, 42, 129, 169, 175, 200, 201

Lowe, Rob, 160

Lucile Packard Children's Hospital, 272

Lululemon, 135, 168, 196, 197

Lusty Lady (peep show), 266

Mac Dre, 68

Machado, Barbara, 128–30, 144

Macy's, 196

Madame Vivien V., 179

Madonna, (Mary, mother of Jesus), *73*, 215, *216*

"Mafioso" (Mac Dre), 68

magic, 224–27

male bias, 9, 25, 75, 184, 199, 209, 244, 248, 253, 276

male gaze
    bras as shield from, 164
    and eye contact, 31
    feminine command of, 22, 32–33, 38, 126, 142
    gay male gaze, 173
    theories of, 31, 99, 149, 238, 252, 267

MAL Entertainment, 261

male supremacy, *See* supremacy, male

mammals, as term, 207–11

Man Ray, 45

Mansfield, Jayne, *96*

Marg, 209, 212–17, 243

Martin, Lindsey, 156–59

Marvelous Mrs. Maisel, The (television program), 19

Mary, mother of Jesus (biblical figure), *73*, 215, *216*

Mary Magdalene (biblical figure), 215

massages, 55

mastectomies, 2–3, 6, 11, 86, 118, 135–36, *137*, 138, 143–45, 149, 209, 238, 274, 275

mastitis, 6

maternity leave, 92, 93, 97

Max (Lange), 239–45

Medela, 82, 84

media
    consumption of, 130–31
    depictions of breasts in, 15–16, 190–94
    mediated breast fetishes, 56

Meisel, Steven, 173

Melonie (stripper), 36

men
    cars purchased by, 150
    dress requirements for, 194, 278
    in medical specialties, 124
    nipples on, 5, 148, 166, 188, 193, *193*, 194, 259
    supremacy of, enforced by religion and science, 210–11

men, breast removal for, *See* gynecomastia

Mendieta, Ana, 47

mental wellness, 128, 129

Mentor (breast implants), 117

Merz, Shawn, 172–74

Meta, 192, 193

#MeToo movement, 9, 262

Metropolis (film), 149

Metzger, Deena, 137, *137*

Miami, Florida, 120

Michigan Womyn's Music Festival, 212

microsurgery, 141

Miles, Margaret, 22, 215–16, 249–50
milk banks, 20–21, 73–109, 252
milk ejection reflex, 76–77
milk kinships, 94–95
Millett, Kate, 26–27
Million Dollar Mermaid (film), 181
Mintz, Sydney, 232–35
misandry, 31–32
Miss America pageant, 25, 161, *162*
Mizuno, Katsumi, 268
MMB, *See* Mothers' Milk Bank of
    San Jose
modeling, 167–76
Monroe, Marilyn, *15*, 16, 40
"moobs" (man boobs), 114, 173
moral judgments, 23, 132–33
mortal sins, 217
Mother Camp (Newton), 19
mothering, 90
Mother Nature (Hrdy), 12
mothers
    education and age of, 268
    and feminism, 23–24
    poverty of, 269
    working, 79
Mothers' Milk Bank of Austin,
    Texas, 105
Mothers' Milk Bank (MMB) of San
    Jose, 75, 77, 81, 83, 84–89, 102,
    106, 107
Motion Picture Association (MPA),
    191
Mötley Crüe, 38
motorboating, 42
Ms. magazine, 253
Mughannam, Paige, 195–99
mugs, as slang, 95
music, in strip clubs, 31
My Story (Kellerman), 181

Nadia (stripper), 36
naked, nude vs., 280, 283
naked male chest, 188, 194, 240, 278

nakedness, 33, 40, 44, 52, 56, 179,
    181, 190, 208, 212–13, 221, 226,
    237–38, 267, 277, 278, 280
National Geographic, 190
National Laboratory, 115
National Organization for Women
    (NOW–NYC), 262
National Task Force on Prostitution,
    50
Natori, 158
Natrelle (breast implants), 8, 117,
    272
natural look, 116–17
Nazis, 95
necklaces, 238
necrotizing enterocolitis (NEC), 89
neo-burlesque, 38, 39–40
Neonatal Intensive Care Units
    (NICUs), 91, 119
Netflix, 192
Network (Nuns on the Bus), 214
Newton, Esther, 19
New York Milk Bank, 268
New York Public Library, 207
New York School of Burlesque, 38
New York Times, 177
New Zealand, 58, 252
NICUs (Neonatal Intensive Care
    Units), 91, 119
Nike, 157, 168, 175, 195–97
"Nipplegate," 192
nipples
    appropriateness of showing, 187–
        88, 195
    in bra design, 160
    censorship of, 188–95, 251, 277
    hiding, with bras, 166
    on men, 5, 148, 166, 188, 193, *193*,
        194, 259
    placement of, 148
    terms for, 21, 178, 188–90
    as third eyes, 231, *232*
nipple torture, 56

"No Humans Involved" (Wynter), 279
nonbinary, *See* gender, nonbinary
nonprofit milk banks, 85
Nora (witch), 212
North Face, The, 157
Norway, 92–96, 106
NOW–NYC (National Organization for Women), 262
nozzles, translation of nipples in Sinhalese, 178
nudity, 47, 180, 213, 264, 280, 283
nuns, 214–17
Nuns of the Bus, 214
Nuru spa, 56
Nussbaum, Martha, 263

Oak, 208
Oak (witch and psychotherapist), 211–14, 217–18, 221–27, 237–39, 243, 244
obesity, 123–24, 273
objectification, 263
obstetricians, 108
Old Navy, *153*, 154–63, 165, 168, 179, 180, 182, 184–88, 195–202
Old Testament, 49, 233–34; *See also* Torah
Olorenshaw, Vanessa, 23–24
One-Piece Bathing Suit, The (film), 181
Opie, Catherine, 173, *174*
original sin, 217
Orpheum Theater, 39
Oslo University Hospital, 92
Our Bodies, Ourselves (Boston Women's Health Book Collective), 269
Our Lady J, 194
Outdoor Voices (apparel), 135
oxytocin, 75, 102, 109, 266

Paradise (stripper), 41, 70
Parks and Rec (television program), 160

Parton, Dolly, 126, *127*
pasteurization, of breastmilk, 84–85, 94, 106, 268
patriarchal perspectives
  and male bias, 9, 25, 75, 184, 199, 209, 244, 248, 253, 276
  masquerading as neutral, 22
patriarchy, 9, 33, 52, 98, 163, 203, 212, *225*, 226, 227, 251, 252, 281; *See also* supremacy, male
Paul, Saint, 220
Paypal, 192
pediatricians, 108
peer-to-peer milk sharing, 268
Peggy L'Eggs, 47
pelvic floor therapy, 96–97
Peña, Cristina Jade, 106–9, 272
people of color
  in medical specialties, 124
  and Neonatal Intensive Care Units (NICUs), 91
  and plastic surgery, 121–22
  and Women, Infants, and Children (WIC) offices, 101
"Perfect Woman, The," 182–84, *183*
personality traits, associated with breast size, 260
"Petite Fleur" (Bechet), 62
Pham, Lily, 81–82
Phrygians, 220
Physical Beauty: How to Keep It (Kellerman), 184
physical bodies, 66–67
physical contact, 57
Pitanguy, Ivo, 128
plastic surgery, 9, 21, 111–51, 252–53
Playboy, 16, 190, 265
Playtex, 161
pleasure activism, 47–48, 263
Pleasure Activism (brown), 263
Pleasure Activist Playing Cards (Sprinkle), 47–48
pole dancing, 58–59, 265

police, 55
Ponte delle Tette (Venice), 51
Porkpie, Jonny, 160
Porn Hub, 192
pornography, 22, 192
Pose (television program), 60
Post-Porn Modernist (Sprinkle), 44
posture, 41–42
Potter, Elisabeth, 135–43
poverty, of mothers, 91, 101, 126,
    269, 271
power dressing, 164
Powless, Yvonne Simone, 169–71,
    170
prehistory excavations, female fig-
    ures in, 227–28, *228*
premature babies, 88–89
prepectoral breast reconstruction,
    275
Price, Amanda, 154–61, 182, 184–
    86, 198, 199
primary sex characteristics, 25
Private Pleasures (phone sex busi-
    ness), 35
privilege, 33, 53, 98, 104, 211, 226,
    264, 271
profit milk banks, 85–86
Prostitute School, 55, 265
prostitution, 49, 264, 265; *See also*
    escort business
Public Cervix Announcement (Sprin-
    kle), 45
PUMP Act, 82
PumpinPal, 84

Quandt, Victoria, 197–200

race, 23, 54, 95, 103, 119, 130, 150,
    164
Ramirez, Elysia, 83–84
rating system, for movies, 191
reclaiming breasts, *See* breasts, rec-
    lamation of

Reclaiming spiritual feminists, 208–
    9, 214, 280, 283
RedBone, 34–38, 41–43, 59, 64,
    68–71, 262
Reddit, 192
registered nurse first assistant
    (RNFA), 113, 115
religion, 21–22, 94–95, 205–45, 253
reproductive choice, 104, 244
Rick's Cabaret, 261
Ritts, Herb, 173
Rivers, Jessica, 86
RNFA, *See* registered nurse first
    assistant (RNFA)
Rochester, New York, 214
romantic relationships, as transac-
    tional, 55–56
Rosie the Riveter, 4, *5*
Rousseau, Jean-Jacques, 270, 279

Sabra (witch), 243
St. David's Medical Center, Austin,
    274
Sakamoto, Pauline, 87–91, 102, 268
saliva, 98, 271
Salomonsen, Jone, 280
Sámi peoples, 210
Santorelli, Ramona, 215
Sarah (biblical figure), 233, 282
Sargent, Dudley A., 182
Sati (goddess), 229–30, 281–82
Sativa (stripper), 70–71
Säugetier, 210–11
Scarlot Harlot, *See* Leigh, Carol
scarring, 117–18, 121–22
Schiebinger, Londa, 207–9, 211
School of Visual Arts (New York), 45
Scythians, 218
secondary sex characteristics, 25
Second Skin bra (ThirdLove), 178
Sekhmet (goddess), 230
self-labeling with slur terms, 21, 248;
    See also speech art

Self-Portrait Nursing (Opie), 173, *174*
Serano, Julia, 24–25
sex (physical trait), 25
sex, as transactional, 55–56
Sex and Social Justice (Nussbaum), 263
sex change operations, 61–62
sexism, 22, 137, 177, 188, 194, 207, 212, 261, 280, 284
sex trafficking, 36
Sexual Behavior in the Human Male (Kinsey), 14–15
sexual freedom, 35
sexualization, of breasts, 13, 15–16
sexual liberation, 194
Sexual Politics (Millett), 26–27
sexual violence, 8–9, 223
sex work, 20, 29–71
    and Black women, 36, 41, 54
    and breast augmentation, 149–50
    coinage of term, 53
    decriminalization of, 48–52, 68, 251–52
    ethical, 55
    in the Old Testament, 234
    sex trafficking vs., 36
    and women's movement, 36
Sex Work (Alexander), 50
Sex Worker Exclusionary Radical Feminists (SWERFs), 32
sex-worker-rights activism, 262
Seymour, Stephanie, 173
Shakti, 230
Sharik, Lisa, 260
Shekhinah, 235
Shelley, Mary, 6
shibari, 56
Showa University Koto Toyosu Hospital, 268
Showtime, 192
Sientra (breast implants), 117
siliconadas, 129
Silverman, Sarah, 194

Sim, Lisa, 199–203
Similac, 90, 272
Sirens Motorcycle Club, 268
Sisters of Mercy (women's religious institute), 214
SKIMS, 169, 180
skin laxity, 123
skin necrosis, 273
Smashbox Studios, 167
Smith, Julie, 100
social class, 23, 55, 81, 119, 121, 126, 131, 208, 273
social media, 192–93
social pressure, 144
Some Like It Hot (film), 16
Spandex, 156
Spearmint Rhino, 261
Special Supplemental Nutrition Program for Women, Infants, and Children, *See* Women, Infants, and Children (WIC)
Spectra (pump), 84
speech act, 19–20; *See also* self-labeling with slur terms
spells, 224–27
spirituality, 21–22, 205–45, 253
sports bras, 195–203, *200*
Sprinkle, Annie, 43–48, 197, 263
stage names, 59–60, 62
Stanford University, 200, 207
Starhawk, 208
Steinberg, Ellen, *See* Sprinkle, Annie
Stephens, Beth, 44
Stockholm Burlesque Festival, 62
Stop Asian American and Pacific Islander hate, 119
Strangio, Chase, 25, *216*, 253
"strap tease," 38
Strattice, 123
Stripchat, 56
strip clubs, 20, 35–36, 42, 261, 262, 266
strippers, 30–39, 57–60, 67–71, 262

stripping, as creative expression, 265–66

Strip Speak (Sprinkle), 45, 47, 263

Stryker, Susan, 148–49

Suckling at My Mother's Breasts (Haskell), 235

suffrage, 23, *24*, 181

Sun newspaper, 195

Sunshine and Health, *189*, 190

Super Bowl halftime show, 191–92

support, in bras, 201–2

supremacy, male, 19, 33, 188, 210, 226, 263; *See also* patriarchy

suturing, 143

SWERFs (Sex Worker Exclusionary Radical Feminists), 32

swimwear, 179–88

Swoosh bra (Nike), 196

symmetry, 121, 131–32

Systema Naturae (*Systems of Nature*; Linnaeus), 209

Talmud, 267, 270

Tara, *205*

Tara (goddess), 241–42, 283

Tarzan the Ape Man (film), 194

taste, 6, 23, 38, 97, 117, 160, 221

technology, 35, 56, 82, 83, 273

Temple Emanu-El, 233

TERFs (trans-exclusionary radical feminists), 212

Tessla (stripper), 67–68

Testino, Mario, 173

Thailand, 60–62

"Thanks for the Mammaries" (exhibition), 193

thelarche, 281

ThirdLove, 155, 167, *170*, 171–72, 175, 177, 178, 184, 201

Thirty-Two Marks of a Good Man, 240

TikTok, 192

Timberlake, Justin, 191–92

tissue, as term, 122

Title IX, 196

Tit Prints (Sprinkle), 47

tits, as term, 20, 34–35, 51

"Tits on the Head" photos, 44

"titty bumps," 42–43

TomboyX, 276–77

top-free, 62, 137, 194, 206, 212, 215

topless, top-free vs., 194, 208

topless protests, 51, 52, 193, 195, 238, 264

Torah, 234, 282; *See also* Old Testament

torso portraits, *236*, 236–38

TRAM flap surgery, 140

trans activism, 25

trans-exclusionary radical feminists (TERFs), 212

trans men, 25, 145

transsexualism, 144

trans terminology, 144–45

trans women, 25, 60–63, 145, 146, *147*, 179–80

Trivia (goddess), 244

Turlington, Christy, 172–73

Under Armour, 168, 197

United Healthcare, 108

University of California at Los Angeles (UCLA), 107–8, 173

University of Texas, Austin, 169

"Up" (Cardi B), 58–59

Updegrove, Kim, 105–6

upper body lifts, 123–24

US Breastfeeding Committee, 88

US Department of Agriculture (USDA), 105, 252

US Food and Drug Administration, 90

Valentina, 57–60, 68, 69

Valiente, Doreen, 224

venial sins, 217

Venice, Italy, 51
Venus de Milo, 182
Venus of Willendorf, 227, *228*
Victoria's Secret, 163, 173, 176–77
Vindication of the Rights of Woman, A
  (Wollstonecraft), 6

Wacoal, 158
Wakefield-Scurr, Joanna, 278
Waking the Witch (Grossman), 209
Walker, Lauren, 179–87
Warren, Elizabeth, 226
Washington DC, 120
"Wave Goodbye to the Patriarchy"
  (Oak), *225*, 226
weaning, 99
Weldon, Jo "Boobs," 36–38, *37*
West, Natalie, 14
West Africa, 223
wet nurses, 13, 80, 97, 210
Wexner, Les, 177
WHO (World Health Organization),
  50, 93
whorearchy, 57, 265
WIC, *See* Women, Infants, and
  Children
Williams, Esther, 181
Williams, Leonna, 175–77, *176*
Williams, Serena, 195
Wimbledon, 195
Wind Hags, 208
Winn, Steve, 267
witchcraft, 224–27

witches, 205–45
Wolf, Naomi, 133
Wollstonecraft, Mary, 6
women
  during Enlightenment, 210
  liberation of, 23–27, 161, 163, 178,
    182, 195, 224, 245
  as strip club owners, 266
Women, Infants, and Children
  (WIC), 101–6, 252, 271
"Women and Cows in France and
  the United States" (Cohen),
  99–100
women's rights, 27, 210, 245, 253–54,
  263
working mothers, 79, 97
World Health Organization (WHO),
  50, 93
Wynter, Sylvia, 279

X (formerly Twitter), 192
XHamsterLive, 262
XVideo, 192

Yale University, 267
yitties, 35
Yitty (apparel), 262
Young, Iris Marion, 133, 273–74
YouTube, 163, 192, 263, 268, 277

Zak, Heidi, 177
Zeus, 221
zonah, 234